Andrew Murray, though d
volume. Walk with this
preparation, great success i
May this book introduce a
God, and stimulate faith that the God of Murray is also our God
and can lead us also to faithful and fruitful service.

ADRIAN WARNOCK
Author of *Raised with Christ* and *Hope Reborn* and prolific blogger at adrianwarnock.com

Andrew Murray: Christ's Anointed Minister to South Africa is the
latest in a series of biographies of the great devotional theologian
and churchman, whose writings still, nearly a hundred years after
his death, bring rivers of living waters into those who wish to know
Christ better. Andrew Murray's many volumes have inspired me
since my early twenties. One of my ministerial mentors, the late
Dr John Reed Miller of Jackson, Mississippi, first gave me one of
Murray's books – *The Spiritual Life* – in the late 1960s, and I knew
that I was onto truth that was alive and transformative. The late
Mary Torrance Wallace (Mrs Ronald S. Wallace of Edinburgh)
said to me some thirty years ago that she saw Murray as filling out
and making further application of the teaching of John Calvin on
Union with Christ, and I have found that to be so.

Murray was certainly in the Augustinian/Calvinist tradition,
and his writings breathe a devotional spirit which have always
cheered me onward. After much careful and appreciative reading of
him I definitely decided that the Puritans' account of the struggles
of the Christian Life (such as in vol. 6 of the *Works of John Owen*)
give a better account of many of these matters than Murray's
'Higher Life' teaching (developed later in his life). Yet his work
is still valuable in so many areas, even though many of us cannot
receive all of it without some exegetical critique.

Vance Christie has done an excellent job on Murray's life.
He shows the experience of a consecrated man of God, without
resorting to unrealistic hagiography. Christie draws together
coherently and clearly the multifarious events of Murray's world-
wide ministry. He also discusses some of the more controversial
aspects of that teaching: not least, Higher Life and Healing. No
one biography can cover everything in one volume, but – given Rev.

Christie's theological perception – I would have been glad to have seen a bit more discussion of Murray's Higher Life views, as well as his writings on prayer, his answer to The Modern Missionary Problem and The Blood of Christ.

This is a fine, relatively brief volume on a huge subject, and I find it accurate and edifying. I shall recommend it to my classes, and to some of the conferences where I speak.

DOUGLAS F. KELLY
Richard Jordan Professor of Theology,
Reformed Theological Seminary, Charlotte, North Carolina

Andrew Murray
Christ's Anointed Minister to South Africa

Vance Christie

CHRISTIAN
FOCUS

Vance Christie is a pastor and author specializing in missionary biographies. He lives in Aurora, Nebraska, and has previously written for the 'Heroes of the Faith' series. He has also written *John and Betty Stam* (isbn 978-1-84550-376-5), *David Brainerd* (isbn 978-1-84550-478-6) and *Adoniram Judson* (isbn 978-1-78191-147-1)in the Historymakers series. His website, www.vancechristie.com, has a complete list of his books in the field of historic Christian biography.

All Scripture quotations are taken from the *King James Version*.

Copyright © Vance Christie 2015

www.vancechristie.com

paperback – ISBN 978-1-78191-600-1
epub – ISBN 978-1-78191-652-0
mobi – ISBN 978-1-78191-653-7

10 9 8 7 6 5 4 3 2 1

Published in 2015
by
Christian Focus Publications Ltd,
Geanies House, Fearn, Ross-shire,
IV20 1TW, Great Britain.

www.christianfocus.com

Cover photograph by Skyler W. Shaw
Cover design by Daniel Van Straaten
Printed by Nørhaven A/S, Denmark

All rights reserved. No part of this publication may be reproduced, stored in a retrieval system, or transmitted, in any form, by any means, electronic, mechanical, photocopying, recording or otherwise without the prior permission of the publisher or a licence permitting restricted copying. In the U.K. such licences are issued by the Copyright Licensing Agency, Saffron House, 6-10 Kirby Street, London, EC1 8TS www.cla.co.uk

Contents

Lake Ngami

DAMARALAND

Walwich Bay

KALAHARI DESERT

GREAT
NAMAQUALAND

BECHUANALAND

Orange River

LITTLE NAMAQUALAND

Clanwilliam

Beaufort West

GREAT KARROO

Saldanha

Tulbagh

Prins Albert

Worcester

LITTLE KARROO

Table Bay

Wellington

Stellenbosch Swellendam

George

CAPE TOWN

Caledon

Cape of Good Hope

Cape Agulhas

R. Zouga

KALAHARI DESERT

ZOUTPANSBERGEN

Limpopo River

Olifants R

° Ohrigstad

°Lijdenburg

Warm Bad

TRANSVAAL

Morikwi River

Zwart Ruggens

MAGALIESBERG

Rustenburg ° PRETORIA

Delagoa Bay

BECHUANALAND

Potchefstroom

Suikerbosrand

Vaal River

Sand R.

ORANGE RIVER SOVEREIGNTY

ZULULAND

° Griekwastad

Harrismith

St Lucia Bay

Modder R.

WITTENBERGEN

°Winburg

NATAL

Bloemfontein

Coledon River

BASUTOLAND

Pietermaritzburg

Durban

Fauresmith °

Bethany

Smithfield

Orange River

Aliwal North

° Colesberg

° Burgersdorp

KAFFRARIA

Graaff-Reinet °

Cradock

BRITISH
KAFFRARIA

George

Sundays River

Grahâms Town

Uitenhage°

Port Elizabeth

SOUTH AFRICA
IN 1852

To our beloved church family members,
present and past,
at the Aurora Evangelical Free Church
with whom it has been our privilege
to share life and ministry for many years
and with deep appreciation
for your unfailing support and encouragement.

INTRODUCTION

In an era that saw many gifted and diligent ministers, missionaries and evangelists being used by God to powerfully advance Christ's Kingdom work in South Africa, Andrew Murray (1828–1917) emerged as that country's premier preacher, devotional writer and Church leader.

From his early twenties till well into his eighties Murray was a dynamic, sought-after preacher. Hundreds and even thousands of people eagerly gathered to hear him preach. His sermons were characterized by overwhelming intensity, depth of spiritual insight and evident empowering by God's Spirit that stirred, instructed and challenged his hearers. Fluent in both English and Dutch, Murray communicated with great effectiveness to audiences in South Africa, Europe and America.

Murray served for fifty-seven years as an active minister of the Dutch Reformed Church in South Africa. He pastored four separate congregations, including his final pastorate of three and a half decades. His ministerial colleagues repeatedly chose him as their leader by electing him to serve six terms as Moderator of Cape Colony's Dutch Reformed Synod. Murray became the foremost minister both in terms of prominence and influence not only in Cape Colony but also in the Orange River Sovereignty (later the Orange Free State), the Transvaal and Natal. He travelled and ministered more extensively throughout all of South Africa than any other minister of any denomination in his day.

As a primary and visionary spiritual leader not only of his denomination but also of his country, Murray actively advanced a wide variety of causes that promoted the well-being, spiritually and in other ways, of both Church and State. He helped establish congregations and recruit pastors to serve in Cape Colony and its neighboring republics. He played a key role in the founding of several educational institutions, not only for the purpose of providing young people of various socio-economic classes with the opportunity to gain an education, but also to train teachers and missionaries. Murray personally carried out several major evangelistic tours of different parts of South Africa, pointing large numbers of people to salvation in Christ. He took the lead in establishing and promoting the work of various foreign missionary societies to carry the Gospel to unreached people groups outside the bounds of the Colony. Murray sponsored and was featured at numerous conferences aimed at calling believers to a higher plain of Christian living and service. He actively supported a number of student ministry organizations as well as home mission works that ministered to military personnel, the poor and moral outcasts. Though Murray did not normally involve himself directly in politics, he sought to lead people in responding appropriately to the sometimes turbulent political events of the day. Periodically he was called on to fulfill a more direct role in working through those challenging situations.

While being a man of seemingly constant action, Murray was also a contemplative individual. His mind constantly probed new avenues and depths of biblical, spiritual truth. His thinking and teaching were deeply devotional in nature. Those who interacted with him sensed that he consistently lived with a profound awareness of the presence of God and a preoccupation with matters spiritual. He was deeply devoted to prayer and tirelessly encouraged all Christians to be as well. He had an appreciation for the writings of certain Christian mystics and has sometimes been classified as being a sane, sanctified mystic himself.

Through his prolific writing endeavors, which saw nearly 240 works (including over seventy books) published, Murray was able to have a worldwide ministry to hundreds of thousands of Christians during his lifetime. To this day dozens of his works continue to be published and read by believers throughout the world. Murray's writings, in fact, are what he is best known for today.

Murray's books divulge his fervent spiritual perspectives. But they reveal virtually nothing about his personal history and ministry. The present volume shows the many events and other factors that went into Murray's personal development and into the formation of his viewpoints and convictions.[1] The current work also reveals that Murray's writing ministry, though truly impressive in its scope, was but one of several major emphases in his remarkably broad and fruitful career of service.

Past Murray-biographies have tended to relate the first half of his life in chronological order, while presenting various aspects of his ministry in the latter half of his life – such as his efforts to promote education, evangelism and missions – in topical (but non-chronological) fashion. The present biography is the first to offer a chronological account of Murray's life from start to finish, presenting the events and developments of his life and ministry in the order in which they unfolded. This has the added advantage of enabling one to gain a clearer understanding of the wide variety of ministries Murray was simultaneously involved in during the different periods of his ministerial career.

Several abbreviations are used in the current volume for various ministry organizations or geographical locations that are referred to repeatedly – for example: CGM for Cape General Mission; CEM for Christian Endeavor Movement; OFS for Orange Free State. One abbreviation, DRC, signifying Dutch Reformed Church, is sometimes used of that denomination and at other times of a local congregation belonging to that denomination. The context makes clear which is intended.

---

1. While this volume naturally gives some attention to Murray's beliefs and spiritual perspectives it focuses on the events and formative features of his life. For a helpful summary of three of the key components in Murray's teaching, see W.M. Douglas, *Andrew Murray and His Message, One of God's Choice Saints* (London and Edinburgh: Oliphants, 1927), pp. 261-344. Douglas reviews Murray's teachings on prayer, holy living and the Holy Spirit.

Slight, inconsequential changes have been made to some of the cited quotations in order to standardize punctuation, the spelling of various words and the form of biblical references. Some Dutch words or phrases were eliminated and only their English translation was retained when it seemed appropriate to do so. Run-on sentences, which were common in Murray's era, have sometimes been divided for the sake of clarity. All these changes in no way alter the meaning of the quotations. Plenty of unique expressions and stylistic features are retained in the citations.

Andrew Murray steadfastly refused numerous requests to record his personal memoirs. He included virtually no autobiographical references in his published writings. He was reluctant even to share his personal testimony of Christian growth lest the attention of others be directed to his experiences rather than to the teachings of Scripture. Instead of drawing attention to himself, Murray habitually pointed people to Christ (His example, presence and power) as well as the empowerment of His indwelling Holy Spirit as the key resources for successful Christian living and service.

Consideration of Murray's personal example in the pages to follow is very worthwhile and beneficial. It can be used of God to inspire and instruct. But as Murray himself would certainly desire, and as is only right, may people comprehend that he accomplished what he did by the power of God working in and through him. Therefore, may God alone receive all the glory.

1

'A GODLY PARENTAGE IS A PRICELESS BOON'
1828–1838

Though born in South Africa, Andrew Murray's influential paternal ancestry traces back to Aberdeenshire, Scotland. There most of his ancestors were farmers and conservative 'Old Light' Presbyterians. Andrew Murray was named after his father, grandfather and great-grandfather, all of whom bore the same appellation.[1] The great-grandfather occupied the sheep farm of Lofthills, near Aberdeen, a farm that had been in the family for several generations.

Andrew Murray, the grandfather, being one of several sons, left Lofthills to operate the mill at Clatt, a village not quite thirty miles northwest of Aberdeen. Scotland was facing arduous economic times at the end of the eighteenth century, and the hardworking miller's family was reduced to painful straits. Flour had to be carefully collected from the mill floor in order to provide bread for Murray's hungry children. Murray was married to Isobel Milne, a woman of great beauty and sweetness of character. Their four children were Anne, John, Elizabeth and Andrew.

Grandfather Murray was a pious individual who died at a relatively young age in 1796. Though he left his wife and children in sadly reduced circumstances, he cherished the confident hope that God would provide for their needs and that his sons and daughters would grow up to lead honorable and useful Christian

---

1. Murray-biographers and descendants have commonly distinguished the primary subject of this biography and his father as Andrew Murray, Jr and Andrew Murray, Sr. Those designations will be used in the current work when needed to distinguish the two individuals.

lives. Isobel survived her husband by twenty-six years and lived to see his cherished expectations for their children fulfilled.

As Murray lay upon his deathbed he was overheard praying in the silence of the night for each of his children by name. This so impressed the oldest son, John, then twelve years of age, that he decided that very night to devote himself to the work of the Christian ministry. By patient endeavor and with the kind aid of an unmarried uncle, John graduated with an M.A. degree from Marischal College, Aberdeen, at age twenty-two. During the subsequent decade he completed the divinity course at the University of Edinburgh, served as an assistant minister in Dundee and was called to pastor Trinity Chapel-of-Ease (later Trinity United Free Church) in Aberdeen.

John encouraged and assisted his brother Andrew, ten years his junior, in completing his education at King's College, Aberdeen. After receiving his M.A. degree, Andrew strongly desired to become a missionary. But his mother was reluctant to part with her youngest and favorite son, being unreasonably convinced that if he became a missionary he would inevitably be eaten by cannibals! In deference to her wishes, he declined an opportunity to serve in St John's, Newfoundland.

Late in 1820 or early in 1821, however, twenty-six-year-old Andrew learned of an appeal from South Africa which he felt compelled to accept. There were not enough pastors and teachers available from Holland to serve Cape Colony's Dutch churches and schools. Scottish clergy and teachers were thought suitable to help fill those positions since the doctrine and practices of the Church of Scotland and the Dutch Reformed Church (DRC) were so similar. Six ministers, Andrew Murray among them, and an equal number of teachers were successfully recruited to serve in the Colony. Of Murray's response to this opportunity, it has been noted:

> [T]he need of that Colony seemed to be so urgent that he could not find it in his heart to dismiss the appeal, while the possibility of doing something on behalf of the natives, and thus taking a small

share in the missionary enterprise, was an additional motive to consider this as a divine call.[2]

After being ordained by the Presbytery of Aberdeen, Murray went to Holland to study Dutch for ten months. Dutch was the primary language he would be using in South Africa as the vast majority of the Colony's residents and virtually all its congregations were Dutch-speaking. Murray sailed from London on 27 February, 1822, and arrived at Cape Town on 1 July. A few days later he received his formal appointment as minister of the Dutch Reformed Church at Graaff-Reinet and proceeded there immediately.

Graaff-Reinet was located some 500 miles northeast of Cape Town on an enormous, arid, elevated plain called the Great Karroo. (The Hottentot word 'karroo' meant 'dry'.) Voortrekkers (Dutch pioneers) had established a settlement at Graaff-Reinet in 1786 due to the availability of water there. The town was surrounded by an amphitheatre of steep rugged peaks called the Snow Mountains. The deep channel of the Sunday River nearly encircled the community. In time Graaff-Reinet became known as the 'Gem of the Desert'. When Murray first arrived there the town's population stood around 1,800. While predominantly a Dutch community, other ethnic groups were represented there as well. Several months after Murray's settlement there, a traveler provided an attractive description of the town:

> It contains now about three hundred houses, almost all of which are neat and commodious brick edifices – many are elegant. The streets are wide, laid out at right angles, and planted with rows of lemon and orange trees, which thrive here luxuriantly, and give to the place a fresh and pleasing appearance. Each house has a large allotment of ground behind it, extending in some instances to several acres, which is richly cultivated, divided by quince, lemon or pomegranate hedges, and laid out in orchards, gardens and vineyards. These are all watered by a canal from the Sunday River, which branches out

---

2. J[ohannes] du Plessis, *The Life of Andrew Murray of South Africa* (London and Edinburgh: Marshall Brothers, 1919), p. 15.

into a number of small channels, and each inhabitant receives his due portion at a regular hour.[3]

The church in Graaff-Reinet had been founded in 1790. Five ministers served the congregation during the thirty-two years before Murray's arrival. A new church building was erected in Graaff-Reinet the year Murray settled there. He developed a special bond with his adopted people that led him to devote his entire pastoral career of over forty years to ministering to that beloved congregation and parish. One of his future children, Maria, later related:

> He cast in his lot so whole-heartedly with his people that his children cannot remember ever hearing him express the wish to visit his native land. How happy he was among his people only his children, who grew up in the presence of that loving intercourse, can testify. Earnest, affectionate and sincere in all his relations, he never forfeited the respect and esteem accorded him by all. How often we have heard him say, 'The lines have fallen to me in pleasant places; I have a goodly heritage' [Ps. 16:6].[4]

In 1824, two years after settling at Graaff-Reinet, Murray returned to Cape Town to attend the Synod of the Colony's DRC. During that visit to Cape Town he also first met Miss Maria Susanna Stegmann, the young lady who would later become his wife. She was the oldest daughter of widower Johan Stegmann. Her mother, Jacomina (Hoppe) Stegmann, had died three years earlier at thirty-five years of age. Both Maria's grandfathers had emigrated from Germany to South Africa. Grandfather Stegmann, a tailor by trade, married Sara Susanna Roux, who was of French Huguenot descent and said to be 'a very pious woman, beloved by all who knew her'. Grandpapa Hoppe, who started a hat factory then a tannery, was a devout Christian and an ardent supporter of missions. His wife, Magdalena Greeff, was of Dutch and

3. ibid., p. 22.
4. Maria Neethling, *Unto Children's Children* (London: T.H. Hopkins & Son, 1909), p. 12.

German descent.[5] When Johan Stegmann married Jacomina Hoppe in 1807 he succeeded to the tannery business of his father-in-law.

Murray and Maria were married in Cape Town in 1825, one year after their first meeting. At the time Maria was barely half Murray's age, he being thirty-one and she only sixteen. Despite the significant difference in their ages, their union proved to be a happy one that lasted forty-one years until Murray's death in 1866. Their first child, a son, was born on 15 September, 1826. The boy was named John, after his father's brother and his mother's father. The Murrays' second son, the subject of this biography, was born on 9 May, 1828. He was named Andrew after his father as well as his paternal grandfather and great-grandfather. Over the next decade Mrs Murray gave birth to six more children: William (1829); Maria, the mother's namesake (1831); Charles (1833); Jemima (1836); Isabella (1837); George (likely 1838).[6]

The Murrays' roomy parsonage was said to be Graaff-Reinet's finest residence, far nicer even than the official dwelling of the town magistrate. The manse stood on a side street, some distance from

---

5. The Dutch established the first European settlement at the Cape of Good Hope in 1652. In 1688 a large number of Huguenot refugees settled in Cape Colony after being driven from their homeland of France. The Dutch East India Company that governed the colony at that time refused to allow the French immigrants to use their native language. Within two or three generations the French were 'completely merged' with the colonists of Dutch or German descent. It has been estimated that toward the end of the eighteenth century around half of South Africa's population was of Dutch descent while one-sixth was German, one-sixth was French and the remainder was comprised of other nationalities. All these spoke a simplified form of Dutch known as Cape Dutch. By the time Andrew Murray, Sr, arrived in South Africa in 1822, Cape Colony had been under British rule for the past sixteen years. Beginning in 1820 some 5,000 British had recently emigrated to South Africa where they received grants of land on the eastern border of the colony. Nearly all the colony's other 40,000 residents were Dutch-speaking and belonged to the Dutch Reformed Church. (See du Plessis, *The Life of Andrew Murray*, pp. 4-7.)

6. Neethling, *Unto Children's Children*, pp. 82-119, provides brief histories of Andrew and Maria's eleven children who lived to adulthood, while ibid., p. 73, lists their five children who died in childhood.

the church. It boasted a spacious yard, outbuildings and a garden. A wide set of stone steps led up from the street to the broad 'stoep' (porch) that ran along the entire front of the house. Eight sets of large, latticed glass windows, all protected by sturdy wooden shutters, looked out from the whitewashed brick front of the home. The front door opened into a sizeable lobby which in turn led to a spacious dining hall. A drawing room, Rev. Murray's study, a smaller dining room, bedrooms and various other rooms filled out the main floor of the home. Murray's daughter Maria describes other features of the house, its yard and garden:

> The front stoep, and also the back stoep, were supported by arches, and underneath the whole house ran a series of rooms corresponding with those above. Some of these were often used as bedrooms when the house was full of visitors. They included the cellar below the big dining-room, the wood room, lime room, chaff room and wagon house. But these arches, with passages beyond, seemed made on purpose for playing hide-and-seek, and often resounded with the voices of the merry, happy children.
>
> From the back stoep, by two circular flights of steps, you went down to the garden. First, the flower garden, then an avenue of orange trees, with tall lilac bushes in between. At the side of the walk was the vineyard, and at the further end of the garden were fruit trees of all kinds, laden in summer time with such fruit as we have never tasted since, and to which the dear children were allowed to help themselves without stint, and regale also their companions who came to play with them. The other half of the garden was sown with oats for the minister's horses, and there was a large plot of lucerne for the cow. On the further side of the lucerne was a row of choice fig trees, and beyond was the boundary wall.[7]

Andrew and Maria Murray raised their children in an atmosphere of earnest piety. According to their daughter Maria:

> The chief characteristic of the household was reverence. We reverenced God's name and God's day and God's Word. The wife

7. ibid., p. 11.

reverenced her husband; the children reverenced their parents;
the servants reverenced their master and mistress. The children
were trained in the ways of the Lord. They were taught to render
obedience in such a way that they never seemed to know it.[8]

Murray was deeply concerned about the spiritual welfare of his
children and that they would come to have a saving relationship
with Jesus Christ. On a Sunday evening, following family worship
when a child came for a goodnight kiss, he would ask, 'Well, dearie,
have you given your heart to Christ yet?' or 'Will you not, before
you go to bed tonight, give yourself to Jesus?' On a child's birthday
he would say, 'This is your birthday. Are you born again?'

Murray impressed spiritual truths upon his children through
other means as well:

> Many sweet words out of God's Word became engraven in the
> hearts of his children by hearing their father repeat them with
> such feeling and emphasis. Indeed, he has left them to us as a
> most precious legacy. The word of Christ did indeed dwell in him
> richly, and he taught and admonished us in psalms and hymns
> and spiritual songs, singing with grace in his heart unto the Lord
> [Col. 3:16]. Many a sweet verse has been imprinted on our minds
> and memories from hearing him repeat it half aloud to himself, as
> he walked up and down the large dining room after supper.[9]

The consecrated mother also played a crucial role in the spiritual
development and general education of her children. She taught
them to read before they were old enough to attend school, and
the hymns and Bible verses they learned at her knee remained in
their memory throughout life. When her husband was away from
home on ministry responsibilities, she listened to her sons rehearse
their daily lessons before they went to school.

In addition to caring for her children and keeping her house, Mrs
Murray did nearly all the sewing for her family. Sewing machines

---

8. ibid., p. 16.
9. ibid., pp. 31-32.

had not yet been invented, so often she stitched from morning to night. Peace and restfulness of spirit, even in the midst of work, marked her life. A regular habit of personal communion with God was the secret to her trust and tranquility. She always took time for her private devotions, and her children and servants knew that when her bedroom door was closed she was not to be disturbed unless absolutely necessary.

The Lord's Day was strictly observed by the Murrays. All Sunday food preparations such as cooking meat, boiling potatoes or rice, baking a tart or gathering fruit were done on Saturday. A walk in the garden was allowed on Sunday, when 'here or there a fruit might be gathered'. But tree-climbing and more significant fruit-picking were not permitted that day.

There were almost always three Sunday church services, in addition to Sunday School, and the older Murray children were normally expected to attend them all. One exception was that the older children took turns staying at home to show their younger siblings 'Sunday pictures' during the afternoon and evening services. In addition, Mrs Murray taught her children the Shorter Catechism on Sunday afternoon, and toward evening the family enjoyed a time of singing together. The oldest Murray daughter would later testify:

> It is sweet to recall those Sundays. Such Sunday keeping has gone out of fashion. Children now would perhaps think it a weariness, yet we cannot remember that we as children ever did. … On looking back upon it all, it does seem almost wonderful that the children did not weary of the long services. For the morning service lasted two hours, and on Communion Sundays three, and we remained to the end. It is perhaps to be ascribed to habit, or still more to the fact that the parents delighted in the worship of God, so the children learned to delight in it too.[10]

Rev. Murray's ministry vision and efforts stretched far beyond Graaff-Reinet. Over the course of his ministerial career he established eight

---

10.   ibid., pp. 65-6.

new congregations. He commonly selected the site for a new town, inducted elders and deacons, planned the building of the church and carried out other ministerial duties until a permanent pastor could be called. Against his expressed wish, one of those towns was named Murraysburg in his honor.

> His parish covered some hundreds of square miles. He established many new congregations ... Until these townships were supplied with their own minister – and that was not easily done then – he remained their preacher and pastor. He had to take long journeys to these places, sometimes being from home for a fortnight at a time for this purpose. At every farmhouse along the road where the minister stopped for the night, he had scarcely dismounted from the large, springless horse-wagon, when the Bible would be produced and he was asked to conduct a service. He always insisted on all the servants and shepherds being called in. And, weary though he was, he rejoiced at being able to break the bread of life to hungry souls. After the death of the Rev. John Evans, the large district of Cradock was also vacant for several years, and our father had to go there every quarter to administer the sacrament, holding three day's services – 'Preparation' on Saturday, 'Communion' on Sunday (six tables to be addressed), and 'Thanksgiving' on Monday. Added to this was the work of catechizing, holding church meetings, attending to cases of discipline, marrying, baptizing, etc. ...
>
> ... One service on Saturday, three on Sunday and one on Monday morning might seem arduous enough, but a very important part of the work still had to be done. This was ... family visitation on Sunday afternoon and Monday morning. This was not, as the name seems to imply, going to the houses; that was out of the question, as the people lived on farms, far apart from each other. The families were admitted in turn to the minister's bedroom, which had to answer the purpose of his study or vestry, and there they were seriously and affectionately exhorted, advised, encouraged or rebuked as the case demanded.[11]

---

11.   ibid., pp. 12-14.

Murray was also able to fulfill his desire of actively supporting the cause of missions through his ministry career. Graaff-Reinet was located about 125 miles northwest of the coastal town of Port Elizabeth, along a main travel route leading to the inland regions above South Africa where missionaries were seeking to reach various tribal groups.

> English, Scotch, French and German missionaries found it not only convenient but most refreshing to rest themselves and their wearied oxen on the long journey between Port Elizabeth and the interior (or on their way back on a visit to Europe) at the Graaff-Reinet parsonage. Men and animals found room in the spacious house and yard, the outrooms affording lodging for a whole host of Bechuana or Basuto drivers and leaders of oxen. The abundance of fruit made it like an oasis in the desert to the missionary children. From the Paris Missionary Society a handsome timepiece was received, in acknowledgement of kindness shown to their missionaries.[12]

Over the years the Murray children met many missionaries in this way, including Scotland's two most prominent missionaries to Africa, Robert Moffat and his even more famous son-in-law, David Livingstone.[13] The children were especially fascinated to hear the 'sprightly' wives of the French missionaries talk so rapidly in an unfamiliar language.

Once every week or two Mrs Murray would pay an afternoon social call to one of her friends in town. After Maria's daughters got home from school around four o'clock, they would put on their Sunday dresses and bonnets and join their mother at the house where she was visiting. The Murray sons also went, if the family being visited had boys their same age, and the boys would romp together in the large garden.

On some holidays or other rare occasions father, mother and children would go for a walk and spend an afternoon in the grassy

---

12. ibid., p. 14.

13. The two oldest Murray boys, John and Andrew, were being educated in Europe when David Livingstone visited at Graaff-Reinet.

veldt with its scattered bushes and trees. Along the way they would sit down to enjoy the 'sixpennyworth of cakes' they had brought along as a special treat. Sometimes in the summer the entire family went to spend a week or a fortnight with their good friends, Mr and Mrs Barend Burger, in the Sneeuwberg, a forested mountain range north of Graaff-Reinet. There:

> The children enjoyed the pleasures of farm life to their heart's content, joining in the delight of harvesting, sheep shearing, fruit gathering, and sometimes spending an hour or two in the schoolroom, where an antiquated schoolmaster reigned supreme, and the town children had an opportunity of showing off their superior learning and accomplishments.[14]

But 'the grand holiday, *the* event in the lives of the family' was the visit once every five years to Cape Town for the meeting of the DRC Synod. Months of anticipation and weeks of preparation went into the trip. The horse wagon was cleaned and freshly painted. Kind elders or deacons loaned ten strong horses to the Murrays for the journey. The wagon was then outfitted with food, water, cooking utensils, bedding and a variety of other supplies needed for the ten-day, 500-mile trek each direction to and from Cape Town. A driver and coachman were hired for the journey, and usually the Murrays were accompanied by a church elder and his family in a separate wagon.

The family set out long before daylight most mornings and stopped for breakfast shortly after sunrise. At the nightly encampment in the veldt, each child gathered an armful of sticks to help in lighting the fire and preparing the meal. 'These outspans were just a series of picnics, brimful of enjoyment for the happy children.'[15] Some nights were spent at hospitable farmhouses but in the Karroo the family slept in and around the wagon. Morning and evening family worship were never missed, and an hour each morning and evening was devoted to singing. They used English

---

14. Neethling, *Unto Children's Children*, p. 68.
15. ibid., p. 69.

and Dutch hymnals as well as 'a little stock stored in the memory of what were called *Slaven Gezangen* [Slave Hymns], compiled for the use of native congregations; so simple and so sweet, they were loved most of all'.[16]

A few years before his death Andrew Murray, Jr, doubtless thinking of the blessed influence of his own parents, wrote in a memorandum addressed to the entire Murray family circle: 'A godly parentage is a priceless boon. Its blessing rests not only upon the children of the first generation, but has often been traced in many successive generations.'[17]

---

16.   ibid., p. 70.

17.   Douglas, *Andrew Murray and His Message*, p. 23.

2

EDUCATION IN SCOTLAND
1838–1845

Opportunities for young people to receive an advanced education were extremely limited in South Africa in the late 1830s. While there were around 100,000 Caucasians in Cape Colony in 1838, not more than twenty-three schools received any sort of government support. As the masters of those schools were paid as little as forty pounds per year, qualified teachers were unprocurable; instructors who offered their services could teach little more than 'the three Rs'. In some of the larger towns, including Graaff-Reinet, parents who desired a better education for their children than the village school could supply joined together to hire a teacher capable of instructing twenty-five students in Latin and mathematics. The parents paid such teachers a more generous annual salary of 120 pounds. Educational conditions were worst in the rural districts where the Boers (Dutch farmers) lived. 'Schoolmaster' was a term of reproach among the Boers because the only teachers available for their children were 'discharged soldiers, who tramped the country from farm to farm, but who were both intellectually and morally incompetent to impart even the most elementary instruction'.[1] There were only two institutions for higher education in the colony at that time and both were located in Cape Town.

Faced with such limited educational prospects for their two oldest sons, in 1838 Andrew and Maria Murray made the painful decision to send the boys to live with their uncle, Rev. John Murray, in Aberdeen, Scotland. There they would be able to obtain a proper

---

1. Du Plessis, *The Life of Andrew Murray*, p. 35.

education. The Murrays accompanied their sons to Port Elizabeth, from which they sailed for Scotland in July. The parting had to be an excruciating one, given the boys' tender ages of ten and twelve as well as the likelihood that parents and children would not see each other again for several years, if ever. Even more sadly, the Murrays' youngest daughter, Isabella, caught a cold on the journey to Port Elizabeth and died shortly thereafter at fourteen months of age.

During the voyage to Britain John and Andrew were entrusted to the care of Rev. and Mrs James Archbell, Wesleyan missionaries who were returning home on furlough. The boys arrived in Aberdeen that autumn. Rev. and Mrs John Murray had one son and three daughters. Years later one of those daughters, also named Isabella, provided recollections of Andrew and John's stay in her parents' home:

> He [Andrew] and his brother, when they arrived after a miserable voyage, were suffering from scurvy ... and I have always thought with pity of the dear little fellow being entered at the Grammar School the first morning after his arrival. But he was very happy there, and had a great teacher in Dr Melvin ... I cannot tell you anything remarkable of his early days with us. He was a bright, lovable boy, extremely obliging, and devoted to his brother John, to whom he owed much. John was studious and thoughtful beyond his years, and seemed weighted with a sense of responsibility, both on his own account and Andrew's. Strange to say, when both boys sat for the entrance examination at Marischal College, it was the younger boy, then only thirteen, who gained a bursary. One remarkable thing I can tell you which applies to both boys: with neither of them had their uncle and aunt even once to find fault during their eight years' stay in our house, and this was due, we believed, to incessant prayer for them in the Graaff-Reinet home. We, the younger members of the family, looked on them as brothers, and were broken-hearted when they left us.[2]

Despite a marked difference in temperament, Andrew and John were always the closest of companions. John, like his father, was

---

2.   ibid., p. 37. Andrew and John actually lived with their relatives in Scotland for not quite seven full years.

quiet, thoughtful, reserved and cautious in word and action. He was disciplined and studious. Andrew reflected his mother's bright, eager disposition. He was active, quick in thought and speech, and exuberant of spirit, though not in the extreme. Andrew the staid older brother would sometimes rebuke him, 'you should not laugh so much; it is not good to laugh so much.' Though less studious than John, Andrew had a retentive mind and was able to assimilate knowledge easily. Like his elder sibling, he was earnest and showed sensitivity to spiritual matters from an early age. Throughout life the brothers' relationship was marked by mutual affection, esteem and support.

In his first letter to his sons after their departure for Scotland, Rev. Andrew Murray provided words of fatherly encouragement and counsel:

> My Dear Boys – ... You may both depend on it, though you are out of our sight you are seldom out of mind. We have been as it were following [you] with our fervent prayers that the God of the ocean may have been your Protector and your Guide, and we cherish the strong confidence they shall have been heard and answered. We also trust that you have not forgotten to cry to this God, 'Thou art my Father, the Guide of my youth' [Jer. 3:4].
>
> You may sometimes think it hard that whilst so many young people you have known, and yet know, enjoy all the happiness of the paternal circle, you should have been sent so far from it. I trust, however, that you will ever remember that this has taken place for your own good. You know God has appointed me my station and my work here. You know also, had my affection for you so far swayed with me as to keep you here, you could never have seen or known the half of the good you are likely to see and know now. It will, however, under the blessing of God, depend much on yourselves whether or not the step we have taken shall be for your real benefit in this life and that which is to come. ...
>
> I rejoice to think that your uncle will not fail to put you in mind of these things. You must try to be always open and candid with him. You may think him sometimes rather too strict, but believe me he will always have your real good at heart. Do not then do or even plan anything you would not like him to know of. Whatever

school he may see meet to send you to, believe it is for your good. Try to keep as far up in your classes as you possibly can.[3]

Throughout their years in Scotland, Andrew and John kept up a regular if somewhat periodic correspondence with their parents and siblings back home in South Africa. It generally took a few to several months for a letter to make its way across the ocean. Rev. Murray's missive to his sons dated 5 March, 1840, reveals that the boys were doing well in school and that stirring spiritual developments were taking place in Scotland:

> My Dear Boys – Your long expected and very agreeable letter of the 7th November gave us all very great pleasure indeed. We were delighted to learn that John had gotten [academic] prizes, and that you, Andrew, stood so near to him. What gave me the greatest satisfaction was that you, John, seemed at least to take pleasure in communicating to us Andrew's respectable appearance in his classes. ...
>
> Nothing could afford me greater delight than to hear of those revivals of religion in the West of Scotland to which Andrew has alluded in your letter. It affords me joy to hear of any number of souls brought to Christ anywhere, and it would increase the joy to think, my dear Boys, that you, though young, begin to take some interest in such things. ...[4]

The primary human agent used of God in igniting the dramatic spiritual awakening then sweeping across Scotland was William Chalmers Burns. One month after Rev. Andrew Murray penned the above correspondence, even before his sons received it, Burns arrived in Aberdeen, where he ministered for several weeks. His ministry there was mightily used by God's Spirit to impact thousands of people, among them Andrew and John Murray.

Burns had graduated from the University of Aberdeen in 1834 at the age of nineteen and subsequently attended divinity school in Glasgow, completing his course of studies there early in 1839. His

3. ibid., pp. 37-8.
4. ibid., pp. 38-9.

public-speaking style was deliberate and wholly unadorned. But he possessed a deep voice of 'vast compass and power' and compelled a hearing by the intense earnestness of his appeals. He devoted much time to prayer and fasting and carried about with him an empowering sense of God's presence.

For years a number of evangelical Scottish ministers had been earnestly praying for a mighty moving of God's Spirit to bring widespread spiritual awakening to their communities and country. The dramatic answer to those prayers began to be manifested on Tuesday morning, 23 July, 1839, when Burns spoke to nearly 1,400 people who had crowded into his father's church in Kilsyth, a town of 3,000 inhabitants located twelve miles northeast of Glasgow. As he discoursed on the theme of 'the day of God's power' from Psalm 110:3:

> During the whole of the time that I was speaking, the people listened with the most solemn and riveted attention, and with many silent tears and inward groanings of the spirit; but at the last their feelings became too strong for all ordinary restraints, and broke forth simultaneously in weeping and wailing, tears and groans, intermingled with shouts of joy and praise from some of the people of God. The appearance of a great part of the people from the pulpit gave me an awfully vivid picture of the state of the ungodly in the day of Christ's coming to judgment. Some were screaming out in agony; others, and among these strong men, fell to the ground as if they had been dead; and such was the general commotion, that after repeating for some time the most free and urgent invitations of the Lord to sinners (as Isa. 55, Rev. 22:17), I was obliged to give out a psalm, which was soon joined in by a considerable number, our voices being mingled with the mourning groans of many prisoners sighing for deliverance.[5]

During the two weeks that followed:

> For some time all business in the town was suspended. Meetings for prayer and preaching of the gospel were held every successive

---

5. Michael McMullen, *God's Polished Arrow, William Chalmers Burns, Revival Preacher* (Fearn, Scotland: Christian Focus, 2000), p. 151.

night, both in the church and in the open-air. There were often thousands who gathered for these times of preaching. Crowds of inquirers flocked at every invitation to the vestry or manse to seek spiritual counsel from Burns or his assistants. Trains from Glasgow and other nearby towns brought thousands of curious and interested people, who swelled the numbers already touched. Prayer meetings for all ages sprang up everywhere in the village and the surrounding areas …[6]

In the months that followed, the mighty reviving work of God's Spirit rested on Burn's ministry efforts in Dundee and Perth, with hundreds of people coming to faith in Christ. For months Burns had received numerous invitations to come and preach in Aberdeen, and he was finally able to honor those requests early in April of 1840. His fruitful ministry there has been summarized as follows:

Sermons to densely crowded audiences in three several [separate] churches on each Lord's Day; prayer meetings in the morning and afternoon, and a public address in the evening of each weekday, with generally an additional hour of counsel, instruction and prayer, for those whose intense anxiety still detained them after the long service was over, with words by the wayside and conferences with inquirers and young disciples at all other available hours, constituted the daily history of his work … for weeks together.[7]

On the evening of 26 April Burns preached in the open air to an immense audience in Castle Street. As he spoke on the willingness of Jesus to save the chief of sinners from the example of the thief on the cross: 'I felt more of the divine presence than on any former occasion in Aberdeen, and labored to pull sinners out of the fire. The impression was very deep, many weeping, some screaming and one or two quite overpowered.'[8] At eight o'clock he adjourned the

---

6. ibid., p. 34.
7. ibid., pp. 50-1.
8. ibid., p. 179.

assembly to Rev. John Murray's North Church.[9] After the latter meeting was dismissed, 'a great many were so deeply moved' that Burns and Murray found themselves unable to get away. The two ministers both addressed the 400 people who had remained at the church before closing the meeting with prayer and singing.

Burns left Aberdeen on 1 May to minister in numerous other locations across the Scottish highlands during the months that followed. After returning to Aberdeen in mid-September, he again held large daily evangelistic meetings. On Thursday, 22 October, Burns related in his journal:

> In the evening I preached in Trinity Church at seven to a full church, from the Pharisee and the publican. The impression was solemn. At an after-meeting a great many remained, and the impression became deeper, many being in tears. We parted at ten, but as we were leaving the session-house many crowded round us, and one mill girl cried aloud, so that I had to return to the session-house with the concourse. The place was filled in a few moments, and almost all fell on their knees and began to pray to the Lord. I continued to pray and sing and speak with these until twelve o'clock, having frequently offered to let them go, but finding that they would not move, and feeling in my own soul that the Lord was indeed in the midst of us. This was the most glorious season, I think, that I have yet seen in Aberdeen. Many poor sinners lay weeping all the night on their knees in prayer, and some of the Lord's people present seemed to be filled with joy.[10]

Hundreds of 'mill girls', young women who worked in the city's numerous mills, attended Burns' meetings and came under pressing conviction. Untold numbers of them were brought to saving faith in Christ.

During his stays in Aberdeen, Burns was a frequent guest in Rev. John Murray's home. Andrew and John had the opportunity

---

9. After serving as the minister of Trinity Chapel-of-Ease for twelve years, John Murray had been called to pastor the North Church in 1828. He was fifty-six years of age at the time of William Burns' ministry in Aberdeen.

10. McMullen, *God's Polished Arrow, William Chalmers Burns*, p. 199.

to converse with the anointed evangelist about spiritual matters and to witness first-hand many of the stirring spiritual events then unfolding in Aberdeen. More than once Andrew was given the privilege of carrying the evangelist's Bible and cloak to church, a great honor for the twelve-year-old boy.

Despite those advantages, neither Andrew nor John was converted under Burns' ministry. Sometime after Burns left Aberdeen for Dundee in early December, both John and Andrew wrote the evangelist. Burns' earnest written reply, dated 13 January, 1841, was addressed to John but intended also for Andrew:

My Dear Friend – I was happy to receive your interesting letter, and I have been attempting in the all-prevailing name of Jesus to commend your soul in its present affecting case to the infinitely merciful and gracious Jehovah. Do not, I beseech you, give way to the secret thought that you are excusable in remaining in your present unrenewed state, or that there is the smallest possible hope of your being saved unless you are really born of the Holy Spirit, and reconciled to the Holy Jehovah by the atoning blood of His only-begotten Son. Search your heart, my dear fellow-sinner, and I am sure that you will find something which you are refusing to let go at the command of God, and look upon this secret reserve in your surrender to Him as the reason on account of which He seems for a time to overlook your case. He is a God of infinite holiness, and cannot look upon iniquity. If we regard iniquity in our heart the Lord will not hear us. But if you are coming in sincerity of heart to Him through Jesus Christ, you will find Him to be a God of infinite mercy and loving-kindness, delighting in mercy and having no pleasure in the death of the sinner. Do not doubt, as your own wicked heart, under the power of Satan, would tempt you to do, that there is mercy for you if you will not willingly harden your heart against Jehovah's voice of authority and love. He will make Himself known to you in good time. Wait on Him. I can testify this to you from my own experience. Often do I think that God has forgotten me, but I find that afterwards He answers prayers which I have forgotten. Oh! dear friend, be not tempted to put off to a more convenient season your entire consecration to Emmanuel. You are enjoying in Jehovah's infinite and most undeserved mercy a convenient season at present; oh! improve it, lest the great God should be provoked and swear in His wrath, 'You shall not enter into my rest.' I will continue to pray for you, and I have hope in the Lord that I may be heard for His own glory. Jesus' service and His presence are indeed sweet.

Burns closed the letter: 'P.S. – Show this to Andrew, whom it may also suit. I got his letter and shall answer it afterwards if the Lord will. Write me again.'[11]

That same year, 1841, Andrew and John took the entrance examination and were admitted to Marischal College, their Uncle John's alma mater. Andrew, then age thirteen, did well enough on the exam to receive a scholarship. That September the boys wrote their father, asking his guidance with regard to what profession they ought to consider. In his letter of response written the following January, the father spoke of a variety of possibilities:

> I should not like, after going from Graaff-Reinet to Aberdeen and to College, to learn a business or trade I could have learned as well at the Cape of Good Hope. I should never wish you to think of the law, as our Bench and Bar and notaries are of such principles and morals, that I should tremble for any contact with them. Should you feel inclined to turn your attention to theology or medicine or mercantile pursuits, I have no doubt there will always be openings at the Cape, as well as at other places. If I were in your circumstances I should cast an eye towards the Indian Missions; there is something *there* worthy of the ambitions of great minds. But even promoting the moral and religious improvement of the rising generation [as teachers] is something more worthy of having obtained a liberal education than turning the attention to any common handicraft.[12]

Andrew and John were always interested to receive the latest news about family members and other acquaintances back home. They not infrequently wrote their father with various questions

---

11.   Du Plessis, *The Life of Andrew Murray*, pp. 42-3.

12.   Neethling, *Unto Children's Children*, pp. 21-2.

they had about their homeland, such as: which histories of South Africa he most recommended they read; Church-State relations in Cape Colony; the polity of the Dutch Reformed Church in South Africa. Conversely, Andrew and John kept their family members informed not only about their personal activities and well-being but also concerning significant religious, ecclesiastical and educational developments in Scotland. The boys sent choice spiritual books they thought their family members would enjoy reading and supplied their father with the latest written reports of Church of Scotland meetings and decisions as they became available.

For years a debate had been taking place between Moderates and Evangelicals within the Church of Scotland over the issues of patronage and the relationship between the Church and the State. Civil law had long authorized a system by which ministers were appointed to their parish charges by wealthy patrons. Evangelicals believed congregations had a scriptural right to select their own pastors and opposed State interference in various ecclesiastical matters. On 18 May, 1843, a Disruption took place within the Church of Scotland. As a result, approximately one-third of Scotland's ministers and parishioners withdrew from the Established Church to form the Free Church of Scotland. Those who affiliated with the Free Church had to make significant sacrifices in order to do so:

> Formidable and disagreeable practical consequences could be anticipated by any ministers who withdrew from the national Church. Government endowment to the extent of a hundred thousand pounds a year would be forfeited. Churches, manses, and schools would all be lost. Not one divinity hall would remain the property of the evangelicals, nor any of the overseas properties of the Foreign Missions which had been built solely by their effort. And not least, ministers would surrender all the advantages and prestige that the parish system had previously given them. The only influences strong enough to counterbalance these losses were the graces of devotion to Christ and faith in the Holy Spirit. ... The ultimate reason why so many ministers in

1843 signed away their earthly possessions, and why the common people followed in such numbers into the Free Church, is that this church was, in the words of one of her ministers, 'nursed in the bosom of religious revival'.[13]

Rev. John Murray led his congregation in seceding from the Established Church. They formed the Free North Church and erected the first Free Church edifice in Aberdeen.

Not long after the Disruption, Dr Thomas Chalmers, one of the foremost leaders among Scotland's evangelicals, visited and preached in Aberdeen. The Free Church there was then meeting in a tent that could hold 2,000 people. Two hours before Chalmers was to preach, the tent was already crowded and thousands more had gathered outside it. The intended service was moved into the open air. Chalmers preached to an audience variously estimated between 6,000 and 10,000 people, 'by whom he was completely heard'. Andrew and John Murray were almost certainly among those listening on that occasion.

That 20 October the boys' father wrote them an earnest letter concerning their need of salvation:

> What John wrote me, at my repeated request, on that most important subject of personal religion, on the whole pleased me much, as showing a state of mind, although not yet sufficiently engaged in the pursuit of salvation as the one thing needful, nevertheless, I trust, candid and at times inquiring. I am well aware, my dear boys, that neither you nor I can ever change the heart; but let me entreat you *both*, with all the intense affection of a Christian clergyman and a loving father, to pray daily that God may in mercy be pleased to do so by His Holy Spirit. Many distinguished students have been taken away by death in the midst of their literary and scientific pursuits. And although I trust God will spare you long to be useful in the world, yet should He take one or other of you away in youth, the consolation of the bleeding hearts of parents would not be that you had excelled in human

13. Iain H. Murray, *A Scottish Christian Heritage* (Edinburgh: Banner of Truth, 2006), p. 110.

aquirements, however important in themselves, but that there was reason to believe that you died in the Lord.[14]

The summer of 1844 found the two Murray brothers studying Hebrew under their uncle's tutelage. Andrew was also taking a botany class, part of which entailed lengthy walking field trips (some as long as thirty miles!) each Saturday to observe and collect plant specimens.

On 1 August Rev. Andrew Murray, knowing that his sons were entering their final year of college, again wrote them about their choice of a profession. This time his remarks were more directive and anxious than had been the case two and a half years earlier:

Young men ought to be decided on that subject before they have nearly finished their course at college. I wrote to you on the 11th April on the subject, expressing my desire, should the Lord incline your hearts that way, that you should devote yourselves to His service and glory first, and then devote yourselves to the service of the Sanctuary. As you have not only received said letter before this time, but I trust have also answered it, I am looking out with intense interest, as you may well conceive, to see what that answer may be. As I am daily entreating God to guide, direct and bless you, I feel a strong confidence that you have not been sent from Africa to Europe to obtain a liberal education, but for some truly worthy purpose.

... I trust you will see not to disappoint our expectations, and enter on avocations you might equally well have acquired here, without having ever left our shores. ... I shall, however, endeavor to leave the matter in His hands who has thus far led us on. You will make the matter a subject of prayerful consideration.[15]

In that same letter Rev. Murray also returned to the subject of their salvation:

Every parent wishes to see his family getting on, as it is termed, but what unspeakable joy for the heart of a Christian parent to have

---

14.   Neethling, *Unto Children's Children*, p. 23-4.

15.   ibid., pp. 24-5.

good ground for believing that his children shall have an eternal inheritance in Heaven! Oh! when may I through the free grace of God have this soul's joy with respect to you both? Do not think I am needlessly anxious. Every letter I write to you may be the last you may receive from me. One of our nearest neighbors spoke to me in tolerable health on Monday, and died on Tuesday ... This is a digression, but with such warnings we ought to live and act, as dying creatures.[16]

Before that correspondence reached Aberdeen, Andrew had written to inform his father that he had decided to devote his life to pastoral ministry. After receiving that desired intelligence on 1 November, Rev. Murray immediately wrote back to his son:

My Dear Andrew – I have been favored this morning with yours of the 7th of September, and am surprised at having received it so soon. ... I have now to congratulate you on your choice of a profession, and rejoice that the Lord has been pleased to incline your heart the way He has done. I trust, however, my dear Boy, that you have given your heart to Jesus Christ, to be His now and His for ever, to follow Him through good and through bad report.

The service in the Church in South Africa does not promise you much wealth nor ease in this world, but a field of usefulness as extensive as you could desire amongst a kind and indulgent people. I may now mention for your encouragement that I have for upwards of twenty-two years enjoyed much happiness in the work, and, I humbly trust, through the blessing of God have had some success in the same.[17]

The more reflective John was somewhat slower in deciding to become a minister. He needed to work through 'conscientious scruples' and 'fears' related to preparing for 'so sacred an office'. But by April of 1845 his parents had received the pleasing news that he, too, intended to prepare for the ministry. Early that same

---

16. ibid., pp. 25-6.
17. Du Plessis, *The Life of Andrew Murray*, p. 52.

month Andrew and John graduated from Marischal College with the Master of Arts degree. Andrew was then not quite seventeen-years-old. John graduated as salutatorian of their class.

3

THEOLOGICAL TRAINING IN HOLLAND
1845–1848

Andrew and John Murray had decided to pursue their theological education at the Academy of Utrecht in Holland. Having been away from South Africa for seven years, they no longer spoke Dutch proficiently. By studying in Holland they would be able to increase their facility in Dutch, which they would use in ministry when they returned to Cape Colony. Their father again wrote them a letter of practical and pastoral advice:

> At Utrecht especially you can get two rooms, furnished, at a moderate rate, also your dinner sent from an eating-house, and the person who hires the rooms provides breakfast and supper, and brushes clothes, shoes, etc. ...
>
> You may soon hear sentiments broached among the students, and even by professors, on theological subjects which may startle you, but be cautious in receiving them, by whatever names or number of names they may be supported. Try to act like the noble Bereans (Acts 17:11). By studying your Bibles and your own hearts I doubt not, under the guidance of the blessed Spirit, you will be led into all truth. One temptation you will be exposed to through companionship is the use of Hollands (alias gin) and water, and smoking tobacco or cigars. Do resist both these abominable customs. If necessary at any time, entertain your friends with tea or coffee, which are both excellent in Holland. Do not be afraid to be singular in such things. ...
>
> Whatever books may be recommended to you, be sure not to neglect the study of the Holy Scriptures. This must be a daily

exercise, and must be attended to with humility and much prayer for the guidance of the Holy Spirit.[1]

Upon arriving in Holland some time during the summer of 1845 the Murray brothers soon discovered that the Dutch Reformed Church there was characterized by 'tepid orthodoxy and chill rationalism'.[2] Pastors and theology professors formally subscribed to the historic formularies of the DRC – the Netherlands Confession, the Heidelberg Catechism and the Canons of the Synod of Dort. But most of those spiritual leaders had largely discarded evangelical doctrine. Theological broadmindedness was the order and boast of the day.

More than twenty years before Andrew and John Murray arrived in Holland, an evangelical revival movement sprang up there which was known by its French name, *Reveil*. That movement originated in literary rather than ecclesiastical circles and was largely confined to the aristocratic and upper middle classes. Willem Bilderdijk, the foremost Dutch poet of the nineteenth century, and his pupils Izaak da Costa and Abraham Capadose, both Jewish converts to Christianity, led the movement in Holland.

Under the influence of the Reveil, five like-minded students at the Academy of Utrecht had banded together in 1843 to form a society known as *Sechor Dabar* (a Hebrew phrase meaning 'Remember the Word'). Their stated purpose was 'to promote the study of the subjects required for the ministerial calling in the spirit of the Revival'. One of those students, N.H. de Graaf, recorded his first meeting of the Murray brothers shortly after their arrival in Utrecht:

> A fair was being held in Utrecht, and it was an excessively busy time. And yet Utrecht was lonely, for the members of our circle were for the most part absent from town. At the house of Madame van Twijll van Serooskerken at the extremity of the new canal, near the plantation, Dr [Abraham] Capadose was to hold a reading. I proceeded thither from my home in Booth Street. Arrived at

---

1. Du Plessis, *The Life of Andrew Murray*, p. 54.
2. ibid., p. 59.

St Jan's Churchyard, I saw two youths in somewhat strange garb walking ahead of me. Their countenances were cheerful, their demeanor unassuming. Was it possible that the two youthful strangers were visiting Utrecht to view the fair? That would be a pity. But no, they walked straight on ... along the new canal, yes, to the very end, and actually entered the house that was also my destination. There, at the entrance to the rooms, I found P.A. van Toorenenbergen [another member of *Sechor Dabar*] talking to them in Latin. He introduced me to the two strangers. They were John and Andrew Murray, newly arrived from Aberdeen, in order to study here and become ministers at the Cape. What a surprise! No fair-trippers, then, but Cape brethren with Scotch blood. From that evening up till now, and for ever, we became friends and brothers.[3]

The following Sunday evening the Murrays joined the members of *Sechor Dabar* at van Toorenenbergen's rented rooms for tea and 'mutual edification'. De Graaf later related:

Discussion was carried on in Latin, for the Murrays spoke only English and very imperfect Dutch, though John assured us, 'As ik jong was, ik sprak de Hollandsch as de jongeling van de straat' (When I was young I spoke the Dutch as the youth of the street). The reading and discussion of a portion of Scripture was in Latin as well, likewise the prayer. Whether the late Cicero and our still living Professor Bouman would have found our Latin classically pure, or even intelligible and endurable, is open to doubt. But it was sufficient that we understood each other.[4]

The members of *Sechor Dabar* took turns hosting their weekly evening meeting. The first three hours of each meeting were devoted to the study and discussion of theological topics. Since nearly all university lectures at that time were delivered in Latin, the society decided to employ that language in its formal discussions as well. Beginning at nine o'clock, the students took turns presenting

---

3. ibid., p. 56.
4. ibid., pp. 56-7.

'improvisations and orations'. Their formal study session completed, they then spent the final two hours of the evening enjoying a simple meal and informal conversation together.

Both in an effort to economize and to set what they considered to be a good example to others, the members of *Sechor Dabar* determined to avoid wine and other liquors, and to drink only coffee, tea and hot chocolate at their gatherings. This decision gained them the ridicule of their fellow students who promptly dubbed their group the 'Chocolate Club', the 'Prayer Club' and the 'pious circle'. Students refused to sit by them at lectures or to associate with them outside the classroom.

Their professors also seemed prejudiced against them, viewing them as too decided and fanatical. Early in John Murray's time at Utrecht, one of his professors advised him 'not to allow the *Sechor Dabar* society to gain too great an influence over him, lest he should expose himself to the danger of fanaticism'.[5] It was customary for the professors occasionally to invite students who had achieved the status of Candidates of Theology to present a popular lecture under the auspices of the Netherlands Bible Society. The honor of such an invitation was never extended to any member of their conservative group.

Some time during his first autumn at Utrecht, Andrew Murray experienced a personal spiritual transformation that he ever afterwards called his conversion. He later testified that he could point to the very house, room and date when his great change took place. In a letter dated 14 November, 1845, he informed his parents of his spiritual rebirth:

My Dear Parents – It was with very great pleasure that I today … received yours of 15th August, containing the announcement of the birth of another brother.[6] And equal, I am sure, will be your delight when I tell you that I can communicate to you far gladder

5. ibid., p. 62.

6. This sibling was named George. He bore the same name as his brother who, at age six, had died of croup and measles not long before. Since Andrew and John had left their parents' home in 1838 three other siblings had been born:

tidings, over which angels have rejoiced, that your son has been born again. ...

When I now look back to see how I have been brought to where I now am, I must acknowledge that I see nothing. 'He hath brought the blind by a way that he knew not, and led him in a path that he hath not known' [Isa. 42:16]. For the last two or three years there has been a process going on, a continual interchange of seasons of seriousness and then forgetfulness, and then again of seriousness soon after. ... But after I came to Holland I think I was led to pray in earnest; more I cannot tell, for I know it not. 'Whereas I was blind, now I see' [John 9:25]. I was long troubled with the idea that I must have some deep sight of my sins before I could be converted, and though I cannot yet say that I have had anything of that deep special sight into the guiltiness of sin which many people appear to have, yet I trust, and at present I feel as if I could say, I am confident that as a sinner I have been led to cast myself on Christ.

What can I say now, my dear Parents, but call on you to praise the Lord with me? ... At present I am in a peaceful state. I cannot say that I have had any seasons of special joy, but I think that I enjoy a *true* confidence in God.[7]

Several months later, on the eve of his eighteenth birthday, Murray again wrote his parents:

Tomorrow will close a year which is certainly the most eventful in my life, a year in which I have been made to experience most abundantly that God is good to the soul that seeketh Him. And oh! what goodness it is when He Himself implants in us the desire of seeking while we are enemies. I rather think that when I last wrote I gave an account of what I believed was my conversion, and, God be thanked, I still believe that it was His work. Since the letter I cannot say that I have always had as much enjoyment as before it, but still there has been much joy in the Lord. Though, alas! there has also been much sin. ... But through grace I have always been enabled to trust in Him who has begun the good work in me, and

---

Isabella (1839, named after her sister who died the previous year), Catherine (1841) and James (1843).

7. Du Plessis, *The Life of Andrew Murray*, pp. 64-5.

to believe that He will also perform what He has, out of His free love before I was born, begun. Oh! that I might receive grace to walk more holy before Him.[8]

In the same letter Andrew provided an update of his and John's several activities with *Sechor Dabar*:

As to our external circumstances here, they are very much the same. We still associate only with our own circle of friends. ... We meet at present every Friday evening for work from 5½ till 10, and then sup together from 10 till 12 – very plainly, of course, bread and butter, cheese, and some sort of coffee. On Wednesdays we meet in a church for oratory, when one delivers a sermon, another speaks extempore, and a third reads a piece of poetry – all, of course, to accustom us a little to the work in which we expect and hope to be engaged. On Sabbath evenings we meet together for reading, singing and prayer, when one generally speaks over a chapter. We have also begun a missionary society to meet twice a month for communicating missionary intelligence, and prayer for the extension of the kingdom of our God and His Christ; ... Most of us also generally spend the Sabbath afternoon in visiting the wretched districts of the town and speaking to the people about their souls, and in teaching a few of their children in our rooms.[9]

In a letter John Murray penned to his parents that September, 1846, he gave full expression to the concerns he had about theological and moral conditions in Holland's churches and universities:

But about this country – I am sure if the people [of Cape Colony] in general, and the ministers too, knew of the doctrines taught here, at Leyden and Groningen particularly, of the contempt with which the most influential ministers (as those of large towns) talk of Dordt orthodoxy, of their alteration of the words of the formulas, for instance that of baptism, they would have done with the relations they maintain with this country. Above all, I forgot to mention the

---

8.   ibid., p. 66.
9.   ibid., pp. 66-7.

scandalous morals of the theological students. I solemnly assure you the name of God is profaned in the theological classrooms, even by the orthodox and respectable students; nor do they lose character by being intoxicated now and then on some festive occasion, provided only it do not take place immediately before the examination for license. And in this I take no notice of grosser offences of which a few are guilty, who though destitute of character and notorious, still become ministers when they are ready.[10]

To that same missive, Andrew added a brief report of their developing missionary endeavors:

I rather think that we also told you of a missionary society that we had erected, to read together a few missionary periodicals in English and German. We are now going to publish a missionary periodical in Dutch – sixteen pages monthly – consisting of extracts regarding the progress of the work of God throughout the whole world. The reason that we (there are eight of us) are going to do this is, that Holland is lamentably deficient in interest in the missionary work, and the two existing periodicals are rather spiritless, and confine themselves to rather small fields.[11]

A third student from the Cape, J.H. (Jan) Neethling, arrived at Utrecht in 1846, to be joined by an additional pair, Nicolaas Hofmeyr and Hendrik Faure, the following year. Each of these was warmly welcomed into *Sechor Dabar*. As several other South African students came to Utrecht in the years that followed, they found in that society an ardent and supportive evangelical fellowship to help nurture their faith. *Sechor Dabar* played a significant role in those students returning to Cape Colony with their evangelical convictions intact and strengthened rather than weakened or shattered.

Some time earlier Andrew Murray had written his father about the possibility of continuing his studies at a more evangelical school in Halle, Germany, following his time at Utrecht. He anticipated

---

10.   ibid., p. 68.
11.   ibid., p. 69.

graduating from the Academy of Utrecht at age twenty, which was two years younger than the mandatory age to be ordained as a minister. He eventually received an unfavorable but not entirely definite response from his father to that proposal. Rev. Murray acknowledged that a probationer normally could not be ordained until twenty-two years of age. But in suggesting that Andrew return to South Africa rather than going to Germany, Rev. Murray assured him, 'There are spheres of usefulness here from the time one arrives, and one is gaining experience before he has all the responsibility of a congregation.'[12]

During one of their vacation periods from school the two Murray brothers greatly enjoyed taking an extended walking tour along the Rhine River. There they met a Pastor Blumhardt whose 'remarkable' ministry of exorcisms and faith healings had sparked a significant revival in the Rhenish provinces of western Germany. This brief association may well have played a part in developing the convictions that Andrew later came to espouse concerning the ongoing operation of God's miraculous healing powers.

By the early spring of 1848 Andrew and John were eagerly awaiting further guidance from their father so they could better determine what their next step, following graduation and ordination to ministry, should be. Andrew's 18 March letter to his parents indicates his desire to remain in Europe for an additional year of study but also shows his trust in leaving the outcome of that decision in the Lord's hands:

> You can conceive that we are anxiously waiting for the letters from home which shall decide the question as to my next year. Although I still feel the necessity of staying, yet I can say that I am prepared for whatever shall be good, trusting that that gracious Father will guide us now, as He has hitherto so kindly led us, and believing that He knows what is best for His Church in that part of the vineyard where I desire to labor. My desire is to place myself in His hands, and He can use me even, although I have not the advantage of an additional year's stay in Europe – perhaps even better than if

---

12.   ibid., pp. 69-70.

I had such an additional stock of human wisdom, which so often proves nothing else than an obstruction to God's way.[13]

Andrew and John were obviously beholden to their father's opinions concerning their educational and vocational decisions. Their sister Maria later explained of Andrew Murray, Sr's influence over his children, even after his sons had become young adults:

Their father's word was law; from his decision there was no appeal; his wisdom was never questioned. It was almost curious to see the reverence with which the young men, after years of study in Europe, and themselves ministers, would bow to their father's decision in every matter where they had asked his advice.[14]

It was customary for DRC ministerial candidates intending to minister abroad to be ordained before setting out for their appointed spheres of service. This ordination was conferred by a group of ministers who formed The Committee for the Interests of Protestant Churches in the East and West Indies. The ordaining council was known more familiarly as The Hague Committee, due to its place of meeting. On Andrew's twentieth birthday, 8 May, 1848, both he and John were examined and duly ordained to the Christian ministry in South Africa. Perhaps due to the pressing need for more ministers in Cape Colony, the committee made an exception in approving Andrew, though he was under the regulation age for ordination.

Sunday 3 July, was Andrew and John's final day in Utrecht. After attending a church service that morning they met with thirteen other members of *Sechor Dabar* in the afternoon to share the Lord's Supper together before parting. At seven o'clock that evening they gathered in the home of N.H. de Graaf's father for a further time of singing, Scripture reading, fellowship and prayer. De Graaf related of the close of the meeting:

---

13.   ibid., pp. 70-1.

14.   Neethling, *Unto Children's Children*, p. 16.

We then knelt down, and I had the privilege of leading in prayer, in which I expressed the gratitude which filled the hearts of us all for the inexpressibly precious blessings we had enjoyed, especially during the past three years ... We then united in singing Psalm 134, standing close round John and Andrew. We wept and embraced the brothers so dearly beloved. John then extended his hands over our heads: 'The grace of our Lord Jesus Christ, the love of God and the communion of the Holy Spirit be with you all. Amen.'[15]

A faithful housemaid who always helped serve the *Sechor Dabar* members when they met at de Graaf's home stood at the front door as Andrew and John prepared to leave that evening. When they attempted to give her a suitable coin as a tip, she protested, 'But, gentlemen, am I the only one from whom you part this evening like a stranger?'

'No, no,' they hastened to respond, 'we look upon you as no stranger, and part from you as a sister.'

'Well then, a sister receives no tip,' she insisted and gave them back the coin.

From Holland the brothers returned to Scotland for a farewell visit to their Uncle John and his family. Rev. Murray invited both his nephews to preach at his church with the result that: 'The family and congregation were divided in opinion as to which of the "twa laddies" was the grander preacher.'[16]

---

15. Du Plessis, *The Life of Andrew Murray*, p. 73.

16. Douglas, *Andrew Murray and His Message*, p. 45.

4

FRONTIER MINISTER
1848–1849

Andrew and John Murray arrived at Cape Town, South Africa, some time during the first half of November, 1848, having been away from their homeland for a decade. They were disappointed that their parents had not been able to travel from Graaff-Reinet to meet them upon their arrival in Cape Town, a prospect with which they had been delighting themselves. But they did receive a hearty welcome from their maternal grandparents[1] who still resided in Cape Town and from their mother's brother, Rev. George William Stegmann. Uncle William, a man of marked piety and evangelical fervor, was then pastoring the 'colored'[2] congregation that worshiped at St Stephen's Church on Bree Street.

The arrival of the two young ministers from Europe created something of a stir, not only in Cape Town but throughout the colony. Their arrival was noted in the secular press, reported in church magazines and discussed in ecclesiastical circles across the country. In addition, as was customary of all newly-arrived ministers at that time, they were both invited to preach at Cape Town's historic Groote Kerk (Great Church), the colony's oldest church. Of this attention Andrew commented in a letter to his parents: 'Especially is the interest which the people of God take in us quite humbling, when I think how little they really know what I am.'[3]

---

1. Johan Stegmann had remarried a number of years earlier.
2. 'Colored' was the common South African designation of individuals of mixed European ('white') and African ('black') or Asian ancestry.
3. Du Plessis, *The Life of Andrew Murray*, p. 75.

The Groote Kerk was a 'large, airy, neat' edifice. Its auditorium could seat 3,000 and possessed a high vaulted ceiling unsupported by pillars. Andrew's sermon at Groote Kerk was based on 1 Corinthians 1:23, 'We preach Christ crucified'. 'But I feel it very difficult not to preach myself,' Andrew admitted to his parents, 'by attending too much to beauty of thought and language, and feeling too little that God alone can teach me to preach.'[4]

While the Murray brothers were in Cape Town they met with the Governor, Sir Harry Smith, who at that time made all ecclesiastical appointments. 'You are the elder,' he said to John, 'and therefore I shall give you the charge of Burgersdorp.' Turning to Andrew, he stated, 'And as you are the younger, I am afraid I shall have to send you to Bloemfontein.' Burgersdorp lay just over 160 miles north-east of Graaff-Reinet, but still within the outer boundary of Cape Colony. Bloemfontein, however, was located some 170 miles north of Burgersdorp, outside the colony in the remote territory beyond the Orange River. Andrew would serve as the first settled minister to the voortrekkers (Dutch pioneers) who lived in that vast region which comprised nearly 50,000 square miles, approximately one-third the size of Cape Colony.

Early in December Andrew and John embarked from Cape Town for Algoa Bay where they were met by their father. Proceeding immediately to Graaff-Reinet, they had a joyful reunion with their mother and siblings, three of whom they had never seen before. Andrew's disposition was so happy and playful that his younger brothers and sisters exclaimed, 'Is Brother Andrew a minister? That can never be. He's just like one of us!'

The Sunday after their arrival back home, Andrew and John preached in their father's pulpit. At the first communion service following their return, the three Rev. Murrays took turns administering the elements to the communicants seated at tables.

> When it was Andrew's turn to dispense the elements and deliver the customary brief address, he rose, closed his eyes, and for some

---

4. ibid., p. 76.

moments seemed lost in meditation and prayer. An almost painful silence filled the building, and a hush of deep solemnity fell upon the great assemblage. When at length the youth – for he was little more than a youth – opened his mouth, the words which he uttered were so evidently sincere, so intense and uplifting, that those who heard him, and had last seen him as a boy of ten, could scarce restrain their tears.[5]

Andrew and John's sister, Maria, later recorded of that special period for their reunited family:

Those were five happy months, when Father, Mother, and twelve children 'went to the house of God in company' [Ps. 55:14]. ... The two sons seemed to have brought a heavenly influence with them, so that when this happy time was drawing to a close, and our hearts were heavy at the thought of our brothers leaving us, Andrew said: 'What! Would you have us make a little heaven here for ourselves, and never want to leave it for another?'[6]

During the 1830s and 1840s, in what became known as the Great Trek, thousands of Boers (Dutch farmers) and their families migrated from Cape Colony to the immense regions north of the Orange and Vaal Rivers.[7] While they did so for a variety of reasons, their primary motivation appears to have been a desire to live where they could be free from British rule, which they found irksome. By the middle of the century, between 10,000 and 12,000 voortrekkers had settled between the Orange and Vaal while an additional 7,000 to 10,000 lived further north in the Transvaal.

When conflicts developed between Boers and two tribes (Basutos to the east and Griquas to the west) in the southern half of the region between the Orange and Vaal, the British government determined to establish its rule over the disputed territory. The

---

5. ibid., p. 77.

6. Neethling, *Unto Children's Children*, p. 87.

7. The following summary is taken from du Plessis, *The Life of Andrew Murray*, pp. 81-84.

township of Bloemfontein was founded in 1846. A British fort was built there under the command of Major Henry Douglas Warden. He was given the unenviable tasks of restraining tribal aggression and conciliating the immigrants.

In 1848 Cape Colony Governor Sir Harry Smith proclaimed Britain's authority over the entire region between the Orange and Vaal, naming the annexed territory the Orange River Sovereignty. Under the command of their celebrated leader Andries Pretorius,[8] the Boers promptly rebelled. They forced Major Warden and his small garrison out of Bloemfontein and demanded that Britain's proclamation of sovereignty over the region be withdrawn. Sir Harry Smith immediately responded by bringing a strong body of troops to deal with the uprising.'A brief but sharp engagement' took place on 29 August in which the Boers were defeated. Pretorius was forced to flee beyond the Vaal, and Major Warden reoccupied Bloemfontein with a considerably larger force of soldiers.

Barely eight months later Andrew Murray began his ministry at Bloemfontein. On 23 April, 1849, the day after preaching a farewell sermon to the Graaff-Reinet congregation, he set out for his new charge. The Bloemfontein congregation had sent a deacon (who was also named Pretorius) with a 'capacious' wagon drawn by a team of powerful horses, to transport the young minister the nearly 270 miles to his new home. As a demonstration of esteem, fifty young men on horseback from Graaff-Reinet escorted the wagon a considerable distance the first day of the journey.

Andrew Murray, Sr, accompanied his son on this journey in order to introduce him to the congregations north of the Orange River. The following Sunday, 29 April was spent at Zendelingsfontein on the Riet River, some 200 miles north of Graaff-Reinet and fourteen miles from the present-day town of Fauresmith. Rev. Murray, Sr, and another minister had established a congregation at

---

8. In just one decade's time, Andries Pretorius had become a hero and gained legendary status among the Boers by courageously leading them in three military confrontations with native tribes and the British. Many Boers on both sides of the Vaal River viewed him as their commandant-general.

Zendelingsfontein about a year and a half earlier while serving as the first-ever commission sent out by the Colony's Dutch Reformed Synod to minister to immigrant Boers beyond the Orange and Vaal Rivers.

From Zendelingsfontein the Murrays and Deacon Pretorius journeyed north-east to Bloemfontein. That town would prove to be Andrew Murray, Jr's home base for the next eleven years. When he first arrived at Bloemfontein it was 'little more than a straggling hamlet, with houses scattered irregularly on both sides of a streamlet known as Bloemspruit'.[9] The Rev. J.J. Freeman, a representative of the London Missionary Society who passed through the region early the following year (1850), left this further description of the town:

> Bloemfontein, the seat of the Government in this Sovereignty, has nothing to recommend it in its natural features. The scenery is extremely uninteresting. There is no wood and little water. ... The foundation of a church is laid. A courthouse and a prison exist. There are about forty or fifty tolerable houses built. There are a few stores and shops, a marketplace with a bell to announce the time when sales take place, and a clerk of the market appointed. A good well has been sunk, and at forty feet depth a supply of water is found ... Here is also a fortress, a few cannon, part of a regiment, a major, one hundred Cape Mounted Rifles [cavalrymen], and barracks, as the usual material of an improving community. There is also a Government schoolhouse, but at the time of my visit without scholars or masters. Religious services are held there on Sunday. Mr Murray, son of the Dutch clergyman of Graaff-Reinet, has received the appointment to the new church. He diligently and laudably employs himself, during a great part of his time, in traveling among the immigrant farmers in the interior, and conducting religious services.[10]

Rev. Murray, Sr, installed his son as pastor of the Bloemfontein congregation on Sunday, 6 May, just three days before the new

---

9. Du Plessis, *The Life of Andrew Murray*, p. 92.

10. ibid., pp. 92-3.

minister's twenty-first birthday. At the installation service that morning Murray, Sr, preached from 2 Corinthians 6:1, 'We then, as workers together with him, beseech you also that ye receive not the grace of God in vain.' Murray, Jr, led the afternoon service, taking as his sermon text 1 Corinthians 1:23-24, 'But we preach Christ crucified ... Christ the power of God, and the wisdom of God.'

On the next two Sundays the Murrays ministered at Winburg and Rietpoort (soon to be settled as the new township of Smithfield). Winburg and Rietpoort were located, respectively, seventy miles north-east and ninety miles south of Bloemfontein. In addition to serving the congregation at Bloemfontein, Andrew Murray, Jr, would be the consulent (acting minister) of the adjoining parishes at Riet River (Fauresmith), Rietpoort and Winburg, until they were able to call their permanent pastors.

Saturday, 26 May, found the two Andrew Murrays at Burgersdorp, for the installation of John Murray as pastor of that congregation. The Burgersdorp congregation was made up of 'Doppers', members of a hyper-conservative sect in the Colony's DRC. Unlike most Cape Dutch, Doppers sang only Psalms and eschewed the use of organs in church. After a full weekend of ministry that included a communion observance, Andrew Murray, Sr, left Tuesday morning to return to his home at Graaff-Reinet while his namesake set out for Bloemfontein. Returning by the most direct route, the latter completed the 170-mile journey from Burgersdorp to Bloemfontein in just three days.

In a letter Murray wrote his brother John the middle of the following month, he related a great deal about his personal and ministry circumstances:

> I am still with Dr Drury, and am very comfortable, except that I am not always sure of my privacy, as his medicines stand in the room which I occupy. The churchwardens have now conditionally bought an erf [piece of property] and house for 400 pounds, which will be ready, it is hoped, in the course of a couple of months. It will be about one of the best houses in Bloemfontein, with three good rooms and pantry, and a large kitchen behind. I have gotten

my servant boy from Winburg, and he pleases very well indeed. ... I got a very good horse for ten pounds, but he has run away! ... For the present I have the use of one of Dr Drury's horses. My dinner I get sent me every day, at the very cheap rate of one pound per month, and though plain it has hitherto been very good. Almost everything can be got here, almost as cheaply as at Graaff-Reinet, so that as to externals I am very comfortable.

But to come to more important matters, you will be anxious to know something about the state of matters spiritual here. As to the Dutch congregation, ... last Sabbath I had a congregation of about seventy, and the preceding Sabbath of about 100. The former will, I suppose, be the average. I cannot describe what I felt on going for the first time into the schoolroom to commence my regular ministrations in the midst of this poor people. ...

On Sabbath afternoon I had an English congregation of about seventy. This cannot be taken as a criterion, as nearly half of the men are away with Major Warden. I feel much more difficulty as to the English than the Dutch congregation as to the preaching, and still more as to the pastoral work. There are only two Dutch families in the village, and some thirty respectable English, besides a number of low English. I hope soon to call on all the families. The officers are all unmarried, rather wild (very often drunk), and two of them are living openly with colored women. I trust that the Lord will give me special wisdom with regard to the English here. I hope next Saturday evening to begin a service for the blacks (there are about sixty of the Cape Corps here), at which there will of course also be an opportunity for the Dutch Boers to attend.

Mr [C.U.] Stuart [the resident magistrate] is very active in doing all he can to promote order here. He is very severe in court, some say by far too severe. He is very busy in improving Bloemfontein – making streets, furrows and bridges. He has four convicts at work, as well as a number of 'drunken ladies', who have to clean the streets from nine to twelve. We may very likely soon have a Teetotal Society here. Next week we hope to begin subscriptions for a library (English and Dutch). With our newspaper we know not how to do, as it would be difficult to get a printer down without being able to secure him a livelihood.[11]

---

11.   ibid., pp. 90-1.

Ten days later, on 24 June, a Sunday school ministry was inaugurated. Of this Murray wrote to his sister Maria in Graaff-Reinet:

> We began our Sabbath school, and had plenty of scholars but no teachers. Near this there is a place where all the Bushmen reside, and from there we had some two dozen grown-up people and as many children. Mr Stuart has been taking great interest in these Kafferfontein people, and when I rode out there with him last week, I invited them to come to church. Accordingly they came, headed by their chief in a cast-off blue coat. The elder ones I took [as a class]. It was really sad to see them. Some of the really old Bushmen could not understand a word of Dutch, and none of them knew much. I tried to make a beginning with teaching them some of the elements of Christian truth, and the first verse of the hymn ... 'God so loved the world'. In speaking of them Mr Stuart always says, 'He is able to save to the uttermost' [Heb. 7:25]. And why should we then despair? May the Lord give grace to work in faith. We have a great lack of teachers. Mr Stuart will most likely take the English Bible Class, with about twenty pupils; Dr Drury the English children who cannot read; and then we shall require one for a Dutch class, and another for the little native children.[12]

The vast plains of the Orange River Sovereignty, including those around Bloemfontein, teemed with a wide variety of game and wild animals: wildebeest, hartebeest, quagga, blesbok, springbok, ostriches, wild pigs and rabbits. Leopards, jackals, wolves and wild dogs were frequently encountered, even in broad daylight, and posed a considerable threat to farmers and their livestock. Lions, too, roamed in the immediate vicinity of the town, prompting Magistrate Stuart to decree that mail was not to be dispatched after 4 p.m. On more than one occasion officers of the garrison shot and killed a number of lions in the surrounding area.

Once while traveling to hold services at a location about seventy miles from Bloemfontein, Murray had to cross a wolf-infested plain, at a time when they were 'very fierce'. After fording a river, he dismounted to rest his horse. When the grazing animal heard

12.   ibid., p. 95.

a pack of wolves approaching, it spooked and ran off. Carrying his pack on his shoulders, Murray had to walk some twelve or fifteen miles to the nearest house. 'How did you do it?' the surprised farmer who lived there inquired.

'I knew I was in the path of duty,' Murray answered calmly, 'so prayed to God to keep me, and walked straight on. The wolves snapped at me but did not touch me.'[13]

Basutoland, to the east of Bloemfontein, continued to experience perpetual unrest due to constant border disputes and regular cattle-stealing raids. Tribal chiefs carried out such raids against white settlers and other tribes. They refused to accept new boundary lines to land which they had historically viewed as their own. Major Warden, with his few hundred soldiers, seemed practically powerless in enforcing order with powerful chiefs and their thousands of warriors. Of the troubled state of affairs on the Basuto border Murray wrote to his father on 27 June:

> From all accounts it appears that matters are wearing a very serious aspect among the Caffres [Kaffirs].[14] Moshesh and his people are very much dissatisfied with the [boundary] line which is making [forming], and declare that they cannot part with such a great piece of their country. It is feared that the disturbance between Moshesh and Sikonyella will give rise to a war between the former and the English. Moshesh has promised to deliver up the cattle taken by his people from Sikonyella within a fortnight, but nobody expects him to fulfill this promise. Major Warden had only about 130 men when dealing with him; they declare that they were very glad when they got away, as Moshesh had 15,000 men in the neighborhood – about 1,000 men on horseback and his own retinue. Of course the

---

13. Douglas, *Andrew Murray and His Message*, p. 54.

14. 'The term *Kafir* – sometimes *Kaffir* or *Caffre* – was used by Muslims to signify a "non-believer" or heathen. The Dutch … adopted this term and brought it to the Cape where it was used to denote heathen Africans. From the twentieth century onwards, it became a highly derogatory term' (Olea Nel, *South Africa's Forgotten Revival: The Story of the Cape's Great Awakening in 1860* [Longwood, FL: Xulon, 2008], pp. 195 and 200). Murray and his contemporaries did not use the term with a derogatory intent.

300 men comprising the garrison here will be able to do nothing against such an enemy, as the Basutos are known never to fight during the daytime. It is also said that great numbers of Zulus are at present marching to join Moshesh. The farmers from the Caledon River [between Bloemfontein and Basutoland] also say that they would not be astonished if the Caffres very soon attacked them there, as they refuse to have anything like a line.[15]

Around that same time Murray was able to return to preach and conduct pastoral visitation in the Riet River region and at Winburg. But his plans to conduct a series of services at Rietpoort (Smithfield) early in August needed to be postponed due to the continued tribal unrest in that vicinity. Murray explained to his family in an August letter:

... [T]here will be no sale of erven [land plots] and no service at Rietpoort. On Friday, the 27th July, the Korannas attacked Molitzani and Moshesh, took all the cattle of the former, and killed thirty-four of their people. Yesterday news was received that there has been another engagement near Platberg, in which a great many lives have been sacrificed. And from Smithfield Major Warden has received a letter stating that the Boers have been in several cases ordered across the Orange River by command of Moshesh.[16]

That August Murray was able to move into his parsonage in Bloemfontein, though only one room was completed. Just then he devoted considerable time and effort to catechizing and interviewing fifteen young people who had applied for church membership. For a full week he thoroughly examined them with regard to their knowledge of the Bible and the Catechism. He then interviewed each candidate personally, trying to ascertain his or her spiritual condition and reasons for wishing to be received as a church member. Finally, he and the congregation's two elders withdrew to collectively consider the spiritual attainments and status of each candidate. By

15.   Du Plessis, *The Life of Andrew Murray*, pp. 94-5.

16.   ibid., p. 97.

their own acknowledgement,' Murray afterward commented, 'they had not yet sought to believe in Christ; or else, while saying that they believed in Christ, their answers showed that they did not even know what they said.' In the end, 'with the full concurrence of both elders', only two of the candidates were accepted as members.[17]

Murray had hoped his brother John would be able to assist him in holding communion services at Bloemfontein that month. But likely due to the dangerous conditions that prevailed in the region, John was unable to come, so Murray fulfilled the considerable responsibility on his own. Communion observances involved extra preaching services and drew large crowds. Farmers who lived at a distance and who normally attended Sunday services only occasionally often made a point of participating in communion weekends. At Bloemfontein two preparatory services were held on Saturday, the Lord's Supper was observed Sunday morning and a concluding thanksgiving service was held that afternoon. The numerous communicants who received the elements Sunday morning were seated around six different sets of tables. Murray ministered to each set with an appropriate hymn and address. The school building was not large enough to accommodate the sizeable crowds that gathered for the services that weekend, so the services all needed to be held out of doors. Murray afterward recorded his gratitude that, though the wind blew strongly, he was able to conduct all the services without sensible strain or fatigue.

Murray and Magistrate Stuart ventured to Riet River for the laying of the foundation stone of that congregation's new church building on Sunday, 1 September. That parish consisted of 'at least 3,000 souls'. Stuart delivered 'a striking address' at the special ceremony while Murray conducted 'the religious services of the congregation'. After returning briefly to Bloemfontein, Murray continued on to Winburg. From there he ventured further east, making a circuit of nearly three hundred miles, in order to visit the recently-founded township of Harrismith as well as the locations where Kroonstad and Bethlehem would be established in future years.

---

17.   ibid., p. 98.

The beginning of October found Murray back in Bloemfontein, though only for a short time. He soon set out for Graaff-Reinet where a Presbytery meeting was to take place the middle of that month. During the fortnight he spent there he had the privilege of baptizing his infant sister, Helen, who had been born 22 September. By 11 November he had returned to Bloemfontein and was making plans for his first ministry venture across the Vaal. In just over six months since first arriving in Bloemfontein, Murray had traveled close to 2,000 miles in carrying out his various ministry responsibilities.

5

FIRST TRANSVAAL MINISTRY
1849–1850

Murray's first ministerial itineration north of the Vaal River lasted just over six weeks, from 7 December, 1849 to 22 January, 1850. During that time he traveled some 800 miles on horseback and by ox-drawn wagon. (Ox wagon travel, sometimes carried out with a span of eight oxen, proceeded at an achingly slow pace of just two miles per hour.) Murray conducted a total of thirty-seven services at six different locations. In addition, he baptized 567 children and interviewed well over 300 young people for church membership, 167 of whom were accepted.[1] It appears he was accompanied throughout much of this journey by three traveling companions, Deacon P. Coetzer, Deacon Caspar Kruger and Frans Schutte.

While Murray would wear a beard throughout most of his adult life, at this time he was still clean shaven and looked quite boyish. He was six feet tall and possessed a slender build. Murray, however, quickly gained the respect of the Transvaal Boers through his serious, confident demeanor, his overwhelming fervency and his willingness to sacrifice himself for their spiritual well-being. Some six decades later a Transvaal Christian would relate of Murray's earliest ministries there, 'The old people in the Transvaal used to tell the most wonderful tales about him, his power of endurance, his great earnestness in preaching, and how frightened people often were of him, though he looked a mere boy.'[2]

---

1. Du Plessis, *The Life of Andrew Murray*, p. 101.
2. Douglas, *Andrew Murray and His Message*, p. 256.

Douglas speaks of the intensity and gravity with which Murray ministered at that time:

> When preaching, so absorbed was he in his message that should he by his violent gestures knock down Bible and reading desk of the impromptu pulpit, he would not notice it. Solemn were the confirmation services when, ... before the final confirmation promise was made, he would lift his hand, and with deep emotion would adjure them not to reject the Savior, saying, 'If you do and promise falsely to be true to Christ, this hand will witness against you in the day of judgment.'[3]

Murray first arrived at the settlement that later came to be named Potchefstroom on the Mooi River approximately seventy-five miles southwest of present-day Johannesburg. He was received with 'the greatest friendliness and apparent confidence,'[4] though there had been doubts on the part of some that the Landdrost (chief magistrate of the district) would allow him to come for fear of British influence. (Such fear sprang from the fact that Murray had been appointed to his ministerial charge by Cape Colony's British Governor, and his salary was paid by the Colonial Treasurer.) Whatever concerns some Boers may have had about Murray were completely allayed through this initial visit. Everywhere he went during this ministry trip, he appears to have been readily received and deeply appreciated.

Of his preaching ministry that weekend he reported: 'The congregation was large, but I found it very difficult to fix their attention, evidently from their long separation from the means of grace. I trust that some impression was produced, if I may judge from their talking about the sermons.'[5] Monday he interviewed sixty-five youth for church membership, with thirty-two of them being approved.

From Potchefstroom Murray and his companions traveled three days north and west by ox wagon to the edge of the Morikwa

---

3.   ibid., p. 57.

4.   Du Plessis, *The Life of Andrew Murray*, p. 102.

5.   ibid.

district. Saturday morning and evening he led preparation services for communion which was then served the following morning, with around sixty individuals partaking. 'Many of these appeared to feel the solemnity of the occasion,' Murray related, 'while others, although I had tried to speak as plainly and faithfully as I could, gave too plain proofs that they came without the proper preparation. I trust, however, that the Lord was with some of us.'[6]

A number of people in the Morikwa area had been unsettled and misled by a group of extremists who called themselves the 'Jerusalem pilgrims'. They interpreted the ten kings allied with the beast of Revelation 17:12 as referring to the rulers of ten western European countries (Holland excepted!) of their own day. The would-be pilgrims were awaiting the Lord's summons, which they anticipated would come soon, to trek to Jerusalem.

On Wednesday, 19 December, Murray traveled from Morikwa to the home of one of his father's friends, Gert Kruger. Following that visit Murray wrote his father:

> Gert Kruger says he considers either John or myself their rightful possession from the promise you made at Mooi River.[7] I really know not sometimes what to answer the people – they do so press me to come here. I must acknowledge that, were I not bound to Bloemfontein, which I have not the least desire to leave, I could not refuse their request. … The field is really ripe for the harvest, and many, many are longing for the preaching of the Word, though with others it is nothing but a desire for the sacraments.[8]

Continuing north and east, Murray crossed the scenic Magaliesberg mountain range, with its beautiful woods, many streams and numerous fruit-laden orchards and vineyards. That Friday he arrived at the home of Deacon Caspar Kruger, in the vicinity

---

6. ibid., p. 103.

7. That is, during Andrew Murray, Sr's earlier visit to that region. Perhaps he had indicated his intention of helping locate a pastor for the Boers in Transvaal; maybe he mentioned one of his sons as a possibility.

8. Du Plessis, *The Life of Andrew Murray*, p. 104.

where the town of Rustenburg would be established two years later. Murray conducted a pair of preparation services on Saturday and spoke with the parents of more than eighty children, whom he baptized that same day. On Sunday he officiated at a communion service for a 'very large' congregation in the open air, which required 'a great deal of exertion' to be heard.

> On Sabbath I was very hoarse, but got on very well, and was enabled to preach and to serve four tables without my voice failing. When I came home, though I did not feel fatigued, I was so worn out that when I lay down for a few minutes I slept full three hours most soundly, and was quite refreshed for the evening service.[9]

After holding another service early the next morning, Murray then 'sat full ten hours' in confirmation interviews of some eighty young people seeking church membership. Of that number, forty-two were approved.

Murray was again deeply moved when the spiritually-hungry people of that area as well as Zoutpansberg, another Dutch settlement about 300 miles further to the north-east, importuned him to come to minister in their locations. To his parents he wrote:

> The impressions which appear to have been produced have made the people still more anxious that I should come here, and some of them have been pleading with me for hours that I should accept a call. On Saturday two men arrived here with an ox-wagon from Zoutpansberg, bearing a letter from the Commandant [Hendrik] Potgieter. They beg me to come thither, as the poverty of many of the people will not allow them to travel thus far, and since it would not be safe to leave the frontier towards [a native region] where they are altogether unprotected. The distance ... from here alone prevented me from going. Potgieter asked me to appoint a time when some other minister, or else myself, should come to them, and I have fixed September. When the men heard that they could not be visited for such a time, they were in tears, as they had hoped I might go with them, and when they left again they could

---

9. ibid.

not speak. I hardly know what to say when the people begin to discourse about their spiritual destitution, and their desire after the Word. ... Suppose another minister ... should refuse to come here, but be willing to take Bloemfontein, what would you think of my coming here? Perhaps you say, Foolish boy! but the way in which some of the people here plead really moves my heart. Many are in a fit state for receiving the seed of the Word. May the Lord in His mercy help them.[10]

From Caspar Kruger's home, Murray and his companion traveled in a south-easterly direction. After recrossing the Magaliesberg range, they came to the home of Andries Pretorius, where they spent the night. A reward of 2,000 pounds was still being offered by the Government for the apprehension of Pretorius.

Of the prominent Boer leader, who was nearly thirty years his senior, Murray revealed: 'He treated me with great kindness and made great professions of sorrow over the decay of religion in the land.'[11] When Pretorius asked if he might receive communion at Murray's next ministry stop, the young clergyman 'spoke as faithfully as I could' in representing scriptural qualifications for participation in the ordinance. Pretorius claimed a 'most earnest desire to serve the Lord' but admitted that he had 'enmity' toward a certain individual who played a prominent role in local politics. 'I am glad to say,' Murray reported after the communion service, 'that he [Pretorius] stayed away from the Table.'[12]

The next set of services was held at the farm of one D. Erasmus, a short day's journey from Pretorius's home. An unusually large number of children, 125, were presented for baptism since the people of that area had not been able to attend religious services for over a year. During that strenuous weekend of ministry Murray caught a severe cold and by Sunday afternoon had come down with a fever that prevented him from preaching that evening. The next morning he conducted a brief service in which he baptized

---

10. ibid., p. 105.

11. ibid.

12. ibid., p. 106.

the children and confirmed the youth who had been admitted as members that weekend. Then, though still not feeling well, 'Immediately after service I had to ride on horseback for several hours, the wagon having gone on early in the morning, since the distance we had to travel to the next church-place did not allow of our losing any time.'[13]

That week they traveled east by north-east to the district of Ohrigstad. The low-lying country through which they passed was thickly wooded and sparsely populated, but they were able to stay at a farm each night along the way. That Tuesday, New Year's Day, they traveled eleven and a half hours in order to reach a farmstead and avoid spending the night in the lion-infested veldt.

A deadly malaria epidemic had led the residents of Ohrigstad to temporarily abandon their town and the 'exceedingly fertile' farmlands that surrounded it. They had relocated to a neighboring plateau which was 'quite bare' but where the climate was more pleasant and healthful. Murray reached the meeting place on the plateau that Friday. Though he still felt 'very unwell', he was able to carry out his ministerial responsibilities. The congregation was not very large because the announcement of his holding services there that weekend had not reached all the families in the expansive parish. While he baptized seventy-five children, he was told that there were even more than that in the district left unbaptized.

The next week Murray and his traveling companions returned to the vicinity of the Magaliesberg Range where he rested rather than holding services on Sunday, 13 January. By the following Thursday they had arrived back at the Mooi River. Fortunately Murray's health had been restored by then, for a major weekend of ministry awaited him there. The Volksraad (regional legislative assembly) was to convene there early the following week, and more than 400 wagons had gathered for the occasion. A very large, partially-open meeting place that could accommodate around 1,000 people had been prepared, but twice that number were present. 'I was really astonished, when I rose in church on Sabbath morning,' he reported,

---

13. ibid.

'to see the multitude that was assembled.' His other perspectives on the weekend of ministry are interesting and enlightening:

> I preached on Friday and twice on Saturday, not without a blessing, I trust, though I cannot say that my own soul was in a very lively frame. I sometimes doubt whether it really be the Lord's assistance by which I am enabled to preach, or whether it be merely natural powers which, when excited, lead me to preach earnestly, and apparently with deep impression on the hearers.
>
> On Sabbath I dispensed the Sacrament, and had by far too many communicants, though I had tried to set forth as faithfully as possible what Psalm 24:4 represents as the way to God. My own heart was somewhat enlarged in speaking on the name of Emmanuel, but I found that very few of the people are in a state to appreciate such subjects. What they want is ... scolding, and if that but produced any good effect, I would willingly [scold]; but I sometimes feel sad at the thought that the blessed Gospel of God's love should be degraded to be nothing else than a schoolmaster to drive and threaten.[14]

At Monday's two services, he preached on texts – 1 John 4:7 and Philippians 1:27 – aimed at promoting love and unity. '[I] tried to speak as plainly as possible on all the contention and enmity which prevails amongst them, especially in reference to the Raad [legislative assembly], where disputes sometimes run very high.' The intentional emphasis appeared to have the desired effect: 'Many professed to be very thankful, and I really think that a good feeling was produced, and that many felt the necessity of striving after peace and unity.'[15] The final service did not begin until 10 p.m. Monday and stretched out till 2 a.m. Tuesday!

After only two hours of sleep that night, Murray set out again the next morning. Crossing the Vaal, he came to the Rhenoster River where he held a service that evening and two on Wednesday. The number of attendees there was very small as many people from

---

14. ibid., p. 108.
15. ibid.

that area had been attracted to the larger gathering at the Mooi. Continuing in a southwesterly direction he arrived at the Valsch River on Friday morning, 25 January. A good-sized congregation had assembled there. Though he felt 'rather unwell', the Lord enabled him to conduct the usual set of communion-related services on Saturday, Sunday and Monday.

While still at the Valsch 'a solemn stroke of the Lord's hand' befell the itinerants:

> Deacon P. Coetzer died there on Tuesday, 29th January, after having been my companion in all our journeyings. He had been ill about fourteen days, and complained of pain in all his members, especially his back. Some say it is the Delagoa [Bay] disease, but this I cannot believe, as we kept far from the district where it has hitherto prevailed. He died trusting in the Lord, and I believe truly one of those who will be for ever with Him in glory.[16]

Two days later Murray reached Winburg, seventy miles north-east of Bloemfontein. Seeing that Murray was unwell and manifesting some of the same symptoms with which Coetzer's illness had begun, the people of Winburg were alarmed. They feared the young clergyman had contracted the same disease that had ended so many lives in the remote Transvaal region. 'Though I could not see any danger myself,' Murray commented, 'yet I could not help thinking of death, and through the Lord's goodness the fear of death was taken from me.'[17] When Murray arrived back at Bloemfontein early in February he was still 'weak, thin and very pale'.

Another incident, of uncertain date, illustrates the influence and reputation Murray came to have among the Transvaal Boers at that time. Arriving one day at the ford of a river, Murray discovered a span of oxen and a wagon stuck in the mud on the river bank. The driver was 'lashing them furiously and cursing and swearing in a dreadful way'. When Murray approached the man and asked him why he swore so, he replied that oxen could never be driven

---

16.   ibid., p. 110.

17.   ibid.

without swearing. 'Give me the whip,' said Murray, taking charge of the situation. Lifting a silent prayer for help, he began cracking the whip and encouraging the oxen. Before long he had the span and the wagon out of the mud. Returning the whip to the driver, he stated, 'Remember, now, you can drive oxen without swearing.' The driver asked who he was and, upon hearing his name, remarked, 'I might have known it by his holy young face.'[18]

During his early years of ministry Murray was sometimes exceedingly hard on himself when commenting, in private correspondence to family members, on his own spiritual condition or endeavors. Of his thoughts while crossing the Vaal at the close of his initial Transvaal ministry tour, he wrote to his father:

> ... [W]hen I looked back at the Lord's leading over the way, all the strength and assistance I had enjoyed, the blessing of which I had been the unworthy channel to not a few, I trust, and the measure of comfort with which He had enabled me to do the work – and when I then thought on the little progress I myself had made in grace, on the want of true love to my fellow sinners, on the hardness and indifference of my wicked heart, on the absence of that true heavenly-mindedness in which an ambassador of Christ ought to live, on all the pride and self-sufficiency with which I had taken to myself the glory which belongs to God alone – surely I had reason to glory and rejoice in God, and to weep in the dust at my own wickedness.[19]

Besides resuming his ministries at Bloemfontein, Murray continued his frequent travels to minister at the neighboring parishes for which he was also responsible. Upon returning from one such ministry trip, he discovered that a new school teacher and his wife, the van der Meers, had arrived from Holland and taken up residence in the Bloemfontein parsonage during his absence. Their presence in his

---

18. Douglas, *Andrew Murray and His Message*, p. 79.

19. Du Plessis, *The Life of Andrew Murray*, p. 109. Douglas, *Andrew Murray and His Message*, pp. 66-9, records a number of other instances of Murray's self-condemning remarks during his opening years of ministry.

house for two or three months, until they were able to purchase a home of their own, lessened his privacy but had the benefits of 'relieving his solitude and adding sensibly to his comfort'. Steady progress was being made on the construction of the Bloemfontein church building and pledges were raised for the erection of a new schoolhouse.

6

'ARE WE TO BE ALWAYS PASTORLESS?'
1850–1852

Murray had indicated his intention to return to the Transvaal in September but a combination of factors beyond his control delayed his desired departure date for several weeks. However, another regional legislative assembly was to convene at the Mooi River in October, and Murray was requested to come and hold services there in conjunction with the gathering. He left Bloemfontein on Wednesday 9 October, and reached 'Mooi River Town' (modern Potchefstroom) nine days later. He was 'welcomed with the greatest joy' by those who had gathered for the Volksraad, which concluded the day he arrived. At least 500 people were present, despite the fact that many had been unable to attend due to a drought and the harvest season.

Murray was pleasantly surprised to discover that the walls of a cross-shaped church building had been erected in the village. Canvas sheets were draped over the walls to serve as a temporary roof, and hundreds of people crowded into the building for services. In addition to holding the usual services on Saturday, Sunday and Monday, Murray baptized seventy-four children, and twenty-four young people were confirmed and presented to the congregation as members.

From Mooi River Murray was accompanied throughout this second Transvaal trip, as he had been during his first itineration of the territory, by Frans Schutte, a farmer from the Magaliesberg range region. On Tuesday 22 October, they traveled nine hours northeastward by ox wagon to the Gats Rand (ridge). There

Murray preached twice to a small congregation but was unable to help a deeply troubled individual:

> A woman was here brought to me to speak to, in distress about her salvation. I cannot imagine a more fearful case of a person under the power of Satan. She has already attempted some five or six times to take her own life. It appears that she was formerly very religious, but now she says she is lost – and such perversity in condemning herself I never saw. When she hears of God's grace or Christ's mercy, it only increases her own misery; for this, she says, will be her condemnation, that she refuses such mercy and her heart rejects such a God. When I came to her she begged of me with clasped hands not to speak to her, as she would have to answer for every word. And when I offered to pray she burst into tears, saying that she would only mock God. Speaking to her one would think that she was in full possession of her reason, and she shows an intimate knowledge of the Bible. I really trembled at the power of Satan, and wondered at the goodness of God in not surrendering more of us, who abuse the day of grace, as she says she has done, to the terrors of His wrath.[1]

Continuing due east for two days by ox wagon, Murray came to the Suikerbosch Rand (where present-day Heidelberg stands). He held services at a farm there Thursday through Sunday, ministering to nearly 200 individuals. By traveling two long days on horseback, in a northeasterly direction and through 'bare and uninhabited' country, Murray reached another farm, where he preached three times on Wednesday 30 October, to a congregation of fifty.

Fourteen additional hours on horseback brought Murray to the tiny settlement of Lydenburg, nestled in a valley between two slopes of the Drakenberg mountain range. There he baptized 109 children and interviewed seventy-nine applicants for membership, forty-nine of whom were received. 'Both on Friday and on Saturday I had to sit late with the work that had to be got through,' he afterward related.[2]

---

1. Du Plessis, *The Life of Andrew Murray*, p. 118.
2. ibid., p. 119.

In addition, he preached with great earnestness to the large, attentive congregation that had gathered, so that by Sunday afternoon he was 'perfectly exhausted'.

As had happened elsewhere, the people at Lydenburg pressed him 'on all sides, and even with tears' to come as a settled minister in the Transvaal. Murray tried to encourage them by stating that he trusted they would soon have a visit from some other minister. To which one man responded, more realistically, 'But is not a year too long a time for us to suffer hunger?' Murray could give no reply.

Throughout the following week Murray and Schutte traveled on horseback in a northwesterly direction. On Thursday, 7 November, they had to pass through uninhabited bush country where they saw rhinoceroses, giraffes, an elephant and 'a multitude of smaller game'. The next day they arrived at 'the Bath at the Waterberg', a mineral hot spring located in the vicinity of that mountain range. There they found only twelve wagons, and those 'standing in lager' (gathered into a camp for safety), due to the potential threat of a Kaffir attack. Most of the Boers in that area had gone to another lager in the direction of the Magaliesberg to the southwest.

'The Bath' had been designated as the location where Murray would hold church services for the inhabitants of the Zoutpansberg region, located about 180 miles to the northeast. He was glad, therefore, when thirteen 'well-loaded' wagons arrived from Zoutpansberg that Saturday evening. Though Murray did not administer the Lord's Supper at the Bath, he did hold preaching services on Saturday, Sunday and Monday. He also baptized thirty-six children. But the young people at that gathering who applied for church membership must have been found wanting in their spiritual understanding and commitment, for of the twenty-five applicants only two were approved.

On Tuesday evening Murray overtook the other lager, which had ended up gathering roughly midway between the Bath and the Magaliesberg. Some of the Dutch farmers in the region had found it necessary to engage in a fight with the Kaffirs. A number at this lager asked Murray to baptize their children, claiming they would not be able to attend his next set of church meetings. He declined, not only because he thought most of them could attend the church services if they desired, but also because: 'I felt too that they were wholly unprepared for the administration of such an holy ordinance, drinking and cursing having been but too much the order of the day.'[3]

Murray and Schutte reached the latter's home on Wednesday and rested there the next day. Friday, 15 November, they rode two hours to the north side of the Magaliesberg, where a new village (the future Rustenburg) had been established. Seven or eight houses were being constructed there, along with a good-sized church building. The large congregation that gathered that weekend could not be contained in the partially-completed structure. Murray held 'the usual services on Saturday, Sabbath and Monday', including communion on Sunday morning. He also baptized 109 children and interviewed seventy-seven applicants for membership, thirty of whom were accepted.

During the week that followed, Murray returned to the Morikwa district, southwest of the Magaliesberg, where he again encountered opposition from the self-styled 'Jerusalem pilgrims'. On Thursday, 21 November, he and his traveling companions were 'suddenly and unexpectedly' stopped less than an hour's ride away from where Murray intended to hold church services that weekend. At a nearby farmhouse Murray was 'detained a sort of prisoner' overnight. Of the next morning's proceedings, he later reported:

I took my seat upon the wagon-box, while some forty Boers stood round to put me on trial. ... [A]ll sorts of nonsensical demonstrations about the duty of coming out of Antichrist were urged, in order to prove that I could not be a true minister till I came out from under the English Government to this side of the Vaal River. Of course there was no arguing with such people, and after answering some of their questions I simply stated the object of my mission, and left them to enjoy an imaginary triumph. The greater part of the people were quite satisfied [with my responses], and those who refused to come to the [subsequent] services were

3.   ibid., p. 121.

but few in number. I felt perfectly calm, but the two churchwardens from Magaliesberg were exceedingly annoyed.[4]

When Murray's traveling companions grew impatient with this interrogation they saddled their horses. As the minister and his friends rode off, their opponents called after them, 'If you cross the Marikawa River we will shoot you!' 'Well, we will shoot back,' the frustrated companions, though not Murray himself, responded. Fortunately, Murray's party was allowed to proceed without further incident.[5]

Nearly 200 people gathered for the church services that were held that weekend. Due to 'the restless state of many' of the congregants, Murray chose to preach three times that Sunday rather than hold a communion observance. The following morning another 'public dispute' was held with the Jerusalem pilgrims. Murray was opposed to having such a debate but a number in the congregation demanded it, since 'a good many were sometimes shaken' by the arguments the extremists set forth for their beliefs. Murray afterward related the mixed outcomes of the public debate:

> They [the Jerusalem pilgrims] exposed their own ignorance most completely ..., and all but their own party were satisfied with the folly of their assertions ... Though the issue of the matter was quite satisfactory, I was very sorry that the meeting took place, as the attention of the people was completely drawn away from the solemn truths they had heard the preceding day, and which had produced some impression.[6]

Murray faced an exhausting travel and ministry schedule in the days immediately following:

> On Monday (25th Nov.) we started about midday on horseback and rode till after dark in south-easterly direction, on our way to

---

4. ibid., pp. 122-3.

5. Douglas, *Andrew Murray and His Message*, p. 64.

6. Du Plessis, *The Life of Andrew Murray*, p. 123.

Schoonspruit, where service had been intimated for Wednesday. We were misinformed as to the distance, and had thus to ride very hard. On Tuesday we were in the saddle by 4 a.m., and at 6 a.m. I held service for a congregation that had previously been appointed to meet us. Then we rode from 9 a.m. till dark to the first farm on Schoonspruit. We were disappointed in not finding horses there, and I was obliged to betake myself to an ox wagon. Traveling all night, we reached the village at sunrise next morning. I was much wearied, and preached only twice that day and once the next to a congregation of tolerable size.[7]

The settlement at which Murray ministered on that occasion later developed into the town of Klerksdorp. Located on the banks of the Schoonspruit, the village was thirty miles southwest of Potchefstroom.

Murray's second Transvaal trip ended with him ministering to 'a small congregation of some 150 persons' at the Vaal River the following Saturday, Sunday and Monday. A drought in the region had led most of the farmers to relocate elsewhere. After the morning service that Monday, 2 December, Murray crossed the Vaal and re-entered the Orange River Sovereignty (ORS). During this seven-week itineration he had traveled several hundred miles, preaching nearly forty times in eleven different locations. He also baptized 451 children and interviewed around 250 youth for church membership, with 121 of those being approved.

Before reaching Bloemfontein, Murray had the joy of meeting and welcoming Rev. D. van Velden, the newly-arrived minister at Winburg. Van Velden, Murray's first pastoral colleague in the ORS, was a Hollander who had served a small parish in Belgium for six years before coming to South Africa. He had just arrived with his wife and children at Winburg and was formally inducted to his new charge by Murray on 9 December. Van Velden assumed oversight of the congregations of Winburg and Harrismith while Murray continued to supervise the parishes of Bloemfontein, Smithfield and Riet River.

---

7. ibid., p. 124.

Shortly after Murray's return to Bloemfontein the congregation at Potchefstroom presented him with a unanimous call to be their pastor. In addition, a memorial bearing 1,100 signatures was sent to the Synodical Committee of the Dutch Reformed Church, urging that council to use its influence in securing the acceptance of the call. Murray had become attached to the Transvaal residents and deeply concerned about their spiritual welfare. He was definitely inclined to accept this invitation but felt constrained to consult his father on the matter. He wrote his father a letter, listing the reasons he was inclined to accept the call. But he ended his letter on a prayerful, submissive note: 'May the Lord direct my dear father in advising me, and may He give His poor servant the comfort of an assurance that he is doing His will.'[8]

As it turned out, Murray's parents were not supportive of his accepting the call to Potchefstroom. They feared that the effort required to minister to so many people scattered over such a vast area would overtax his limited strength and health. Doubtless they had concerns about him ministering in a region that was even less stable than the ORS. Though likely somewhat disappointed, Murray concluded he could not overrule his parents' definite advice. As a result, on Sunday 9 March, 1851 he announced, to the great joy of his Bloemfontein congregants, that he had decided to remain among them.

But Murray's concern for the welfare of the Transvaal Boers remained undiminished. Consequently, just two months later he crossed the Vaal for a third visit to that region. He was accompanied by his brother John and John's wife, Maria.[9] This itineration was a shorter one, lasting less than four weeks, and saw the Murrays venture to only two locations, Potchefstroom and Rustenburg, where newly-completed church buildings were duly dedicated. Though sizeable edifices, they were unable to contain the large congregations that gathered on those occasions. Andrew Murray's

---

8. ibid., p. 126.

9. John had married Maria Ziervogel the previous year. At the time of this trip they were twenty-five and twenty years old respectively.

heart had to be pained when the people again pleaded, 'Are we to be always pastorless?' His repeated reminders that the Lord would provide obviously failed to comfort them.

December of the previous year had brought the commencement of the Eighth Kaffir War (1850-1853), the longest, bloodiest and most costly of the protracted conflicts that took place between South African tribal groups and European settlers between 1779 and 1879.[10] Various tribes, dissatisfied with continued encroachments and confiscation of their lands, initially launched a series of attacks against British forts and settlers on Cape Colony's eastern frontier late in December. In the months that followed, unrest spread to tribes in all parts of the country, including the Basutos in the southeastern portion of ORS.

Circumstances became so threatening that Major Henry Douglas Warden thought it necessary to carry out a punitive expedition against the Basuto chief Moshesh. Warden summoned all able-bodied burghers (free citizens) to Bloemfontein to form a commando (militia) and aid the 160 British soldiers then stationed there. Not more than 150 men responded to this summons, as the Boers of the ORS generally thought Warden should leave the various tribal chiefs alone and let them 'compose their own quarrels'. With this small combined force and upwards of 1,000 tribal warriors who joined them en route to Basutoland, Warden engaged Moshesh's much larger army. On 30 June Warden's forces suffered a humiliating defeat and were forced to retreat to Bloemfontein.

Some of the ORS Boers then took matters into their own hands by inviting Andries Pretorius, who was still wanted as an outlaw by the British government, to return from Transvaal and act as a mediator in the present conflicts in the Sovereignty. Next, on 3 September, they went to Moshesh and made an agreement. The Boers promised to refrain from interfering in tribal quarrels while Moshesh consented to leave the Dutch farmers and their possessions in peace. Unfortunately, some of the Boers at that

---

10. These are also known as the Xhosa Wars, the Cape Frontier Wars and Africa's 100 Years War.

gathering urged Moshesh to have a commando of Kaffir warriors attack the British troops who were then making their way westward from the region of Natal to the ORS.

Word reached Bloemfontein late in September that Pretorius had decided to accept the invitation to come to the ORS as a mediator and that he 'intended coming with nothing but the most peaceable intentions'. Murray thought that Pretorius sincerely desired to be a peacemaker. But he also believed Pretorius would 'so far mix himself with the enemies of the Government, that he will be obliged to assume a hostile position towards it, and will thus ensure vengeance on himself and his people'. After careful thought and prayer, Murray concluded it was his duty to attempt 'to prevent what may be the cause of much bloodshed' by meeting with Pretorius and persuading him not to come to the ORS.[11] Despite 'frequent detentions owing to heavy rain', Murray was able to make his way to Potchefstroom in the week that followed, arriving there on Saturday 4 October. Murray's mission on this occasion was successful, for Pretorius, after meeting with the young clergyman, decided not to interfere in ORS affairs.

That same day, and perhaps with Murray's assistance, Pretorius wrote a letter to Major Warden stating the desire of the Transvaal Boers to establish a lasting peace treaty with the British Government. Warden forwarded Pretorius's communication to the Colony's Governor, Sir Harry Smith, who in turn sent two Assistant Commissioners to establish such a treaty.

Upon reaching Bloemfontein toward the year's end, one of the Commissioners' first official acts was to rescind the sentence that had earlier been pronounced against Pretorius. The Commissioners also asked Murray to act as translator when they met with twelve Transvaal delegates 'a little beyond Sand River' (about ninety miles northeast of Bloemfontein, near present-day Ventersburg), on Friday 16 January, 1852. The following day the Sand River Convention was signed by the Commissioners and Andries Pretorius. The agreement 'guaranteed to the immigrant farmers

---

11.   Du Plessis, *The Life of Andrew Murray*, pp. 129-30.

beyond the Vaal River the right to manage their own affairs and to govern themselves according to their own laws, without any interference on the part of the British Government'.[12]

On Monday, 1 March, Murray set out on what would prove to be his longest and, until much later years, final ministry trip to Transvaal. He was away from Bloemfontein just over three months, until 3 June. Murray was accompanied on this itineration by his friend J.H. (Jan) Neethling,[13] minister at Prince Albert, located nearly 250 miles east of Cape Town. Initially following the same course as Murray's second Transvaal tour, they traveled northeast to Potchefstroom on the Mooi River, east to the Suikerbosch Rand and northeast to Lydenburg. As on previous itinerations, all arrangements for the transportation of the ministers by ox wagon or on horseback were made by elders, deacons and other supportive individuals at the various places where they ministered. At every stage of this journey Murray and Neethling were accompanied by other traveling companions who counted it an honor to escort them for a couple of days or even a week and to help supply their needs along the way.

The native servants on the journey observed the 'great kindness' and 'eager politeness' the farmers along the way gave the ministers. One evening, the African who led their oxen sat beside the fire with his chin resting on his knees. After staring at the two clergymen for a long time, he then remarked to Neethling in broken Dutch that they 'must surely be very great chiefs' since everywhere they went the Boer bazen (masters) removed their hats and invited them into their dwellings. He noted further that long before the ministers arrived, a fresh span of oxen was already collected in the kraal. As soon as the evangelists came, the new oxen were yoked to the wagon and the master called out, 'April, loop!' (April, hasten!).

---

12.   ibid., p. 131. Just a year and a half after the signing of this treaty Pretorius died of natural causes at his home in Magaliesberg at fifty-four years of age.

13.   Johannes Henoch Neethling attended the Academy of Utrecht and was a close associate of Andrew and John Murray the last two years the brothers were in Holland. Later in 1852 he married Murray's sister, Maria.

On another occasion a Kaffir watched Murray closely as he preached with his habitual fervency. The native did not understand a single word of what he heard but afterward stated his impression of what he had observed: 'I never thought that the white men stood in such dread of their chiefs. Look at the young chief yonder [Murray]. He points his finger at the people; they sit quiet. He threatens them; they sit quiet still. He storms and rages at them; they sit as quiet as death!'

Murray had promised to visit the Transvaal's northernmost Dutch settlement, located on the southern slopes of the Zoutpansberg Range, during that fourth tour. But when word came that the settlers at that location were suffering from repeated attacks of malaria and that several individuals had already died, the ministers were strongly advised not to proceed into that unhealthy region. Since arrangements had already been made for the services there, however, Murray and Neethling considered it their duty to fulfill their obligations. From Lydenburg they traveled eleven days to Zoutpansbergen, arriving there on Friday, 9 April.

Nearly sixty wagons had gathered in lager there. The ministers soon learned that in recent weeks 24 of the 150 settlers at Zoutpansbergen had perished from malaria, 18 of those within a fortnight of contracting the disease. No home had been spared from death. The majority of these isolated people had not had access to religious services for several years and were overjoyed with this opportunity. 'For the poor people of Zoutpansberg,' Murray testified, 'it was a veritable feast, the very children rejoicing at they hardly knew what.' Murray was pleasantly surprised at the scriptural knowledge of the candidates for membership; twenty-four of forty applicants were approved. Forty infants and young children were baptized. 'We did not dispense the Lord's Supper,' Murray reported, 'on account of the state in which many of the people live, though I must confess that I was agreeably disappointed in not finding them so careless as was represented.'[14]

From the Zoutpansberg the ministers made their way southwest to the Magaliesberg, pausing along the way at Warm Bath. Reaching

---

14. Du Plessis, *The Life of Andrew Murray*, p. 136.

the Magaliesberg range the last day of April, they discovered that malaria had invaded the least populated portion of that region as well. In 'a small patch of country behind the mountain'[15] some thirty people had died and many were still seriously ill. The ministers remained at Rustenburg for over a week, holding three services on Sunday and two every weekday. Between the early morning and evening services Neethling ministered to the catechumens and Murray visited the sick and those who were 'in apparent anxiety of soul'.

Upon reaching Potchefstroom at the Mooi River, Murray 'had to perform the painful duty' of visiting a criminal named Pieterse who was imprisoned under sentence of death for having murdered his nephew in a drunken rage. 'Poor man,' Murray wrote of the prisoner, 'he appeared to deceive himself with some hope of pardon as a ground for postponing conversion.'[16] The death sentence pronounced on Pieterse after a trial by jury was confirmed by the Volksraad and subsequently carried out by a three-man firing squad.

---

15.   ibid., p. 137.
16.   ibid.

7

In Service of Church and Country
1852–1855

In October, 1852, Murray attended the quinquennial Synod of the Colony's Dutch Reformed Church when it met in Cape Town. At those meetings Murray actively participated in public discussions about such issues as incorporating the Transvaal congregations into the Synod (that request of the Transvaal churches was approved) and the pressing need of establishing a theological seminary in South Africa to supply the DRC with orthodox ministers.

That November a Hollander named Dirk van der Hoff arrived in South Africa for the express purpose of ministering to the pastorless Boer immigrants. From the time he settled in Potchefstroom the following May, controversy surrounded his ministry. According to the regulations of the DRC in both Holland and South Africa, a minister's connection to his congregation was not considered officially finalized until he was formally installed to that position by the pastor who had been serving as the consulent (acting minister) of the vacant congregation. Murray was the acknowledged consulent of Potchefstroom, and 31 July, 1853 was set as the date for him to induct van der Hoff there. On 15 June, however, van der Hoff wrote Murray, informing him that 'a general assembly' of representatives from Transvaal congregations was going to meet early in August to discuss van der Hoff's induction, and requesting 'Your Reverence [Murray] to postpone your visit somewhat longer'.

Both that General Assembly and the Volksraad (legislative assembly) met separately at Rustenburg on 8 August and passed similar resolutions to sever their connection with the DRC of Cape

Colony! A separatist body claiming to be The Dutch Reformed Church of the Transvaal was formed. It was further decided that since van der Hoff had already been legally ordained as a minister of the DRC while still in Holland, a formal installation service was unnecessary and would not take place. Sadly, this series of decisions brought to a sudden halt the heretofore positive and beneficial ministry relationship Murray had enjoyed with the Transvaal churches.[1]

Meanwhile, momentous events had continued to unfold in the Orange River Sovereignty. By then Sir George Cathcart had replaced Sir Harry Smith as Governor of Cape Colony. Cathcart managed to bring to a close the protracted and costly Eighth Kaffir War early in 1853 but only after another nearly disastrous conflict with the Basuto late in 1852. In November Cathcart led 2,500 British troops into the ORS as a show of force to the tribes there. Losses sustained by farmers of the Sovereignty through the depredations of tribesmen were assessed at 25,000 pounds. As Moshesh, the powerful Basuto leader, was viewed as responsible for the majority of those losses, he was ordered to make reparations of 10,000 head of cattle and 1,000 horses.

After Moshesh produced only a fraction of that recompense, the British attacked the Basuto stronghold, Thaba Bosiu, near Berea Mountain, early in the morning on 20 December. The Basutos put up strenuous resistance. The British managed to capture a

1. Du Plessis, *The Life of Andrew Murray*, pp. 139-45, contains a fuller account of these events involving van der Hoff and the Transvaal congregations. The people who made these decisions were motivated by a desire to gain not only ecclesiastical but also political independence from Cape Colony, and this ecclesiastical schism hastened the political division that followed shortly thereafter. While the Lydenburg congregation was initially persuaded by van der Hoff to join in this separation, it soon regretted its decision and asked to have its affiliation with the Cape Synod restored, leading to its inclusion in the Presbytery of Transgariep (Trans-Orange River). 'And in this manner was the D. R. Church of South Africa reestablished in the Transvaal territory, where it has not merely maintained itself until this day, but has steadily grown in numbers and influence, until now it holds the premiere position among ecclesiastical bodies north of the Vaal' (ibid, p. 145).

few thousand head of cattle but were nearly forced to retreat from the battle. Moshesh, satisfied that his honor had been preserved through the strength and courage his tribe had shown in the conflict, then sent a conciliatory letter to the British commander asking for peace. Cathcart was mightily relieved to speedily grant that request.

Of these events Andrew Murray wrote his brother John from Bloemfontein on 30 December:

> Most of our poor townspeople will spend anything but a happy new year. All is doubt and uncertainty. The Governor has had a fight with Moshesh, in which the former was almost obliged to retreat, though he took some cattle. Immediately afterwards he concluded a peace – all the officers begging to go and punish the Basutos, and the officials, I believe, protesting. … Everybody thinks it certain that he [Cathcart] intends sacrificing the Sovereignty. And meantime it is confidently expected that Moshesh will soon come to retake the cattle. I hardly know what to think of matters.[2]

The months that followed revealed that the British government was indeed ready, even eager, to relinquish its control of the troublesome ORS. Sir George Russell Clerk, a former Governor of Bombay, was sent as Special Commissioner to superintend the withdrawal of British authority from the Sovereignty. He arrived in Bloemfontein in August, 1853, and immediately called for a meeting there on 5 September, involving elected delegates from each of the ORS's five districts. The stated purpose of the conference was 'to decide upon some form of self-government'.

Initially many, if not most, ORS residents opposed Britain's 'abandonment of the Sovereignty'. English colonists had invested a significant amount of capital in the territory and now saw their investments endangered. Missionaries feared that a change of government would further destabilize conditions in the Sovereignty and have a strong adverse effect on their efforts to bring Christianity to area tribes. Even many Dutch farmers thought the British

---

2.   ibid., pp. 147-8.

government should not desert the Sovereignty until it had restored a good degree of order to the region.

The meeting of delegates took place at Murray's church in Bloemfontein Monday through Thursday, 5-8 September. Murray declined nomination to serve as one of the delegates for the Bloemfontein district but he played an important part in the proceedings. Mr Joseph Orpen, one of the representatives from Harrismith, provided an interesting description of the opening day's activities:

> There were ninety-five of us, including the field cornets,[3] and of these seventy-six were Dutch and nineteen English. The church in which we met was a big T-shaped building, with a pulpit on a low platform opposite the shank. It had a clay floor and no seats. A table which had stood in front of the platform was moved a little to the right. The delegates, with a crowd of spectators, stood, half filling the church.
>
> When Sir George Clerk arrived, he was taken up to the little platform by the Rev. Andrew Murray, the young, eloquent, earnest and greatly respected clergyman of the Dutch congregation. ... Sir George's Commission was first read out in English and in Dutch. ...
>
> After the reading of his Commission, Sir G. Clerk read an address to us, which directed us in Her Majesty's name to prepare ourselves to take over the government of the territory whenever British jurisdiction should be withdrawn. Practically he advised us to elect a chairman at once, and then to draft the outlines of a republican constitution; and then, as the drought and the weather made it difficult to stay longer away from our homes, to appoint a Committee, which would remain in office till we could reassemble, and would consult about details.
>
> On finishing his address he made the regulation three bows to the assembly, preparatory to retiring. At once a big babel of voices arose. ... Nobody could understand anybody else, till the

---

3. Field cornets were civilian officials in local government districts. They served under a Landdrost, the chief magistrate of an entire district. Field cornets were empowered to act as local magistrates.

Rev. A. Murray, who was still on the little platform, raised his hand demanding silence. He told us we should find tables and seats prepared for us there in the afternoon, when we could meet, elect a chairman and proceed to business.

We met accordingly, and found a T-shaped, four-foot-broad table … in the west end of the church, with forms [benches], mostly of planks, placed around it. Mr Murray kindly translated between us. When the votes for a chairman were counted, sixty fell to Dr [A.J.] Frazer[4] … He accordingly took the chair, while Mr Murray continued to give his kind assistance in translating. He sat or stood at Dr Frazer's right hand, and next to him on the right was Mr J.H. Ford, who was elected secretary. Next to him was Mr J.P. Hoffman, future first President of the Free State. Mr Hoffman at once took a prominent part in the proceedings.[5]

In the following three days the delegates passed a unanimous resolution to forward to Commissioner Clerk a protest against the British Government's decision to abandon the ORS. They drafted eleven conditions[6] that they insisted must be met in order for them to be willing to assume the self-governing of the Sovereignty. The delegates also appointed a twenty-five member committee to confer with Sir George Clerk, and gave the committee strict instructions not to consider any proposals for the formation of an independent government until their eleven conditions had been settled by the Commissioner 'to their entire satisfaction'.

After most of the delegates had dispersed, the 'Committee of Twenty-five' continued to meet for a few more days. Before the Committee members left Bloemfontein, they asked Dr Frazer and Rev. Murray to go to England as delegates, to present to the British

---

4. Frazer was a British army surgeon who had settled in the Sovereignty.

5. Du Plessis, *The Life of Andrew Murray*, pp. 149-50.

6. The eleven conditions are recorded, ibid., p. 151. They had to do with such issues as: determining an agreeable boundary line between the Sovereignty and Moshesh; gaining the promise of non-interference on the part of the British government into future affairs of the Sovereignty; sharing in the customs dues levied at Cape and Natal ports; having permission to purchase munitions of war and to transport them, unimpeded, from the coast.

Ministry 'an extensively-signed petition against abandonment'. Of this request, Murray wrote his father on 20 September:

> The matter is this: two delegates are to be sent to England from the Sovereignty. Sir George Clerk appears to waver, and there is still hope that it may not be too late, as we have reason to believe that the decision of the Ministry was not so final as it was represented to be. An opinion has been very generally expressed that the minister of Bloemfontein ought to be one of these delegates ... You may imagine that there is much that is pleasing in the prospect, especially if the possibility of doing the country any good be held out. My own health would also plead for going. I have felt far from strong during the past four or five weeks ... A weakness in my back, legs and arms, with a sort of nervous trembling in my hands, make me believe that I would be the better of rest; and I had resolved to ask for three months' leave of absence during the heat of summer. This object could now so well be obtained by the voyage to Europe and back.[7]

This correspondence is significant not only with regard to the commission to go to England but also because it marks the first-ever recorded reference to a neurological affliction that Murray would live with the remainder of his life. At this time he was still but twenty-five years of age.

Murray eventually accepted the nomination to go as a delegate to England. Leaving Bloemfontein in November, he first went to Graaff-Reinet, where he briefly visited his family and was joined by Dr Frazer. They promptly proceeded to Cape Town where they were detained for several weeks. On 21 January, 1854, they sailed for England aboard the steamer *Queen of the South* and reached their destination late in February.

They were granted an appointment with the Duke of Newcastle, Secretary of State for the Colonies in the Aberdeen Ministry, in mid-March. Of that meeting and their subsequent efforts, Murray informed his father:

---

7.   ibid., p. 152.

As regards our mission here, on the 16th of March we had an interview with the Duke of Newcastle. He received us most kindly, but informed us that the matter was so far settled that he expected the first mail to bring him the report of the arrangements being completed, as final orders had been dispatched in November last. We felt there was very little hope, and were almost prepared to give up the question, were it not for the fear of being afterwards accused of doing so little. On putting ourselves into communication with Mr Adderley, he advised us to get a legal opinion as to the power of the Crown to abandon without consulting Parliament.[8]

Murray and Frazer had no way of knowing that, through a surprising turn of events, the matter had indeed been settled in South Africa before they ever set foot in England. Back in Bloemfontein, Sir George Clerk, the Special Commissioner, had begun actively using his influence to persuade the citizens of Orange River Sovereignty to oppose the Committee of Twenty-five's protest of Britain's intended abandonment of the ORS. Patriotic Dutchmen encouraged their fellow countrymen to accept independence and to take up self-governance. As a result, several of the Twenty-five, including the prominent and influential J.P. Hoffman, resigned from the Committee.

A republican party led by Hoffman quickly formed. It favored taking over the governance of the Sovereignty and rightly claimed that it now represented the majority of settlers in the ORS. When the Committee of Twenty-five, by then reduced to only thirteen members, declared themselves as the only legally-constituted representatives of the Sovereignty's inhabitants, Commissioner Clerk accused the Committee of being 'obstructionist' and promptly disbanded it! He then met for several days with the republican group to draft the terms of an agreement by which the residents between the Orange and Vaal would govern their own territory. That agreement, the Convention of Bloemfontein, was signed on 23 February. The Orange River Sovereignty thus became the Orange Free State (OFS). The first Volksraad met in March. Two

---

8.   ibid., p. 156. C.B. Adderley was a member of the British House of Commons.

months later Josias Philip Hoffman was selected by plebiscite as the first President of the OFS.

Around that same time, on 9 May (Murray's twenty-sixth birthday), MP C.B. Adderley raised in the British House of Commons the issue of Britain's abandonment of the Orange River Sovereignty. Not a single other legislator joined Adderley in requesting that the decision be reconsidered.

Throughout his time in London Murray received a number of invitations to preach, including as the interim minister at the prominent Surrey Chapel. Most of these invitations he needed to decline, as he explained in a correspondence to his father:

> As to my engagements here, they are not so frequent as they might otherwise be, as we have often to wait at home, to be ready for any official calls of duty. ... Surrey Chapel ... has become vacant ... The Rev. Newman Hall ... does not come for three months, and I have been applied to to take charge of it for May and June, with the offer of a parsonage, etc. I have, of course, declined the offer. Several other invitations to preach I have also declined. I suppose, however, that I shall be engaged about once every Sunday.[9]

To one of his sisters he further revealed a few weeks later:

> As regards my health I cannot speak very favorably, and you may imagine that I now long for rest. Perhaps I ought not to preach at all. I find it difficult to refuse altogether, and preaching is in fact most refreshing to myself. On Sunday evening, for instance, I preached at Surrey Chapel to a congregation of some 3,000 from the words, 'I beheld, and lo! in the midst of the throne a Lamb, as it had been slain' [Rev. 5:6]. The subject has been most edifying to myself. ... I think the Lord gives me favor in the sight of the people [of Surrey Chapel], though my violent manner [of preaching] is much against me.[10]

Murray was able to spend ten days in Holland during the middle of April. There he visited his brother Charles, who was then a student

---

9.   ibid., p. 157.

10.   ibid., pp. 157-8.

at Utrecht, as well as a number of former friends and acquaintances in a few different cities.

Throughout May Murray remained in London, wrapping up his responsibilities in connection with the thwarted political mission. He then left for Scotland where he had a happy reunion with Uncle John and his family in Aberdeen. In both Aberdeen and Edinburgh Murray tried unsuccessfully to find young men who would be willing to go to South Africa as ministers and teachers. His uncle informed him that during the past two years the Free Church of Scotland had supplied various British colonies with some forty ministers and now faced a shortage of ministerial candidates to fill its own pulpit vacancies.

Murray's health continued to be a serious concern. He related in a letter:

> I feel my strength so worn, that I do not believe that even perfect rest for three or four months would restore me, and a single summer in Africa would lay me prostrate. The doctor says that my whole system has been much more seriously affected than I have any idea of, and that prolonged rest is necessary to restoration. And even then the system will remain very weak, unless allowed time to gather strength. He disadvises my leaving England before the winter.[11]

At his doctor's recommendation, Murray underwent several weeks of hydrotherapy at a prominent treatment center in Yorkshire, but with little physical benefit. In September he returned to Holland for about a month. There he visited another doctor who advised him to undergo another course of hydrotherapy, this one at Boppart (modern Boppard) on the Rhine in Germany. From there he wrote his family:

> Here I am, trying a second water-cure establishment. In Holland I found I was still so far from strong, and so incapable of bearing the least excitement or exertion without fatigue, that I consulted a medical man, who positively advised me to stay over the winter in

---

11.   ibid., pp. 161-2.

Europe, and thought that a few weeks' continued trial of the cold-water cure might do me good. What I chiefly suffer from is the pain in the hands and arms. Half an hour's lively conversation, or earnest application to anything that requires thinking, immediately makes itself felt there. I cannot even write a note without feeling the pain in my arms; and the pain in the arms is but the index of a general weakness of the nervous system. The doctor says that the whole constitution must be strengthened before the pain can be removed.[12]

November found Murray back in Holland, where he stayed till the following January. As had been the case in Scotland, so in Germany and Holland Murray did not succeed in finding qualified men who were able and willing to venture to South Africa to serve as pastors or teachers. In mid-January, 1855, Murray left Holland to return to England. Though he intended to depart from London for South Africa almost immediately, the winter was severe and his vessel was detained by inclement weather till 9 March. Murray reached Cape Town in the fourth week of May. There, unknown to him, he was about to make a life-changing acquaintance.

---

12. ibid., p. 162.

8

EMMA
1855–1856

Shortly after arriving in Cape Town Murray was introduced by a Dr Philip, secretary of the London Missionary Society's work in South Africa, to Howson Edward Rutherfoord, a respected and influential Christian merchant, philanthropist and politician in the metropolis. Rutherfoord had come from England to Cape Town in 1818 as a young man of twenty-three. In his new setting he prospered as a shipping agent and eventually helped support a number of charitable causes. In 1854 Rutherfoord was elected as a member of the Legislative Council of the Cape Parliament.

Rutherfoord, his wife and five children belonged to the Church of England and for many years were members of Holy Trinity Church in Cape Town's Harrington Street. Though they were devoted to their own denomination, the Rutherfoords' Christian sympathies were broad and they were well-known for their generous hospitality to missionaries of every society and denomination. Upon meeting Murray, Rutherfoord promptly invited the young clergyman to join his family for dinner at their home on Herschel Estate[1] near Claremont, one of the southern suburbs of Cape Town. After that Murray was a regular and welcome guest at the Rutherfoords' home and table. As the hospitable Mr and Mrs Rutherfoord were wont

---

1. The nine-acre estate, with its large Cape Dutch style house, several out-buildings, sizeable garden, orchards, vineyards and one acre of natural forest, had previously belonged to English astronomer Sir John Herschel when he stayed at the Cape during the 1830s.

to do with some of their guests, before long they invited Murray to stay in their home for a time.

Murray, who had just turned twenty-seven years of age, soon began to be attracted to the Rutherfoords' twenty-year-old daughter, Emma. She was her parents' third child and second oldest daughter. Her older sister, Mary, had married a Mr Reeves, and they now lived in India where he was in the Bombay Civil Service. Emma also had an older brother, Frederic, and two younger sisters, Ellen and Lucy.

Since the time of Mary's marriage three years earlier, Emma had inherited the title of 'Miss Rutherfoord' and carefully carried out her duties as the eldest daughter at home, paying calls with Mama and helping her to receive visitors, giving out the household stores [to servants] each morning and keeping the weekly household accounts, and being an example to her younger sisters.[2] Following in the footsteps of her mother, Emma taught children's classes first at Trinity Church and later at the High Church School in Claremont. She also regularly carried out 'district visitation' to the sick and poor as well as a tract distribution ministry.

While her brother, Frederic, had been sent to England to obtain his education, Emma and her sisters were taught at home by their mother and visiting governesses and masters. Besides studying such basics as reading, writing, grammar, literature, arithmetic, history and geography, the Rutherfoord girls also received lessons in French, Italian, German and Dutch. At the outset of her study of the latter language late in 1852, Emma optimistically stated, 'I began my first Dutch lesson on Monday and don't expect much difficulty in picking up enough to speak.'[3] At that time she had no way of knowing what a prominent role the Dutch language would come to have in her future life and ministry. Emma and her sisters were also trained in skills that were considered essential for accomplished young women in the Victorian era – music (both singing and playing the piano),

---

2. Joyce Murray (Ed.), *In Mid-Victorian Cape Town, Letters from Miss Rutherfoord* (Cape Town: A.A. Balkema, 1953), p. 5. Joyce Murray was Emma Rutherfoord Murray's granddaughter.

3. ibid., p. 37.

fancy needle work as well as drawing and painting. Emma was an avid reader and had an appreciation for a wide variety of books.

As Murray observed and learned more about Emma he was impressed with her and his heart was drawn to her. Though he had known her less than a month, he concluded he desired to marry her. He further decided to propose to her straightaway, apparently presuming she would be receptive to that.[4] As it turned out, he was completely mistaken.

Besides the fact that his proposal was totally unexpected, it was also poorly timed. Emma and Ellen were right in the middle of helping with a large children's birthday party for the five-year-old son of some neighbors, Mr and Mrs Boyle. Mr Boyle was Aide-de-camp to Cape Colony's new Governor (since the previous December), Sir George Grey. In addition to a sizeable group of children, the party was to be attended by Sir George and Lady Grey themselves. As a special surprise, the two Rutherfoord sisters spent hours decorating a Christmas tree with tapers, sugar plums and flowers.[5] Young Mordaunt Boyle's birthday was on Thursday 21 June. After spending that entire morning at the Boyles' house finishing the decorating, Emma and Ellen returned to their own home. They planned to be back for the party the latter half of the afternoon and, as its climax, to light the tree as evening came.

Murray had left the Rutherfoords' home that morning but returned 'most unexpectedly' early that afternoon. Finding Emma

---

4. Sixteen months later, Emma would write of her newly-wed husband's approach to a ministry-related venture: 'My husband is so bold, he carries the day. ... never fear is his motto, I think. He never anticipates difficulties or refusals ... [W]ith Andrew an idea suggests itself, approves itself to his judgment and then he never rests till it is carried out' (ibid., pp. 45-6). This appears to have been Murray's general outlook on and approach to life. While such a confident outlook and bold approach often brought him success, they likely contributed to his failure in this first proposal of marriage.

5. 'This must have been one of the first Christmas trees at the Cape; certainly very few have been decorated and lit in June – but what a sensible idea for a winter party!' (Murray, *In Mid-Victorian Cape Town*, pp. 93-4). June is wintertime in the southern hemisphere.

alone, he presented her with a rather businesslike proposal of marriage. She was so completely stunned by it that she was unable to make any reply. Instead, she fled to her bedroom and locked herself in. When Ellen, who had gone out riding, returned home, she found her sister, very uncharacteristically, in an overwrought state. As a result of these unfortunate developments, both sisters were too upset to return to the Boyles' for the party and the lighting of the tree. While there is no record of Andrew Murray's response to all this, likely he retreated from the Rutherfoords' home feeling confused, distressed and embarrassed at what he had unintentionally precipitated.

The next morning Emma composed a written refusal to Murray's proposal:

> Dear Sir, It was with feelings of perfect astonishment and wonder that I received your communications yesterday, which on further consideration quickly changed into those of deep pain and regret. A proposal of marriage after so short an acquaintance shocked me much. It seemed to me that there could be no mutual sympathy, and no clear knowledge of character necessary for so close, so holy a relationship. With these sentiments I feel obliged to decline any further acquaintance. But wishing you a safe journey and much prosperity in your future labors, Believe me, yours truly, Emma Rutherfoord.[6]

In a letter written that same day to her sister Mary, Emma further revealed:

> I cannot tell you what pain and suffering this has cost me. And more so I cannot help feeling that if left to himself he would not have proceeded with such haste but that he has been spurred on [by] the Rev. Mr Long and his Uncle Rev. Mr [G.W.] Stegmann, as up to that unfortunate day his conduct had been such as to put me perfectly at ease. And if the thought ever flitted across my mind that I might be invited to the Sovereignty, it was in such a vague manner and at so remote a period as not to cause me the slightest uneasiness. Our intercourse hitherto had been so pleasant

6. ibid., pp. 94-5.

and I had entertained such a respect for his character, felt that his mind was no ordinary one, that his want of appreciation and consideration has wounded me most painfully.

To my real character I feel he is as perfect a stranger as I am to his. And if I loved him with all my heart, it would be a bitter trial and a great sacrifice to leave such a home as mine, and enter into a field – certainly it might be of great usefulness, but of much hardship and self-denial. Of all this he seems to have made no note. While I feel it must be a love passing anything I have yet known, to keep me from fainting under the trials and sorrows of wedded life – a love that I feel in my inmost soul that I am capable of and therefore will never marry anyone till I feel it awakened. No respect, no ideas of usefulness (for they would be false where my heart was not) shall ever induce me to leave my home.

Cannot you imagine the sort of cold chill and shock I have experienced. ... It will soon be like a dream and I have had great comfort in dear Papa's and Mama's kindness as well as Ellen. Lucy I have enraged exceedingly. She will scarcely speak to me, as she has conceived a great affection for Mr Murray and thinks I ought immediately to have accepted him. And I cannot convince her that it would be a much greater unkindness to accept than to refuse if I do not love him.[7]

Three days later, on Monday, 25 June, Emma concluded her letter to Mary:

Mr Murray called on Papa today to know if my answer was decisive and negative. I feel so fashed [vexed], so wearied about it. It pains me that one of no ordinary mental capacity and vigor of piety should be so totally devoid of proper feelings on this one point. And then I get vexed with myself for feeling so pained ... Sad that one whose mental superiority and whose work is all I could desire, should so want heart cultivation.[8]

Emma again wrote Mary the first week of July. The correspondence reveals that, despite her strong front, Emma was having difficulty

---

7.   ibid., pp. 95-6.

8.   ibid., pp. 96-7.

putting the unsettling developments with Andrew Murray out of her mind:

> Mr Murray has left Cape Town today. He called on Papa on Saturday, and said that he felt that his conduct had been very wrong, did not seek to extenuate it, under any circumstances it had been wrong, but that his mind had been very harassed and pressed, his people constantly urging his return. He had only left them for ten months and had been absent twenty. He felt at the same time the disadvantage and pain of his entirely lonely condition, no one he could associate with or make a companion, and that he had acted hastily without due consideration for me. He expressed extreme regret. Papa said he was evidently agitated and his mind overpressed, and also said he felt how entirely proper and just my conduct had been, that it had only heightened his esteem, and begged to be allowed to send me his very best regards.

> And so our intercourse has ended. Whether we shall ever meet again is a problem I do not wish to pierce or think of at present. But I am not quite happy in many ways. Papa and Mama have both such an extremely high opinion of him whilst I am not satisfied. I have received such a shock. It seemed so businesslike a thing and there seems to me a want, I don't know what exactly to call it, perhaps a refinement of heart. I don't think I could ever do without it. ...

> A missionary life is one I have always looked forward to and I have always thought that they of all others ought to have resources in themselves and be well educated. Still I have many, very many doubts as to whether this is the path appointed me, so I am going to dismiss it entirely from my thoughts. If it is to be it will be, and no thinking upon it now can do good. If it is not to be, [thinking about it will] perhaps do harm. I want to keep my judgment unbiased and heart free, and then leave everything. I don't think the latter will give me much trouble, and now Farewell to this subject. ...

> I don't feel quite happy in a variety of ways, but however I am trying to think of nothing but the present day and its duties. For to myself I seem moving in the midst of clouds, though I daresay to others all looks bright around me. ... I feel very harassed though I ought not to be and should not be if I were living above the world.[9]

---

9. ibid., pp. 103-6.

After leaving Cape Town Murray first made his way to Prince Albert and Graaff-Reinet to visit family members. His father accompanied him from Graaff-Reinet to Bloemfontein, which he reached in August, having been away for twenty-one months. 'I feel quite ashamed at all the warmth of friendship and kindness with which I have been received,' he reported, 'and I fit more easily into the Bloemfontein life than I had expected.'[10]

A letter he penned to his brother John around that same time contained additional interesting perspectives and news:

> I am very thankful that I feel so well and comfortable. I was able yesterday to preach with more composure than I have ever yet done. I trust the course of sermons which I have announced on the Mosaic Worship will aid me in my endeavor to cultivate calmer habits in the pulpit. May the great secret of success in this matter – the quieting influence of God's presence and peace – be mercifully vouchsafed.[11]
>
> In domestic matters everything is going on well. I feel wonderfully at home and enjoy the quiet. My hopes as to a possible restoration of my strength begin somewhat to revive. I yesterday received a letter from Henry Faure, enclosing a call from Ladysmith.[12]

Ladysmith, located in the province of Natal, was not the only church to have recently contacted Murray about coming as its minister. While still in Europe he had received a similar invitation from the congregation at Colesberg, just south of the Orange River.

Two months after his return to Bloemfontein, Murray attended the meeting of the Presbytery of Transgariep (the Orange Free State region) which was held at Winburg. One significant item of business considered by the Presbytery was an offer from Sir

---

10. Du Plessis, *The Life of Andrew Murray*, p. 164.

11. In time Murray would learn (as all seasoned preachers do) that it was neither possible nor desirable to alter his natural preaching style. His exceedingly passionate sermon delivery was the unaffected outcome of his intense emotional makeup and fervent spiritual convictions. His exceptionally zealous preaching style was one of the primary reasons he was such a popular, effective preacher.

12. Du Plessis, *The Life of Andrew Murray*, pp. 165-6.

George Grey, Cape Colony's new Governor, to aid the OFS in establishing a college to train men for the teaching profession. The Governor proposed to donate, from imperial funds at his disposal, 1,500 pounds for the erection of a building that could house thirty boarders. The Presbytery would serve as the institution's board of management. The Governor's generous offer was gratefully accepted and further action was turned over to a committee of which Murray was selected to be the head. Less than two weeks later, three land plots were purchased in Bloemfontein as the future site of the college.

Meanwhile, back at Herschel Estate, Emma Rutherfoord was still finding it impossible not to think about Andrew Murray and what might have been, as some of her letters to her sister Mary betray:

September 28 – How very quickly you answered my June letters. Don't be alarmed about me, though you cannot, not knowing, appreciate the intellect, originality, earnestness and goodness of my friend [Murray]. Yet I never allow my mind to dwell on the subject long without feeling a sort of shudder for a want inexplicable. And whenever any of his good qualities come in view, still this feeling drives me from relenting in any way. Yet there was much that was pleasant in the anticipation of the realization of so many of my daydreams, which seem to me now completely shattered. It seems as though my desire for a missionary life can never be realized. I don't know that I am fitted for it, certainly not if there must ever be that want in them.[13] … [Mr Murray] has a far larger and more comprehensive mind and I do trust he will get a good wife. He may pick and choose from all the young ladies in town, Dutch or English, for they adore him. And perhaps I have done him good and schooled his heart a little, for he seemed to have appreciation of my reasons, which I scarcely at first anticipated. Perhaps the next time he falls in love he will act in a different manner. I don't know

---

13. By this last phrase, 'if there must ever be that want in them', Emma appears to refer to a lack of a romantic outlook on the part of missionaries. She is still put off by the businesslike nature of Murray's proposal to her. She was, of course, making a wrong assumption about Murray and most missionaries.

where he is to get a companion in his wife, but I earnestly hope he will have a good one and a helpmeet. Many things now make me feel it would not have been desirable for either party. And yet I have rather a dread, to speak the truth, of becoming moss grown and dank and slimy and rusty before my time ...[14]

October 30 – I must say I very nearly lost my heart and had not that fault betrayed itself, I certainly should have quite [lost it]. And still [I] think if you and Mr Reeves [Mary's husband] had been here you would have both acknowledged there was much to captivate, much that Mr Reeves himself would have admired and which quite blinded Papa. But now I begin fully to see I never should have been fit for such a life. I do not possess the mental or bodily strength for it. ... But now I feel quite reconciled. I should have been no help, no comfort to him, on the contrary very likely a care and anxiety. Then how I should have regretted it. And I am determined not to listen to those who try to work on my feelings by accounts of his delicate health and ever telling me that he will return and that they are sure he has not forgotten.[15]

Indeed, Murray had not forgotten Emma. He still desired to marry her. Some time early in 1856 (probably February) he wrote 'a very kind letter' to ask her forgiveness for past offenses and to learn if he might have some hope of winning her as his wife in the future. In a 20 March letter to Mary, Emma revealed of her response to Murray:

I wrote I am conscious but a cold answer to a very kind letter. I think both Mama and Papa would have wished it somewhat kinder. But I must and do still refuse to decide without further acquaintance. And he only asks forgiveness of the past, and some hope for the future. Whether the very small degree [of hope] I felt justified in giving him he will consider enough to venture on returning to Cape Town, I know not. He will have much to hazard. But if he does not, I cannot think more on the subject. ... I am sure he does not really know me. Who can get acquainted with anyone so timid and shy in three weeks? ... And yet if he does not come soon, I shall feel that

14.   Murray, *In Mid-Victorian Cape Town*, pp. 114-15.
15.   ibid., p. 123.

in justice to myself I ought to dismiss the subject from my mind.
I cannot possibly hear his decision for three weeks. I assure you
my letter was perfectly cool enough to make him quite happy in
terminating the acquaintance if he feels inclined.[16]

Less than two weeks after penning the above words, Emma received
a reply from Murray which persuaded her of his genuine attachment
to her and broke down her resistance. Somewhat surprisingly, she
set aside the condition she had just given him that they must first
become better acquainted through an in-person visit. Instead, she
promptly indicated her willingness to marry him and to return
with him to Bloemfontein. Her 5 April letter to Mary brings to
light some of the sentiments Murray had shared with Emma that
led to her change of heart:

He is very romantic and German in his disposition. All sorts of
things that in reading German poetry and plays I had put down
to German mystery and romance, I find he fully sympathizes in.
I thought no one in this matter-of-fact age did, that it was only the
philosophy of poets. I was so amused before I received his letter,
driving down to Kalk Bay one day, I began expatiating on German
poetry and some passages particularly in the Bride of Messina,
and was trying to explain to Mama the doctrine of sympathies
and strange union of spirits unknown to themselves, etc. ... That
evening Mama gave me his letter to her, in which there was more of
that spirit than in any living person's writing I had seen. I must say it
seems very odd that he should have fallen in love with me in so short
a time, excepting that he explains it by these mysterious sympathies
which made him love me the first time we met and drew us together.

He acknowledges he did wrong in acting on impulse and
forgetting my feelings in the first instance, when he found he must
leave. But [he] hopes that various reasons that he gives, such as not
being able to forget, etc. will convince me that they were not mere
transitory feelings and impulses, etc. He expatiates on the sacrifices
he asks from me, etc.[17]

---

16. ibid., p. 140.

17. ibid., pp. 148-9.

EMMA

Murray had also stated in his letter that he 'fervently' hoped to return to Herschel Estate 'very soon'. But he posted the missive immediately, even before arrangements could be worked out for him to leave Bloemfontein for a time. As a result, Emma did not know if he would be able to come the following month or not for several months. In addition, reports had just reached Cape Town of renewed unrest among the Kaffirs and war again being imminent along the border of Cape Colony and in Orange Free State. 'At such a juncture I could not wish Mr Murray to leave his people in the event of an attack,' Emma wrote. 'Who can tell the issue, or when it may end. ... Doubtless this sudden rupture has perplexed him and disturbed all his future plans.'[18]

Of her anticipated future with Murray, Emma again wrote Mary in mid-May:

> I only comfort myself that he wants [needs] a drag, instead of a spur, or he will wear himself out. I am not going to let him take those long journeys alone. I shall get into the cart too, as everyone says he wears himself out with work. But if I am with him he will be obliged to rest.
>
> ... I think eventually we may very likely be in Cape Town. The various congregations here are very anxious to persuade him to stay in town, but I am rather glad not to be in town at first. I should not like him to become what is called a popular preacher. I think it is much better to be a father to the poor and infant commonwealth, to superintend the erection of a new village, to take an interest and lead in the improvement of a young and rising population, [rather] than to be a town demagogue or oratory idol. I did not, when he was down here, like the way in which old as well as young flattered him. I think he thought it great tosh himself and was glad to get away from it.[19]

In response to the recent conflicts with native tribes in OFS, a commando was sent to 'punish' Witse, the son of Moshesh, as well as a chief in the Harrismith district who had committed 'numerous

18. ibid., p. 152.
19. ibid., pp. 157, 159.

acts of depredation and robbery'. The commando succeeded in recovering around 4,000 head of stolen cattle. Murray was then able to set out for Cape Town, arriving at Herschel Estate on 31 May after completing the journey, which normally took three weeks, in just thirteen days.

As it would likely be at least another year before Murray could return to Cape Town, Emma consented to a short engagement and to go with her beloved to Bloemfontein immediately after they were married. Their wedding took place on Wednesday morning, 2 July, 1856, at the Dutch Reformed Church in Wynberg, not far from Herschel. Rev. G.W. Stegmann, Murray's uncle, officiated at the service in English for the sake of the Rutherfoords and their acquaintances, most of whom understood little Dutch. Following the ceremony, the bridal party made its way to Herschel where the family and a few friends enjoyed 'a beautiful breakfast' together. That afternoon the newlyweds traveled thirty miles east to Stellenbosch on the first leg of their journey to Bloemfontein.

9

Newly-wed Life and Ministry
1856

Andrew and Emma Murray did not at all have a conventional honeymoon. But their newly-wed journey to Bloemfontein was doubtless infused with special joy for both of them. For Emma it was filled with many fascinating new sights and experiences. They needed a Cape Cart and a wagon to transport themselves and Emma's belongings, including her piano, select pieces of furniture, china dishes, table linens and other household goods, clothes and cherished books. A team of mules drew the wagon, and four horses were brought to take turns pulling the cart. They were accompanied by a few men to assist them along the way and by Mrs Henly, an 'English' servant whom Mrs Rutherfoord had hired to help Emma in Bloemfontein.

They followed a northeasterly direction through the first few days of their journey. At Paarl on Friday 4 July, Emma attended her first Dutch church service. 'One thing impressed me very much,' she observed afterwards, 'they often sing a hymn in the midst of the sermon to wake people up again. I said I thought it was time to leave off when the hymn was sung.'[1] The next evening at Ceres she heard her husband preach in Dutch for the first time. Murray preached twice there on Sunday as well. The church did not have a settled minister at the time, so people came from all parts of the surrounding country for this rare opportunity to attend Sunday services, packing out the little church building. 'After the two services on Sunday,' Emily related, 'my husband and I walked up into the kloof [canyon

---

1. Joyce Murray (Ed.), *Young Mrs. Murray Goes to Bloemfontein, 1856-1860* (Cape Town: A.A. Balkema, 1954), p. 12.

or ravine] to enjoy its beauty and quiet. And there we read and sang together till sunset, enjoying the grandeur and loneliness of the place.'[2]

Something else impressed Emma throughout the trip:

One thing I have remarked in traveling is the multiplicity of children and the size of the babies. Each house has its baby, if not two, and ten or twelve children is the ordinary number. ... I never saw such a marrying and children loving people. If you want to get to their hearts, nurse the baby or talk to the children. My husband is a great adept at both. He understands quieting a baby far better than I do. But then he has even now a little sister of six months old and has always had some little brother or sister to play with.[3]

Of their crossing the Karroo, Emma wrote:

The next three days and nights were to me great fun. We had been traveling through high mountain ranges, Alps upon Alps, and now we suddenly came upon a wide open plain with nothing but very distant mountains to relieve the monotony, no houses. We halted at night, lit a fire ... and boiled coffee. The men meanwhile unharnessed the mules and horses ..., the cart and wagon were fastened together, the former prepared for my bedroom, and very snug and comfortable it was. We took out our cakes, bread, butter, milk and cold meat, and enjoyed a supper by the fireside in the bright moonlight. The men established themselves at another fire a little distance off. I used then to sing hymns while the wagon was being prepared by Mrs Henly, a most excellent servant. We then had prayers and I retired to rest by the light of a carriage lamp. ... Getting up in the morning is the most difficult thing for then my hands used to get quite useless and it was really very cold. Sometimes we traveled on in the moonlight till 10 o'clock. We had two or three adventures of losing our way and then rejoicing in the bleating of sheep or barking of dogs as indicative of some sheep farm where we could learn our direction.[4]

---

2. ibid.

3. ibid., pp. 13-14.

4. ibid., p. 14.

The following weekend brought them to Beaufort West, which Emma described as a 'sweet little oasis in the desert'. There on Sunday, 13 July, she participated for the first time in a Dutch communion service: 'It was to me a very impressive and beautiful service.'[5]

Two more days of desert travel, now in an easterly direction, led them to Graaff-Reinet so Murray could introduce his new bride to his parents and several of his younger siblings: Catherine (aged fifteen), James (13), George (11), Helen (7), Maggie (3) and baby Elizabeth. Reported Emma:

> ... I was most warmly received by all Andrew's relations. His father ... has quite the Scotch manners and appearance. And [his mother] is a quiet, gentle person much loved by all her children, quite a pattern of a mother and wife, makes her husband's and children's clothes, superintends the baking, washing and candle making, yet looks after the lessons of the children. Andrew is one of sixteen, the youngest a baby of six months old, a sweet little creature. I should have enjoyed my stay there very much had we not been overwhelmed by visitors.[6]

Traveling north and east again, they came to Middelburg where Murray's brother William ministered. The previous year William had married Elsabe Gie. Murray's sister Isabella was living with William and Elsabe at the time. At Fauresmith, midway between the Orange River and Bloemfontein, they visited Murray's sisters, Maria and Jemima, along with their husbands. A year earlier Jemima had wed Andries Adriaan Louw, the minister at Fauresmith. Jan and Maria Neethling were visiting from Prince Albert. During

---

5. ibid., p. 15.

6. ibid., p. 18. Andrew and Maria's one other son was named Robert. The dates of his birth and death have not been preserved. He died of meningitis at age four. He is known to have died 'some years' after the death of his brother George in 1844 (Murray, *Unto Children's Children*, p. 73). As no mention is made of Robert in the recorded references to siblings at this time (1856), it appears he had already died.

Andrew and Emma's brief visit at Fauresmith, Jemima, attended by Maria, gave birth to her first child.

Another day and a half of travel in the latter part of July brought the Murrays to Bloemfontein. They were immediately assailed with visitors, people doubtless eager to welcome Murray back and to meet Emma. 'It is indeed true that a predikant [DRC minister] is public property and everyone's friend,' Emma reported in a letter to her mother on 15 August. 'From six in the morning till nine at night we are never sure of not having visitors.'[7] Emma quickly made a favorable impression with the people of the church and town:

> I believe that the people are pleased that I look happy and contented and praise Bloemfontein and try to talk to them, as they were afraid of my being too fine and discontented, and trying to persuade Mr Murray to leave. And they are willing to build us a nice house, at least enlarge this.[8]

Nearly a century later, Joyce Murray provided a fuller description of her grandparents' early home at Bloemfontein:

> Like most of the other houses in the village, the parsonage had a thatched roof and mud floors, the latter because of the expense of flooring boards, there being a complete absence of local timber. I am told these mud floors kept the houses beautifully warm in the bitter Free State winters. The surface was smeared periodically with cattle dung, applied with the palm of the hand in a circular movement. This gave the floor a lovely polish and color, and though the smell was overpowering at first, the next day it was not at all noticeable. The carpets could then be laid, and apart from sprinkling a little water over the floor before sweeping each day, no more care was needed. Emma found this a little primitive, and was delighted to find the kerkraad [church council] agreeable to the suggestion that a couple at least of the rooms should be floored. They promised to build on two more

---

7.   ibid., p. 20.

8.   ibid., pp. 23-4.

rooms, and she ordered new all [wall]papers, and grates for two more fire places.[9]

The parsonage property was a large one on the south side of the Bloem Spruit, the stream that flowed through the town. Both Andrew and Emma helped tend their sizeable vegetable and flower gardens. The entire garden was surrounded by a high stone wall that during the summer was covered with vines. In addition to 'a great variety' of fruit trees, two willows and a grape arbor grew on the property. Murray also planted some blue gum trees, the seeds of which they had brought from Cape Town.

To increase her usefulness, Emma set herself to learning the Dutch language. She hoped to start a Sunday school and a weekday school for primary children as well as to establish a lending library. Before long she had become the regular church organist. Of the church music, services and building, Emma wrote to family members:

> There are always four slow Hymns sung at both services. I do so enjoy the Dutch singing, the hymns and psalms are exceedingly beautiful and simple … and as a people they generally sing so heartily. … They have many of them splendid voices and the effect of 3 or 400 voices all joining heartily and earnestly in a solemn, plaintive, almost German Psalm is very fine.
>
> Between ourselves I think the Dutch Church services too long, three hours in the morning, two in the afternoon and the whole fatigue resting on the Minister. But then there is much truth in my husband's argument that many of the people come in perhaps only once a month or fortnight, some less frequently, and living in a tent or wagon there is so much opportunity for waste of time, and levity or business talk among the villagers … The excitement of the new [worship] form and language, the new scenes in a country church, the want of quiet reverence owing to the people carrying their own chairs, often on their back etc, all distresses me and renders the service far more fatiguing than an English one.
>
> I am glad to say we are daily expecting seats from Cape Town. And when these are finished and the ceiling accomplished (at

---

9. ibid., p. 27.

present swallows and occasionally owls whirl over our heads) my husband is going to preach a sermon on order and reverence. They are very attentive when he is preaching.[10]

Several months after Emma penned those words, the 11 July, 1857, edition of a weekly newspaper entitled *The Friend of the Free State and Bloemfontein Gazette* had a lead article on 'Progress in Bloemfontein'. The editor who wrote the article reported of Murray's church:

> During the last six months ... our plain but commodious church building has been much improved by a set of neat dealwood pews, sent up ready-made from Cape Town, which added to a complete wooden-vaulted ceiling, now render this place of worship, which was formerly, during at least three winter months, so intensely cold, as to be all but unbearable to aged persons and invalids, one of the most comfortable churches in which we could desire to sit.[11]

The church was originally built in 1852. An attractive-looking structure with four gables, it was the pride of the community. It was located in the center of town but, less conveniently, was a considerable distance from the parsonage on the opposite side of Bloem Spruit. After a heavy rainstorm the stream sometimes flooded, leaving the Murrays temporarily cut off from the town and church.

Besides preaching twice on Sunday in Dutch, Murray preached at an English service each Thursday evening. He invited Emma to critique his sermons, as she revealed to her mother in a 11 September, 1856, correspondence:

> I often wish my sisters could hear his weekday English services; they are much to the young. I am obliged to listen very attentively to all his sermons for he makes me critic, and always expects to know just what I think. I tell him it is good for him that he has a simple congregation to whom it is an effort for him to simplify his

---

10.   ibid., pp. 71-2.

11.   ibid., pp. 72-3.

ideas and bring them down to their comprehensions. He is obliged to clip his wings or else I think there is some danger, if he had a clever and intellectual congregation, of his becoming too fanciful or too new, if I may use this expression, in his sermons. Now they are plain and practical and shorn of the new, varied, and perhaps a little wild, interpretations and symbolic meanings he favors me with.[12]

In another letter written several weeks later, Emma related further of her husband's characteristic, conscientious sermon preparation: 'He has been very much pressed for business this last week, and has had little time for himself. And though when journeying and circumstances necessitate it, a good extempore preacher, he is never satisfied at home without study and a well digested sermon.'[13]

Andrew and Emma truly were happy in their new life together. Emma again wrote her mother in late September or early October:

You might tell Mary not only that you hope I may learn great and holy lessons here (which I do hope too, and do feel it is a large sphere of usefulness), but I have never known such overflowing happiness in my life hitherto. And this you will not think any bad compliment to yourself. Certain it is happiness and joy beyond my expectations and our deserts, and we both feel this, it is far greater than our warmest feelings ever anticipated. It is strange what perfect sympathy and suitability there seems to be in our characters.[14]

An auspicious event took place in Bloemfontein on Monday, 13 October, 1856, when the foundation stone of Governor Grey's proposed college building was laid. By that time the Governor had indicated his intention to increase his contribution to 4,500 pounds so that, in addition to the erection of the building, the salary of the school's headmaster would be guaranteed from interest accruing on the principal. The ceremony of the laying of the foundation stone

---

12.   ibid., p. 38.

13.   ibid., p. 79.

14.   ibid., p. 43.

was officiated by Jacobus Nicolaas Boshof, the second President of the Orange Free State.[15]

President Boshof, Rev. Andrew Murray and Mr J.D. Griesel, an elder of Bloemfontein, were appointed as the first trustees of the college. As Bloemfontein had no bank, Murray agreed to act as banker for the initial 3,000 pounds the Governor had provided for the undertaking. In order to gain additional income, a portion of those funds was loaned out at six percent interest.

Writing to her sister Mary early in November, Emma shared intimate thoughts of appreciation, admiration and affection for Murray:

> I am anxious to be a good housekeeper, especially as Andrew never finds fault with anything I do. And I am afraid I don't understand being economical quite yet, though he never says so, or even hints that things might be better. Sometimes I wish he would, as I know so little. And yet he always listens to the smallest little household trouble and tries to find me a remedy, and does everything I ask him and gets what I wish. You cannot imagine a more sympathizing, loving husband, so tender and gentle to his little wife.
>
> And yet [he] seems made to command, a sort of Bishop or little pope, amongst the people. I tell him I sometimes feel afraid when he is talking to other people but never for myself. He had so early to command and act decisively for himself and others that it has imparted a great amount of decision and strength of character.
>
> But you will think I am always praising my husband. I only wish you knew him; I feel sure you would love him.
>
> I certainly never knew before I could be so bound to anyone or love anyone so much. It seems a new faculty I had been perfectly unconscious of, and almost overwhelming in its strength and depth of joy.
>
> The only tinge of sadness is in yet what I scarcely wish otherwise – that deep earnestness and feeling which often exhausts his physical strength and reminds me he is human and life uncertain. Yet I know 'man is immortal till his work is done', and trust he may be long spared to be useful in his day and generation.[16]

---

15.   Boshof served as OFS President from 1855 to 1859.

16.   Murray, *Young Mrs. Murray Goes to Bloemfontein*, p. 58.

In mid-November Bloemfontein suffered the most violent thunder, lightning and hail storm that residents had ever recalled seeing there. Emma related:

> ... the hailstones the size of plums nearly, battered so against the roof I thought it must surely come through. In the corners of the garden it lay a foot thick. ... In the course of an hour, or more, the garden was a miserable wreck, flowers [and] leaves torn to shreds, apples, plums and peaches strewing the ground. All our lettuce and spinach beaten down to nothing, everything stripped, vines torn down, bunches of grapes strewing the ground. It was a melancholy spectacle.[17]

To make matters worse, during recent construction work on the parsonage, the drain for water off the back roof had become clogged. As a result, during the storm a foot of water collected against an exterior door and 'finally broke into' the house, flooding the kitchen and an adjacent sitting room with a few inches of water. It was three or four in the morning before the Murrays finished sweeping and bailing water out of the two rooms. 'As the rooms are mud floor,' Emma wrote afterwards, 'you may imagine what a sight they were next morning and are still.' The Murrays were blessed to promptly find a small, vacant two-room house about a five-minute walk from the parsonage and were able to move into it temporarily the day after the storm. One benefit from the storm was that it was decided that wood flooring would be put into all four of the parsonage rooms as soon as the mud floors had dried out.

For several months deep animosity had been brewing between the Dutch and English elements of Bloemfontein in connection with a tragic set of murders and the contentious trials that followed in that immediate vicinity. The murders involved an Englishman named Charles Cox, who lived on a farm about two miles from Bloemfontein and who had married the daughter of a neighboring Dutch farmer named Bouwer. On 26 April of that year, 1856, Cox's wife and two young children were found dead, apparently having

---

17. ibid., p. 65.

been murdered. Cox was arrested and charged with the murders, though he vociferously proclaimed his innocence. Most of the English inhabitants of Bloemfontein and throughout OFS believed Cox to be innocent while the vast majority of Dutch were equally convinced of his guilt.

Since the OFS did not yet have a regular court of justice, the case was brought before a special tribunal consisting of the Landdrosts (chief magistrates) of Bloemfontein, Smithfield and Winburg, as well as a jury. Due to 'so many irregularities and informalities', the initial court proceedings were declared a mistrial. Cox was retried by a Court of Landdrosts who found him guilty and sentenced him to death. That sentence was approved by the Executive Council of the Volksraad and Cox was executed the end of October. Throughout the course of these tumultuous events, feelings ran very high and many angry words were exchanged by opponents on both sides of the issue.

For their part, Murray and Emma sought to be peacemakers. On 3 December Emma wrote about the situation:

> I am glad I have been with Andrew during the last few months. There has been so much outwardly to worry and trouble him, which I think had he been alone must have weighed more heavily upon him. This sad business has stirred up the evil passions of men on both sides so much, for neither are without blame. To a certain degree one sympathizes with both and feels there has been a great need of forbearance. ... I am sorry to say their [English] clergyman, to say the least, has acted very foolishly, omitting in the church service the prayers for the President, and preaching a sermon from Hebrews, comparing Cox's death to that of Abel.[18] ... Through anonymous letters the English have threatened Mr Boshof's life. One which came through Andrew, it was just directed to the Minister of the Dutch Church, and then inside was an awful letter vowing that the writer's arm could not lie cold in the grave without the President's life. ... It is sad, too, to think how all this

---

18. Emma here refers to the Sunday minister of the English congregation in Bloemfontein. Murray ministered to that congregation on Thursday evenings.

strife must tell on the children of all concerned, witnesses of their parents' ill feelings towards each other. We still live in hopes that time will provide a remedy and that nothing further may occur. Few can tell the moral evil of such a state of things. How much we need wisdom – my husband for his sermons, to preach the truth and warn them of the sins they are committing, without alluding to politics, to teach them lessons of mutual forbearance and charity and submission to those in authority. On Thursday evenings he is going through the Lord's Prayer, principally to preach on 'Forgive us our trespasses as we forgive them that trespass against us', without incriminating their own pastor to the English, and yet to convince them of their own sin in that Sunday weekly exposition of evil feelings even in God's house.[19]

Murray's ministerial duties took him into the country three or four days every fortnight. While he was away Emma kept herself busy doing a good deal of parish visiting in town, especially among the English tradespeople. She and others had established a Sunday School for both Dutch and English children. In addition, aided by three or four other ladies, Emma started 'a school for colored people', with classes being held three times a week. That venture was not popular with most of either the Dutch or English residents of Bloemfontein. In his absence, Emma also assisted her husband with the local banking responsibilities he had agreed to oversee.

Murray and Emma made many pastoral visits together. Of that shared ministry and the warm response of their parishioners to it, Emma informed her mother:

We sometimes are out walking and driving till 8 [p.m.] or near it. I am getting acquainted with those farms within two hours of Bloemfontein. The people are delighted to see us and we must generally outspan for an hour. I hope it will give me greater influence and encourage their visits to the parsonage besides bringing them to church. We often bring home offerings; they are a most hospitable people. At first I did not know how to thank them and did not like receiving so much – vegetables, a sheep, a

---

19. Murray, *Young Mrs. Murray Goes to Bloemfontein*, pp. 63-4.

115

pair of ducks or hens, eggs, etc. – much more according to their dispositions than means.[20]

When Emma wrote her sister on Christmas Eve Day she had special news to share:

My darling Mary, I hope you won't be shocked when I tell you that I intend to present [Andrew] with another little temptation and interruption to study in the shape of a little son or daughter next April, if all is well. It is very soon to begin [a family] certainly, and I was a little shocked at myself at first, but now conclude it is but doing my duty as a poor parson's wife, whose families are always the largest, but I hope they will not prove the other adage true. But seriously, I cannot yet realize the idea or imagine myself a mother …[21]

---

20.   ibid., p. 75.
21.   ibid., pp. 79-80.

10

FINAL YEARS AT BLOEMFONTEIN
1857–1859

Emma gave birth to her namesake on 20 April, 1857. Murray wrote his brother John: 'I have to communicate to you the glad tidings of the birth of a little daughter last Monday morning. God has been very kind. Emma has suffered little, and the babe is doing well.'[1] Around that same time Murray's teenage sister Catherine, nicknamed Kitty, came to stay with them for several months.

In mid-September the Murrays, accompanied by Kitty and Mrs Henly, set out for the DRC's Synod meeting in Cape Town. For the Murray clan the Synod, which commenced on 13 October, provided the opportunity for a grand family reunion. Emma, with her baby, relished the opportunity to stay with her family at Herschel during the six or seven weeks they were in the Cape Town vicinity.

At that Synod it was decided to establish a theological seminary for the training of ministers at Stellenbosch, located thirty-one miles east of Cape Town. The possibility of starting a divinity school in South Africa had been discussed for years but for one reason or another had repeatedly been delayed. Some of the older ministers at the Synod strongly opposed the proposal, fearing that such independence from Holland and its universities would lead to intellectual and spiritual loss. Despite their opposition, a large majority of the delegates voted to proceed immediately with the

---

1. Murray, *Young Mrs. Murray Goes to Bloemfontein*, p. 89.

founding of a South African seminary. Since numerous attempts to obtain qualified professors from Holland had failed, the Synod determined to select two of its own members to serve in that capacity. In the end, John Murray and Rev. N.J. Hofmeyr were nominated and approved.[2]

Another significant issue addressed at the Synod was the need for an increased effort on the part of the Dutch Reformed Churches to carry out missionary work among 'coloreds' and 'blacks' both within and beyond the Colony's borders.[3] Ever since the second meeting of the Synod in 1829, the official position of Cape Colony's DRC was that church attendance and membership were to be open to all, regardless of race or social status. Due to deep-seated prejudice, however, many white Afrikaners[4] (most of whom were professing Christians) were opposed to seeing dark-skinned servants and tribesmen evangelized, baptized and confirmed as church members. The vast majority of South Africa's DRC congregations left it to the various missionary societies to evangelize servants and tribesmen in separate mission chapels but did not financially support such missionary endeavor.[5] Even when servants were permitted to attend Dutch Reformed churches they found it nearly impossible to become official members due to the requirement that members had to be able to read the Bible in Dutch.

---

2. Nicolaas Hofmeyr had been an intimate acquaintance of Andrew and John Murray as well as a member of their evangelical fellowship group *Sechor Dabar* at the Academy of Utrecht in Holland. Hofmeyr served as pastor of the DRC at Calvinia for six years prior to assuming his responsibilities as professor at Stellenbosch. Calvinia was located about 230 miles north of Cape Town, near the Kalahari Desert.

3. Much of the description to follow of this missions issue is gleaned from Nel, *South Africa's Forgotten Revival*, pp. 47-9, 64-5.

4. Afrikaners were South African natives of European descent, especially Afrikaans-speaking descendants of seventeenth-century Dutch settlers.

5. Between 1857 and 1860 forty-five of South Africa's seventy-one DRC congregations failed to contribute 'a single penny' towards missions (Nel, *South Africa's Forgotten Revival*, p. 68).

N.J. Hofmeyr wrote a series of articles that had appeared in *De Kerkbode* (The Church Messenger)[6] in which he argued that colored people should be able to become church members even if they did not know how to read or write at all. He proposed a compromise solution, which he called 'the middle way', by which churches could work through this thorny issue. Each congregation would be required to build a separate chapel for colored people to attend. While that daughter church would have its own missionary, it would be administered and supported by the mother congregation.

Hofmeyr, Andrew Murray, Jr, and J.H. Neethling urged the Synod to increase its emphasis on mission work. They, along with P.K. Albertyn (an older clergyman intended to moderate and offset their youthful enthusiasm and inexperience), were elected to form a new Missions Committee, charged with the responsibility of obtaining missionaries from overseas to serve in South Africa. Nel relates further:

> Although no session had been scheduled to debate Hofmeyr's 'middle way', a question posed by Robert Shand on this topic sparked a blistering debate. It resulted in the division of the Synod into two distinct camps: those who pleaded for the unity of all believers [in unified congregations] and those who argued that a more pressing issue was at stake, namely, the unhindered ability to evangelize the colored community in a way that addressed their special needs [in segregated congregations].

At the close of the debate, a compromise motion was accepted by the majority. It was put forward by Andrew Murray, Sr, who had been subjected to ongoing opposition in his own attempts to evangelize the coloreds [servants] and Africans [tribesmen] in his parish of Graaff-Reinet. His motion reads as follows:

> The Synod regards it as desirable and scriptural that our members out of the heathen be received and incorporated into existing

---

6. *De Kerkbode* was the official magazine of South Africa's DRC. This was the common abbreviation for the periodical's original title, *De Gereformeerde Kerkbode* (The Reformed Church Bulletin).

congregations, particularly where this is possible. But where these measures, due to the weakness of some, stand in the way of the progress of Christ's cause among the heathen, the congregation established from the heathen, or still to be established, should [be allowed to] enjoy her Christian privileges in a separate building or establishment.[7]

While this compromise may seem inadequate or even inappropriate by contemporary Christian standards, it was an honest and reasonable attempt at reaching a workable solution to a deeply perplexing and vexing situation.

Andrew Murray, Jr, and his family left for Bloemfontein at the beginning of December. Mrs Henly had accompanied them to the Cape but did not return with them to Bloemfontein. Her place was being taken by 'a very superior colored girl' named Charlotte. They were also accompanied by a Miss McGill who intended to start a small school in Bloemfontein. Kitty Murray apparently returned with her parents and siblings to Graaff-Reinet from Cape Town.

The Murrays planned to take a week longer than usual in getting back to Bloemfontein but as Emma related, 'Indeed I much dislike the work [preaching] arranged for him [Andrew] all along the road, which will render this journey no holiday.'[8] They traveled in an easterly direction, with Murray ministering at Swellendam, George and Oudtshoorn along the way. A coachman drove the wagon while Murray usually navigated the cart. Sometimes Emma was able to leave the baby sleeping in the wagon and could enjoy the quiet company of her husband as well as assist him with the driving of the cart.

After leaving Oudtshoorn the Murrays and their party encountered two extremely trying days of travel. Emma afterward related:

The next day [Thursday, December 16] we left Oudtshoorn through Meirings Poort [a mountain pass] on our way to Prince

7. Nel, *South Africa's Forgotten Revival*, p. 65. The bracketed words are Nel's.

8. Murray, *Young Mrs. Murray Goes to Bloemfontein*, p. 104.

Albert. The day was intensely hot. Our road lay through a deep ravine winding through a mountain range, with lofty cliffs on each side and apparently in front. ...

Before we were quite out of the labyrinth, a thunder-storm came on. We were benighted and lost our way, not being able to see the road. Only every now and then a vivid flash of lightning would reveal some trees. At half past nine at night, we (Andrew, Baby and I) in the cart discovered a light and made for a house. But you perhaps can imagine better that I can describe how we were tossed about, jerked here and there, often I thought we must upset, over stones and bushes, through streams. However we very gladly reached the house in safety. Those in the wagon had to sleep out all night. Fortunately the storm passed over with only one shower, and we saw them come in safety with some joy the next morning.

The mules, however, were lazy or tired, and we had hard work the next day. ... The road was over the summit of a hill, on one side as steep as the side of the kloof [canyon or ravine], and a cornfield below. The little brutes did not want to go, so when Andrew beat them they took us down this side. ... Andrew just fortunately ran them into a bush or we should certainly soon have begun rolling over. I then got out and laid Baby under a bush while I led the mules and Andrew beat. And with tugging and beating we at last got them back. But Baby lay screaming and I had the pleasure of carrying her all down the hill. We arrived at Prince Albert at 10 at night very tired.[9]

Sad news awaited them at Jan and Maria Neethling's parsonage in Prince Albert. Andrew Murray's four-year-old sister, Maggie, had suffered sunstroke as her family traveled home from the Cape and died, apparently from meningitis, several days after they reached Graaff-Reinet. Andrew, Emma and their small party arrived at Graaff-Reinet on Christmas Eve. The joyous family reunion they had anticipated there was overshadowed by this sorrowful development. Early in January, 1858, the younger Andrew Murray family was back in Bloemfontein.

Marked tensions had continued to exist between white settlers and Basuto tribes along the border of the Orange Free State.

---

9.   ibid., pp. 110-11.

The Basutos still felt portions of their tribal land had wrongly been sold by the British government to European settlers and continued to carry out cattle thieving raids against them. In the middle of March, 1858, the OFS Volksraad declared war and a commando of burghers (free citizens) drove the Basutos back into their mountainous strongholds. In turn, however, bands of Basuto horsemen swiftly descended on defenseless portions of the OFS, destroying homesteads and driving off large herds of cattle. As a result, the burghers immediately broke camp and hurried back to their homes.

A letter that Emma wrote to her sister Mary at the end of June revealed the stress and anxiety the inhabitants of Bloemfontein had experienced as a result of the crisis:

> The state of this country has been and still is very distressing, although better than it was a few weeks since. The moral effect of the political excitement and war has been very deleterious. … Many are the sad stories of murdered families till my mind gets quite depressed and sometimes nervous. These barbarians are in our very midst. I sometimes imagine wrong even of those in and around the village, but this is wrong and I try to conquer all morbid fears which are apt to depress me in my husband's absences. But God's redeeming Providence was very marked when our Boers retreated, when if they [the Basutos] had liked nothing could have prevented them overrunning and destroying Bloemfontein. For ten days we remained in this defenseless condition, everyone looking with amazement at the other, no one knowing what might happen. Even Andrew admitted the possibility of an attack, and many expected it as a certainty.[10]

Joyce Murray further relates:

> To prevent complete disaster, [President] Boshof asked both the Colony and the Transvaal for help, and with Sir George Grey as mediator, an unsatisfactory peace was patched up. It was generally felt that the Free State was too weak to stand alone, but they

10. ibid., pp. 121-2.

were unwilling to be ruled by the Transvaal, and Sir George Grey's proposals for a Federation with the Cape Colony were not approved by the Imperial Government. Two more costly wars were waged against the Basutos, and only in 1868 was the vexed question of the boundary between the two countries settled when Britain definitely annexed Basutoland, and the Free State could then stabilize its Republic.[11]

In a letter to Mary early in September, Emma also divulged something of the financial stresses their family was presently facing as well as some of the contributing factors:

> ... [Dutch clergymen] are called upon to work hard and always be the entertainers of strangers of all sorts and classes on a scanty pittance of 250 pounds per annum. There are no inns as you know in these villages and everyone thinks he has a claim on the minister's hospitality. ... With this war, painful claims press on us, every article is most enormously expensive. And my husband gives to the utmost farthing, or asks some unfortunate here [to our home], and then comes with the apology: 'I do not know what you will say, but I could not help it.' I make the best of it now and make beds everywhere, and give out stores without a sigh. And somehow we manage to keep straight and don't suffer any personal inconvenience nor get into debt I hope.[12]

Just a couple of weeks after Emma wrote those words, the ministerial couple experienced an instance of the Lord's ever-faithful, providential provision for their needs. On Friday 17 September, the English-speaking citizens of Bloemfontein held a 'public Tea Meeting' in the Murrays' honor. As a token of their appreciation to him for having conducted a weekly religious service in English throughout the past three years they presented him with a purse containing seventy-five gold sovereigns (worth the same number of British pounds).

---

11.   ibid., p. 121.
12.   ibid., pp. 129, 131.

Around that same time a minister of the Separatist Reformed Church of Holland, Rev. Dirk Postma, arrived at the Cape. He had been commissioned by his denomination to investigate current conditions of the Transvaal Boers and to engage in mission work among indigenous tribesmen. After a cordial meeting in Cape Town with several prominent ministers of the Colony's DRC (including Professors Murray and Hofmeyr, Rev. J.H. Neethling and others[13]), Postma proceeded to Natal en route to the Transvaal.

Some time in October or early November Andrew Murray went to Natal at the request of the Winburg churchwardens with their invitation to Postma to become their minister. Postma said he could not give a positive answer until he had spent several months across the Vaal, after which he would see if he felt at liberty to join the Dutch Reformed Church. One of Postma's key reservations toward the DRC was its use of hymns other than those from the Psalter in its worship services. After returning from his meeting with Postma, Murray wrote in a 30 November letter to his brother John: 'I spoke very seriously to him on the danger I thought there would be in his establishing a body of Separatists across the Vaal. I must confess I am not without very serious apprehensions as to the result of his mission.'[14]

Construction work was completed on Bloemfontein's college building and student boarding house by the end of the year. Two teachers, one Dutch and the other English, had been procured for the school but not a suitable Rector to oversee the students' spiritual development. Murray was eager to see the institution get off to a good start, so offered to serve as Rector himself for a year. In that position he would not be responsible for any classroom teaching. But the Murrays would serve as dorm parents, take their meals with the students (all boys) and conduct morning and evening 'prayers'

---

13. By that time John Murray, N.J. Hofmeyr and J.H. Neethling had begun ministering in Stellenbosch: Murray and Hofmeyr as professors at the fledgling theological seminary and Neethling as the new minister of the DRC congregation there. These three leaders became commonly known as the Stellenbosch Triumvirate.

14. Du Plessis, *The Life of Andrew Murray*, p. 176.

with them. Of this new responsibility and its desired effect with the boys, Murray revealed to John: 'I [have undertaken] it with the strong desire that to some of them at least it may be made the means of salvation.'[15]

Andrew and Emma Murray's second child, a daughter whom they named Mary Ellen (after two of Emma's sisters), was born on 14 December. Early the following year, 1859, the Murrays moved into the school's boarding house on the college property not far from their parsonage. The house began receiving 'Boarder-Pupils' on Thursday 13 January, and the school officially opened the following Monday.[16] At the beginning of March fourteen students were residing in the house and by the end of April that number had grown to twenty-two. The boys ranged in age from nine to eighteen. An additional twenty students attended the school during the day and returned to their own homes at night.

A letter of 8 March to his brother John revealed another significant development and blessing in Andrew Murray's ministry just at that time: the publication of his first book, a life of Christ for children written in Dutch and entitled *Jezus de Kindervriend* (Jesus the Friend of Children). The small quarto volume was fifty-four pages in length and contained a number of illustrative prints. It was eagerly welcomed by parents and children who could easily understand its simple language. Of his first impressions upon seeing the book, Murray shared with John:

> I have just received the first copy of the *Kindervriend*. I like it, but am disappointed that it is not more simple. It is to myself intensely interesting as containing the expression of what filled my mind some time ago. There are passages that I hardly believed that I myself had written.[17]

---

15. ibid.

16. This was only the third institution of higher education to be established in South Africa, the first two having been founded in Cape Town. The Bloemfontein school was later named Grey College in honor of Sir George Grey who had played a vital role in its establishment.

17. Du Plessis, *The Life of Andrew Murray*, p. 177.

Both Andrew and John Murray desired to do what they could to help supply worthwhile reading materials in Dutch for their own and other congregations. At that time in South Africa there was a dearth of Christian books and pamphlets in the Dutch language. Andrew had already translated a few English tracts into Dutch and had them printed for use by his congregation.

Two years earlier, in 1856, John had published an Abridged Catechism and his *Kinderbybel* (*Children's Bible*). The latter was a free translation of *Line upon Line*, an English work 'on which generations of Victorian children were brought up'.[18] John's *Kinderbybel* was an immediate and abiding success, with 3,000 copies selling in its first six months of circulation, and one edition following another into the later years of the nineteenth century.

The Murray brothers covered the cost of having their own first books published, then sought to recover that expense as the volumes sold. John had assisted Andrew in the publication process of his first book. About these matters Murray wrote his older sibling:

> What do you think from your experience would be the time needed to get in the capital that has been laid out? You have never yet let me know what the printer's bill comes to. I would be sorry that you should suffer the least inconvenience in making my money arrangements. Only let me know betimes, and I will manage.[19]

Four months after the publication of *Jezus de Kindervriend* Emma wrote to a relative:

> I like this book writing very much when we can find time for it, for I am my husband's amanuensis. ... The last book he published, *The Kindervriend*, is selling well and should pay its own expenses soon. And then in perhaps eighteen months there may be a little profit, enough to invest to set our next publication off. ... John has been very much blessed in his publications, which have some of them been extensively circulated, gone through several editions and been

---

18. Murray, *Young Mrs Murray Goes to Bloemfontein*, p. 45.
19. Du Plessis, *The Life of Andrew Murray*, p. 176.

much blessed. And he, cautious quiet Scotchman that he is, has always made them pay themselves. What he loses on one he is sure to gain on another.[20]

Within two months of Dirk Postma's arrival at Rustenburg in the Transvaal late in 1858 or early in 1859, he did what Andrew Murray had feared he would, and seceded with 300 members from the Dutch Reformed Church and launched a Separatist church movement in South Africa. The Transvaal Volksraad was 'greatly exercised' over this development, knowing the strife that religious dissension would likely produce. The legislative council invited ministers and representatives from all the Transvaal churches to a general assembly at Potchefstroom on 26 April, 1859 in hopes of repairing the breach. After days of discussion that assembly agreed to accept Postma as minister of Rustenburg, 'leaving him at liberty to sing what he liked'.

At that assembly Postma appeared to be in agreement with the efforts to heal the breach that he had brought about in the Transvaal. But immediately after, he proceeded to Bloemfontein and Burgersdorp where he promptly established Separatist congregations! Postma paid Murray a short five-minute call while in Bloemfontein. But when Murray requested a longer visit, Postma declined, claiming he did not have the time. Murray, for his own part, had become accepting of rather than perturbed by these developments, as he indicated in a letter to his brother John on 1 May:

> I sometimes think that it may do good that our [DRC] monopoly is brought to an end. As to myself, the words have sometimes occurred very strongly, 'He will let out the vineyard to other husbandmen, which shall render Him the fruits in their season' [Matt. 21:41]. We have never been able, even when willing, to reach the real, stiff Dopper mind. Our language was strange to it. These new ministrations, possessing their confidence, may reach hearts that appear to us quite closed against the Gospel. ... I look upon the whole thing as the direct work of Providence, and though

---

20. Murray, *Young Mrs Murray Goes to Bloemfontein*, pp. 140-1.

I would have been anxious to open our church for psalm-singing congregations and ministers, yet as no opportunity for acting in the matter was afforded, I am content.[21]

Murray's open-minded perspective on these matters led him and the Consistory of his church to invite Postma to preach at their DRC in Bloemfontein sometime in the months that followed. This resulted in a rebuke being issued against Murray and his church leaders by the Presbytery of Transgariep at its meeting in mid-October. The official resolution read:

That in view of the actions of Rev. Postma, in view of the condition of our Church, and in view of the significance and influence of the act of the Consistory and Minister of Bloemfontein, the Presbytery feels itself compelled to disapprove of the neutral attitude of that Consistory in admitting Rev. Postma to the pulpit, as incautious and harmful.[22]

---

21.   Du Plessis, *The Life of Andrew Murray*, p. 178.

22.   ibid., p. 179.

11

Prelude to Spiritual Awakening
1860

A number of congregations had continued to approach Andrew Murray about coming to serve as their minister. In 1858 he received pastoral calls to Robertson, Prince Albert and twice to Burgersdorp, while in 1859 such invitations came from Victoria West and Pietermaritzburg. While Murray gave very serious consideration to the call from the latter church in Natal, in the end he declined it as he had all the others. The thought of returning to minister in the Transvaal still appealed to him, and he had begun contemplating the possibility of offering to go there himself if a DRC missionary was not found soon to minister in that needy region.

But then toward the end of 1859 Murray received a call to become the minister of the DRC congregation in Worcester. Located about seventy-five miles northeast of Cape Town, Worcester was already considered an important educational center. Both his father and his brother John affirmed his inclination to accept this opportunity. On the last Sunday of the year Murray announced his acceptance of the Worcester call to his Bloemfontein parishioners, who received the news with 'undisguised dismay'.

Emma's parents were planning to return to England before long due to her father's poor health. Emma and her girls were able to spend two delightful months, February and March, with her parents and younger sisters at Kalk Bay, then the fashionable seaside resort for Cape Town. As it turned out:

> The family never gathered together again at the Cape, though the Rutherfoords had intended to return. Mr Rutherfoord died in

England a couple of years later, and his wife remained there. Ellen and her [newlywed husband] Henry [Rudd] went over about this time and Lucy went with them, and later trained as a Nurse in Miss Nightingale's School for Nurses at St. Thomas's Hospital in London, a very 'modern' thing for a well-brought-up girl to do.[1]

Meanwhile, Murray wrapped up his affairs in Bloemfontein. He had made arrangements for a group of teachers to come from Holland, and five of them arrived 'in a batch' at Bloemfontein just at that time. Murray was responsible for seeing that they were provided for and gotten to their respective teaching sites. Rev. George Brown from Alice, in the Eastern Cape of South Africa, was secured to succeed Murray as Rector of the college.

While Murray looked forward to his new ministry opportunity, he dreaded the painful final parting from the flock he had shepherded for eleven years. He divulged in a letter to Emma:

I think daily of Worcester, but there is a dark cloud to pass through before reaching it. The parting here hangs heavily upon me. I have more than once read Acts 20 and 1 Thessalonians 2, and mourned. That 'ye know' and 'ye are our witness, and God' I cannot use. There are many people I dare not look at, because I have been unfaithful.[2]

Murray was ever hard on himself when it came to his evaluation of his own spiritual condition and ministry efforts. One of his daughters later divulged of this period in his ministry:

The photographs taken of him at this time represent him as a stern looking man, and his wife often speaks of his hard criticisms of and deep dissatisfaction with himself. He would say: 'My work seems vain, the people have no real consciousness of sin, no real dread of it; there is so much frivolity and lightheartedness, they come so

1. Murray, *Young Mrs Murray Goes to Bloemfontein*, p. 147.
2. Du Plessis, *The Life of Andrew Murray*, p. 180. Murray alludes to Acts 20:18 and 1 Thess. 2:10 where the Christians whom Paul had served, as well as the Lord Himself, could testify of the Apostle's consecrated, blameless ministry among them.

thoughtlessly before God and to His table, with no real preparation and no deep heart-searching.' He himself was constantly probing his own heart and blaming himself because of the unreality and want of consecration in his hearers, though we know he was much respected and loved at Bloemfontein.[3]

On 30 March the townspeople held a farewell tea in his honor in the old government schoolroom. A cash gift was presented to him along with many expressions of personal esteem and appreciation for his years of faithful, capable service. Unfortunately, the meeting was brought to a rather abrupt end by an approaching thunderstorm.

The town of Worcester had been established some forty years earlier. Its physical setting differed markedly from the flat, barren environs that Murray was leaving behind at Bloemfontein: Worcester was flanked by majestic mountain ranges on three sides. The town was located on a spacious, well-watered plain. To the southeast the Breede River made its way toward the ocean. The Hex River, a tributary of the Breede, not only provided Worcester with an abundant supply of fresh water but also carved out the mountain pass to the Great Karroo to the northeast. Worcester stood at a major crossroads, with highways stretching from the southwest to the northeast and from the northwest to the southeast.

Murray's Bloemfontein parish had measured 120 miles west to east by 80 miles north to south. There the closest neighboring churches lay seventy or more miles away. Many of his Bloemfontein parishioners were livestock farmers whose ranches covered thousands of acres apiece and were sparsely scattered over a wide area. In the Breede River valley, Murray's closest ministerial colleagues were located just thirty miles to the southeast at Robertson and not much further to the northwest at Tulbagh. Most of his Worcester parishioners were agriculturists whose farms were a couple of hundred acres in size and were located within a few minutes' drive of each other.

The DRC at Worcester was formed in 1824 and welcomed as its first pastor Rev. Henry Sutherland, one of the original six Scottish

---

3. Douglas, *Andrew Murray and His Message*, p. 83.

clergymen (including also Andrew Murray, Sr) recruited to serve in South Africa. Sutherland had faithfully served the Worcester congregation for over thirty-five years. While being a man of 'great piety and devotion', Sutherland had never succeeded in mastering the Dutch language and confessed that he was 'better at prayer than at preaching'.

The theological seminary at Stellenbosch had officially opened in November, 1859. The ministers present on that occasion authorized the Stellenbosch Triumvirate of John Murray, Nicolaas Hofmyer and J.H. Neethling to issue an invitation to members of all Christian congregations (regardless of denomination) in Cape Colony to attend a conference at strategically-located Worcester the following April. The intention of the conference was to address and discuss some of the pressing issues facing churches in South Africa at that time.

When the conference took place on 18 and 19 April, 1860 some twenty churches were represented. An anonymous member of Worcester's DRC reported: 'We counted 374 strangers [including] ministers, elders, deacons, retired members of church councils and [ordinary] church members.'[4] Of the sixteen DRC ministers in attendance, seven were either sons or sons-in-law of Rev. Andrew Murray, Sr, who was himself also present. The four non-DRC ministers represented the Scotch Church, the Wesleyan Church and the Rhenish Mission. Papers were read and public discussions ensued on such topics as 'Revivals', 'Christian Philanthropy', 'Literature for the People', 'The Hallowing of the Sabbath', 'Missions', 'Christian Governments' and 'Education'.

Toward the end of the second day of the conference, as suggested by Andrew Murray, Jr, DRC representatives met on their own to discuss the pressing need to supply qualified ministers for their churches throughout South Africa. Murray reminded them that twenty-six congregations were presently without a pastor and several more were expected to be within the next few years. Only two ministers currently served in the Orange Free State and just

---

4. Nel, *South Africa's Forgotten Revival*, p. 78.

one in Natal, while six congregations remained pastorless in each of those provinces. Despite the fact that the governments of OFS and Natal had agreed to provide the salaries for a total of eight ministers and twenty-five school teachers, individuals could not be found to fill those positions.

Murray proposed that a DRC deputy be sent to Holland, Germany, Scotland and, if necessary, America, to recruit ministers, missionaries and teachers to serve in South Africa. Dr William Robertson, minister of the DRC congregation at Swellendam, was selected to carry out the assignment. Murray, Nicolaas Hofmyer and Elder J.A. le Sueur of Cape Town were appointed as the committee that was to: promote interest in and collect funds for the undertaking; correspond with congregations and individuals who desired assistance in obtaining a minister or teacher; communicate necessary instructions to the deputy. In the months that followed Murray was kept busy fulfilling those responsibilities.

Robertson sailed for Europe the following June. In the end his mission was a great success. He recruited: nine ministers (two from the DRC in Holland and seven from the Free Church of Scotland) to serve in Cape Colony; two missionaries (Scotsman Alexander McKidd and Swiss Henry Gonin) to minister in Transvaal; two 'thoroughly qualified principals' for a pair of public schools; two teachers for a private parish school; four 'pious catechists' from Holland. Nearly all the individuals recruited went on to serve in South Africa for many years.

Another significant focus at the Worcester conference was the one on revival that was taken up in the opening session. In the address that William Robertson delivered on that theme, he recalled some of the many occasions in Scripture and subsequent history when God had visited His people with a fresh outpouring of His Spirit in prayer as well as 'a great revival of vital religion'. The conference participants listened intently as Dr James Adamson provided an account of the remarkable Prayer Meeting Revival that had swept across the United States in 1857 and 1858.

Also designated the Businessmen's Revival, that mighty moving of God's Spirit began at what would become famously known as the Fulton Street Prayer Meeting in New York City. Jeremiah Calvin Lanphier, a neighborhood missionary for NYC's North Dutch Church, began holding a noon-hour prayer meeting each weekday with local businessmen. The number of participants and prayer meetings grew rapidly. Within months numberless daily prayer meetings involving countless thousands of people had sprung up in cities, towns and villages throughout the U.S. Several hundred thousand (in a nation then numbering thirty million) were brought to faith in Christ and many communities experienced dramatic moral reform. As many as ninety college revivals, including at many prominent universities, occurred across America between 1857 and 1859. Virtually every Protestant denomination was touched by the awakening and shared in its blessings. In 1859 the revival spread to Northern Ireland where 100,000 conversions were reported.[5]

For more than thirty-five years Andrew Murray, Sr, had devoted every Friday evening to praying for revival in his own parish and throughout South Africa. 'His children will never forget,' related Murray, Sr's daughter Maria, 'standing outside his study door and listening to the loud crying to God and pleading for an outpouring of His Holy Spirit.'[6] Once, after reading of a minister who prayed for a revival for forty years before it came, Murray, Sr, stated, 'Aye, and that is longer than thirty-six!'

After Dr Adamson concluded his revival report at the Worcester conference, the senior Rev. Murray rose to share his own perspectives on this subject which was so much on his heart. He was, however, quickly overwhelmed with emotion and unable to continue. All this made a deep impression on the conferees. They returned to their home parishes with a deepened desire and a heightened hope that God would graciously choose to bring bona fide spiritual revival to their own churches, communities and country.

---

5. Collin Hansen and John Woodbridge, *A God-Sized Vision, Revival Stories That Stretch and Stir* (Grand Rapids: Zondervan, 2010), pp. 77-97, provides an excellent summary of the Prayer Meeting Revival.

6. Neethling, *Unto Children's Children*, p. 33.

This was not the first time of late that South African DRC congregations had been urged to prayerfully seek revival. A pair of articles published by two separate sets of pastors in *De Kerkbode* in August and October of 1859 had encouraged such prayer. The latter call to prayer, undersigned by fourteen clergy (including Andrew Murray, Sr, and his brother-in-law, G.W. Stegmann) concluded: 'We earnestly beseech you to faithfully and fervently pray one hour every week – with others or alone – that God by His grace may visit our land and give us the blessing of the outpouring of the Holy Spirit just as He is presently doing in other parts of the world.'[7]

In addition, an eighty-five page booklet entitled *De Kracht des Gebeds* (The Power of Prayer) was being distributed in many congregations. It described the revival in America and emphasized the necessity for prayer both before and during a spiritual awakening. Jan Neethling not only distributed the booklet to his parishioners but also published several articles on revival in the local church bulletin *De Wekker* (The Alarm) late in 1859.

Andrew Murray assumed his responsibilities as the new pastor of Worcester in May, 1860, the month he turned thirty-two years of age. His formal induction service was not held until Whitsunday (Pentecost) on 27 May. His brother John delivered the charge from Acts 2:1. That afternoon Andrew took as his preaching text 2 Corinthians 3:8, 'How shall not the ministration of the Spirit be rather glorious?' Large congregations attended these worship services, including many members from neighboring congregations.

---

7.   Nel, *South Africa's Forgotten Revival*, p. 73.

12

Revival!
1860–1861

The same month Andrew Murray began his ministry at Worcester, revival ignited in Cape Colony. The sudden awakening started in the village of Montagu, located nearly fifty miles southeast of Worcester. At the time Montagu did not have a resident minister. Likely in part due to the encouragement received at the recent conference at Worcester, a spirit of prayer and expectation started to grip Montagu. So many people began streaming to prayer meetings that former locations for those gatherings were unable to accommodate all who wished to participate. Separate prayer meetings were held daily for men, women, boys and girls; prayer meetings multiplied and convened up to three times daily.

Two months later a pair of ministers from the towns of neighboring Robertson and more distant Tulbagh came to conduct the quarterly communion service at Montagu. Afterwards it was reported:

On Sunday evening (22nd July) a prayer meeting was conducted by Revs Shand [of Tulbagh] and de Smidt [of Robertson], when the spiritual fervor was so great that people complained that the meeting ended an hour too soon. A year ago prayer meetings were unknown; now they are held daily, and sometimes as frequently as three times a day, and even among children. Some have doubted whether this be the work of God's Spirit; but we have witnessed cases in which a man has come under strong conviction of sin, and on that account has suffered indescribable anguish, from

ANDREW MURRAY

which nothing was able to deliver him but prayer and simple faith
in the expiatory sufferings of our Lord Jesus Christ.[1]

Another contemporary of those events related:

> It was a time when many truly longed for salvation. A time when the
> youth shared abundantly in God's blessing and many heathen were
> saved. A time of great activity and undertakings for the Kingdom
> of God. A time especially of great earnestness and an increasing
> interest in spiritual matters and fervent prayer.
>
> Early each morning and evening, people would make their
> way to prayer meetings. Children and young people would come
> together pleading for mercy. Their hearts were warmed and
> charitable towards missions, and each sought the redemption of
> his unsaved brother.[2]

Rev. Servaas Hofmeyr, the younger brother of Professor Nicolaas
Hofmeyr, had been called as Montagu's pastor but did not arrive
and begin his ministry there until the end of September. He later
reported:

> Extraordinary scenes were witnessed in those days. Anxious cries
> were uttered, heavy with fear. Heart-rendering testimonies of
> conversion were heard. Visions were seen and troubled dreams
> dreamt. Here in corporate prayer, elsewhere in quiet dwellings,
> even behind bushes and rocks, on mountains and in ravines, men,
> women, grayheads, children, gentlemen, servants – all kneeling on
> the same ground crying for mercy. And none of this expected by
> anyone, nor prepared by anyone, nor worked up or preached by
> anyone – it was all the Spirit of God; and not for a few hours or
> days, but months long.[3]

Nicolaas Hofmeyr, who conducted his brother's installation service
at Montagu, testified of the revival there:

---

1.   Du Plessis, *The Life of Andrew Murray*, p. 194.

2.   Nel, *South Africa's Forgotten Revival*, p. 91.

3.   ibid., p. 93.

In Montagu, especially, where I had ample opportunity to speak to many of those who had been awakened, I was firmly convinced that a powerful work had been carried out by the Spirit of God. When I was there, the feeling of anguish and distress had generally subsided. The soul had been able to appropriate to itself the offered pardon in the blood of Christ. Love had banished fear. But some had still to carry on a hard conflict caused either by their wavering faith or by their outbursts of native depravity.

For two or three weeks, when the awakening was in full strength, cases of heartfelt conversion occurred daily. A pious man told me that during that time the awakened were so much increased in number, and felt so anxious for spiritual advice, that he could scarcely allow himself bodily rest.

Scarcely a house in the village is to be found where the awakening of God's Spirit has not been felt by one or more individuals. The religious indifference for which this place has been known has given way to a tone of earnestness, which is diffused throughout society. The aspect of this place is entirely changed. Even those who do not approve of the revival have told me that the general improvement in the conduct of the inhabitants, within a few months, has been quite marvelous.[4]

The revival was not long in spreading to Worcester where Murray had begun his new ministry. C. Rabie was a teen in the Worcester congregation at that time who later went on to become a DRC minister. Years afterward Rabie described spiritual conditions at Worcester at the time of Murray's arrival as well as the new minister's powerful preaching ministry:

Mr Murray arrived at Worcester just at the right time. The congregation had been faithfully served by old father Sutherland, but the religion of the majority was merely formal. Only one or two of the oldest members used to engage in prayer, nor was it permissible for women to take audible part in the prayer meeting. No one would venture at that time to affirm that he was converted or regenerated; that was held to be a great presumption. ...

---

4. ibid., p. 97.

When Mr Murray commenced his ministry on the 27th May with his sermon on 'The Ministration of the Spirit,' there was a general movement among the dead bones. His preaching was in very deed in the ministration of the Spirit and of power. It was as though one of the prophets of old had risen from the dead. The subjects were conversion and faith; the appeals were couched in terms of deadly earnestness. Let me mention some of the texts. 'What meanest thou, O sleeper? Rise and call upon thy God' (Jonah 1:6). 'He that believeth not shall be damned' (Mark 16:16). At a sacramental service: 'Friend, how camest thou in hither, not having a wedding garment?' (Matt. 22:12). His pulpit manner was very violent, and bookboard and Bible were soundly belabored.[5]

The awakening at Worcester, however, did not come as a result of Murray's powerful preaching. He himself later pointed out that he did not intentionally use his preaching ministry to promote the revival until it had already been underway for six months.

Instead, awakening began on the farm of David Naude in the Breede River ward of the Worcester parish. There three individuals – Naude's son Jan, Jan's cousin Miss Van Blerk and an old native farmhand named Saul Pieterse (who was also known as 'Saul the Prophet') – had been faithfully meeting weekly for several months to pray for revival. Miss Van Blerk taught the 'coloreds' on the farm and was particularly distressed over their spiritually needy condition. She became so burdened for them that she prayed almost continuously for a week. Then one evening shortly thereafter, God's Spirit moved suddenly and mightily on a meeting she was holding for them. The spiritual distress of the people became so great that she ran from the meeting place to seek help with the situation. The emotional strain of the sudden, ongoing awakening soon overtaxed Miss Van Blerk and she retreated to Worcester for a week. Upon her return to the farm, the workers came out, singing, to greet her. Reportedly nearly everyone on the farm was converted.

---

5.   Du Plessis, *The Life of Andrew Murray*, p. 199. Presumably the pulpit and Bible were 'soundly belabored' by plenty of pounding.

As news of these developments quickly spread, people from neighboring farms promptly began streaming to the previously-neglected prayer meetings: 'young and old, parents and children, white and colored, flocked to the gathering, driven by a common impulse to cast themselves before God and utter their souls in cries of penitence.'[6] Andrew Murray came to lead one of the meetings not long after the revival first broke out. But after giving his careful instructions and inviting individuals to pray one at a time, the whole group immediately burst into simultaneous prayer, pleading for mercy and forgiveness. According to one witness, at that point old Saul jumped up, faced Murray and Naude, and challenged them, 'Try now to throw a dam wall around if you can.'[7]

Members from other parts of the parish and even from other congregations began to arrive at the Naude farm in carts and wagons. For three months the Naudes needed to suspend their farming activities to assist the many people coming to seek salvation. It was there that teenager C. Rabie came to faith in Christ and subsequently determined to enroll in the theological seminary at Stellenbosch.

Not long after Murray officiated at the meeting at David Naude's farm, the awakening spread to Worcester itself. J.C. de Vries, another young man from Worcester who later became a DRC minister, provides the following eye-witness account of the dramatic developments:

> On a certain Sunday evening there were gathered in a little hall some sixty young people. I was leader of the meeting, which commenced with a hymn and a lesson from God's Word, after which I engaged in prayer. After three or four others had (as was customary) given out a verse of a hymn and offered prayer, a colored girl of about fifteen years of age, in service with a farmer from Hex River, rose at the back of the

---

6. ibid., p. 194.

7. From a pamphlet by F.J. Liebenberg entitled *Herlewing in Suid Afrika* [*Revival in South Africa*]; *Montagu en Worcester – 1860*, as recorded in Nel, *South Africa's Forgotten Revival*, p. 101. Liebenberg interpreted Saul's statement to mean, 'Seeing you want to contain the Spirit – just try if you can.'

hall, and asked if she too might propose a hymn. At first I hesitated, not knowing what the meeting would think, but better thoughts prevailed and I replied, 'Yes.' She gave out her hymn verse and prayed in moving tones. While she was praying we heard as it were a sound in the distance, which came nearer and nearer, until the hall seemed to be shaken, and with one or two exceptions, the whole meeting began to pray, the majority in audible voice, but some in whispers. Nevertheless, the noise made by the concourse was deafening.

A feeling which I cannot describe took possession of me. (Even now, forty-three years after these occurrences, the events of that never-to-be-forgotten night pass before my mind's eye like a soul-stirring panorama. I feel again as I then felt, and I cannot refrain from pushing my chair backwards, and thanking the Lord fervently for His mighty deeds.)

At that time Rev. A. Murray was minister of Worcester. He had preached that evening in the English language. When service was over an elder (Mr Jan Rabie) passed the door of the hall, heard the noise, peeped in, and then hastened to call Mr Murray, returning presently with him. Mr Murray came forward to the table where I knelt praying, touched me, and made me understand that he wanted me to rise. He then asked me what had happened. I related everything to him. He then walked down the hall for some distance, and called out, as loudly as he could, 'People, silence!' But the praying continued. In the meantime I too kneeled down again. It seemed to me that if the Lord was coming to bless us, I should not be upon my feet but on my knees. Mr Murray then called again aloud, 'People, I am your minister, sent from God. Silence!' But there was no stopping the noise. No one heard him, but all continued praying and calling on God for mercy and pardon. Mr Murray then returned to me, and told me to start the hymn verse commencing ... 'Aid the soul that helpless cries'. I did so, but the emotions were not quieted, and the meeting went on praying. Mr Murray then prepared to depart, saying, 'God is a God of order, and here everything is confusion.' With that he left the hall.

After that the prayer meetings were held every evening. At the commencement there was generally great silence, but after the second or third prayer the whole hall was moved as before, and every one fell to praying. Sometimes the gathering continued till three in the morning. And even then many wished to remain longer, or returning homewards, went singing through the streets. The little hall was soon quite too small, and we were compelled to move to the school building, which also was presently full to overflowing, as scores and hundreds of country folk streamed into the village.

On the first Saturday evening in the larger meetinghouse Mr Murray was the leader. He read a portion of Scripture, made a few observations on it, engaged in prayer, and then gave others the opportunity to pray. During the prayer which followed on his I heard again the sound in the distance. It drew nearer and nearer, and on a sudden the whole gathering was praying. That evening a stranger had been standing at the door from the commencement, watching the proceedings. Mr Murray descended from the platform, and moved up and down among the people, trying to quiet them. The stranger then tiptoed forwards from his position at the door, touched Mr Murray gently, and said in English: 'I think you are the minister of the congregation; be careful what you do, for it is the Spirit of God that is at work here. I have just come from America, and this is precisely what I witnessed there.'

One Saturday evening Hessie Bosman, who was afterwards married to Rev. McKidd, the missionary, came to the village. At that time she had a school in Boschjesveld, and when she came to town she lodged with my parents. I said to her at once that she must not think of going to the prayer meeting, as it would be too much for her in her weak state of health. She replied: 'No, I must go, even if it should prove my death; for I have prayed so much for these meetings, and longed so much to take part, that I cannot remain away. No, come what may, I am going!' She attended, and was the third to engage in prayer that evening. While she was pouring out her heart the whole meeting broke forth into prayer, while she fell unconscious to the ground. I carried her out to the parsonage, where they were some time in bringing her round. That night she had to remain the guest of the parsonage, and next day she was herself again. ...

The fruits of that revival were seen in the congregation for many years. They consisted, among others, in this, that fifty young men offered themselves for the ministry. And this happened in days when it was a difficult matter to find young men for the work of the ministry. ... [8]

---

8.   Du Plessis, *The Life of Andrew Murray*, pp. 194-6.

From the above accounts it seems clear that initially Murray had some reservations about the revival, especially its emotional aspect which was, at times, overwhelming and uncontainable. To see a whole congregation of people bursting out simultaneously in prayer, crying out for God to have mercy on their souls, seemingly unaware of their surroundings and unable to control themselves, did not fit with his lifelong training and notions that God is not the author of confusion and that divine worship is to be conducted decently and in order (1 Corinthians 14:33, 40). He may have also had reservations about a purported mighty moving of God's Spirit coming primarily through prayer rather than in conjunction with a pronounced emphasis on the proclamation of God's Word. From the statements made by and about other ministers involved in the early stages of the South African revival it is evident that Murray was not alone in his cautious initial responses.

In a letter to her mother, Emma Murray further described the revival at Worcester:

> We are having many visitors from the surrounding places who come to see us on account of the revival meetings, and they go away blessed, saying that half has never been told. It is a solemn thing to live in such a congregation at such a time. I feel sure the Lord is going to bless us even more, and yet there are heavy trials before us; the work is deeply interesting and yet some things are painful. In the midst of an earnest address a man drove a dog into the church with a tin tied on its tail and frightened the people. Andrew came down the aisle and prayed a most solemn, heart-searching prayer, that if the work was not of God, He Himself would put a stop to it. The people were terrified as the excitement was very intense and some even fainted. ...
>
> The prayer meeting last night was very full and ten men decided for Christ, but fifty undecided left the building about twelve o'clock. We had no idea of the time. Two souls afterwards came through who were wrestling in agony for a time, but got into the light in their own houses. Some go through a fiery struggle. Two sisters have both passed through, are now bright and rejoicing. ...
>
> Last night again the church was full and Andrew preached so powerfully and yet so simply on 'the Lamb of God'. He is so

very discreet in dealing with souls. About twenty came forward, and others stayed behind to be talked to. We do feel and realize the power and presence of God so mightily. His Spirit is indeed poured out upon us.

Andrew is very tired after the meetings but is generally able to sleep well and feels refreshed in the morning[9]

Murray's father visited Worcester at that time and praised God for the opportunity to witness and speak at such meetings. 'Andrew, my son,' he said, 'I have longed for such times as these, which the Lord has let you have.'

A number of prayer meetings spontaneously sprang up at Calvinia, far to the north, in August. (That congregation had remained pastorless since Nicolaas Hofmeyr moved to Stellenbosch two years earlier.) Several weeks later a member of parliament who had known the residents of Calvinia for years and who was currently visiting there wrote his wife, stating that he could not adequately express to her how wonderfully the townspeople had improved since he last saw them the previous year.

One day a farmer in that area heard the distant, heart-wrenching cries of an individual obviously overwrought with grief. Following the sound, he was deeply moved when he came upon one of their young servant girls – a member of the Fingo (Mfengu) tribe of South Africa – earnestly engaged in prayer. She was pleading with God for the forgiveness of her sins in the name of Jesus Christ. Returning home, the farmer asked his wife whether the servant had previously manifested any concern over the salvation of her own soul. His wife related that only the day before she had been asked by the girl if Christ had died for her also and if she too, like others, could obtain pardon.

Several other towns were visited and transformed by the revival around that same time. The Consistory at Wellington, a congregation Murray would later pastor for many years, reported to the Presbytery that the parish had made greater moral and spiritual progress in recent weeks than throughout its entire previous history

9. Douglas, *Andrew Murray and His Message*, pp. 88-9.

of nearly two decades. The church leaders at Stellenbosch enthused of revived spiritual conditions in their community, 'The whole of society has been changed, yes, turned literally upside down!' The towns of Tulbagh, Ceres and Robertson, the rural Klein Drakenstein district of the Paarl parish, and the Rhenish Mission Society station at Schietfontein also shared in the revival blessings at that time.

Toward the end of the year God began to use Murray's preaching ministry in even greater ways than he had previously experienced. Some thirty-five years later, while sharing his testimony at a Keswick Convention, Murray related: 'In 1860, when I had been six months in the [Worcester] congregation, God poured out His Spirit there in connection with my preaching, especially as I was moving about in the country, and a very unspeakable blessing came to me.'[10] Of the extent and effect of Murray's Spirit-anointed preaching ministry at that time, Du Plessis reveals:

> Andrew Murray contributed in no small degree to the diffusion of the blessings of the revival. He was invited to be present at conferences held at such widely-separated centers as Cape Town and Graaff-Reinet, and wherever he spoke the impression was immediate and profound.[11]

At the latter conference in April, 1861, he preached at the closing session, taking as his text 2 Chronicles 15:12, 'They entered into a covenant to seek the Lord God of their fathers with all their heart and with all their soul.' One auditor afterward effused:

> We refrain from offering any observations on this most impressive discourse. Much had been told us of the talents of the young preacher, whom we were privileged to hear for the first time, but our intense expectation was far surpassed. We cannot but reiterate the heartfelt conviction, to which one of the daily papers has given utterance, that it would be the greatest of blessings for the D. R.

10.   Du Plessis, *The Life of Andrew Murray*, p. 448.
11.   ibid., p. 200.

Church of South Africa if she possessed a dozen Andrew Murrays of Graaff-Reinet to give to the Church as many and such-like sons as he has given.[12]

During 1861 the awakening continued to spread across South Africa, impacting some two dozen additional parishes,[13] including Bloemfontein and three other towns in the Orange Free State, Ladysmith in Natal and Hartebeesfontein in the Transvaal. After revival came to Graaff-Reinet beginning the middle of April, Maria Neethling wrote to a younger sister still living at home: 'I can imagine Papa's joy. I think he must be saying with Simeon: "Lord, now lettest Thou Thy servant depart in peace, for mine eyes have seen Thy salvation" [Luke 2:29-30].' When the letter was read to the senior Murray his eyes welled up with tears and he replied, 'It is just that.'

At a Graaff-Reinet prayer meeting that was held one Sunday evening during that period of revival, scoffers who had come to the meeting merely out of curiosity soon fell under heavy conviction of sin. God's Spirit worked so powerfully on that occasion, the meeting continued non-stop until midday on Tuesday! Only then did farmers from outlying areas return home with their families.

Some of the communities first awakened in 1860, including Worcester, continued to be powerfully impacted by the revival in 1861. Early in September of the latter year Nicolaas Hofmeyr visited Worcester. He was on a collection tour to raise funds for missions but also wanted to observe for himself the 'vehement, excited and confused prayer meetings' he had heard were taking place at Worcester, purportedly as an inevitable outcome of the powerful work of God's Spirit.

Murray was away at the time of Hofmeyr's arrival at Worcester, so the latter attended a prayer meeting with a church elder. As Hofmeyr opened the meeting in prayer he heard a few people moan.

---

12. ibid.

13. Nel, *South Africa's Forgotten Revival*, p. 144, provides a complete list of those revived congregations.

Then when a youth who had been powerfully converted began to pray in emotional tones, the assembly broke out in a bewildering verbal tumult. Due to their emotional distress, people tended to pray in short outbursts: 'Lord, won't you pour out your Holy Spirit?' 'Yes, Lord, do it!' 'O Lord, convert the unconverted!' As soon as the young man's emotional prayer came to an end, the commotion stopped. But when other individuals subsequently prayed with great fervor the same type of group response took place.

Hofmeyr was convinced that such behavior was not of God's Spirit, was unedifying and needed to be stopped. As soon as Murray arrived home, Hofmeyr expressed his concerns and suggested that Murray put an immediate stop to the questionable behavior.

According to Hofmeyr's journal, we have the following brief outline of what took place:

> [Murray] told Hofmeyr that he was in no position to accurately judge a whole movement by observing it during its middle phase rather than from its commencement. He then went on to explain that he had tried to put a halt to the emotional behavior, but had been unable to. He also found that these prayers from the heart served as the most powerful proof that the Holy Spirit was at work. It was for this reason that he was reticent to squash any manifestations with force.[14]

This incident certainly shows the change of perspective Murray had come to have concerning his own role in the midst of revival. He was now seeking not to interfere with, rather than to moderate, the mighty moving of God's Spirit. To Hofmeyr's credit, he did not press the issue further.

---

14. ibid., pp. 107-8.

13

CHALLENGING SYNOD RESPONSIBILITY
1862–1864

Andrew and Emma Murray's third child, a daughter named Catherine (Katie), had been born on 12 August, 1860, about three months after they settled at Worcester. Emma gave birth to their first son on 14 March, 1862. The boy was named Howson Rutherfoord, after his maternal grandfather who passed away around that same time. Another boy, Andrew McCabe, was living with the Murrays at that time while he pursued his education. The Murrays had brought McCabe with them from Bloemfontein, and he lived with them for six years. Douglas reports:

> From this onward, for the next sixty years one or more young people, chiefly boys, lived in the parsonage, being educated in the hope of supplying the need for Christian workers. It was wonderful to see how Mrs Murray opened her heart to these children. In her home letters one can hardly distinguish between the interest in the formation of the character of her own and her adopted children.[1]

C. Rabie's perspectives on Murray's personal pastoral ministries during his Worcester years are enlightening:

> Mr Murray was a man of power in his catechizations. I was one of those privileged to be confirmed by him. He carried his catechumens to the Bible, and made them read and explain it. When the class was over, two or three were directed to remain behind, in order that

---

1. Douglas, *Andrew Murray and His Message*, p. 96. These sixty years commenced in Bloemfontein in the late 1850s and continued till Andrew Murray's death.

ANDREW MURRAY

he might speak with them about the condition of their soul. These
were moments never to be forgotten. Not a few date their spiritual
birth from those talks.

His pastoral visitation carried terror to the hearts of his
parishioners. If his preaching was like thunderbolts from the
summit of Sinai, what would personal rebuke be like? People felt
under the earnestness of his individual dealing that they were
being ground to powder. On one occasion, at the close of a prayer
meeting, he proceeded to deal with each individual present. One
lady, observing how her pastor drew nearer and nearer to where she
sat, became gradually more and more uneasy, until, as Mr Murray
turned to her, she fell upon her knees, ejaculating, 'O Lord, into thy
hands I commend my spirit.' This, however, I must add: that there
is a wide cleft between the stern Mr Murray of those days and the
loving and gentle Mr Murray whom we knew in later years.[2]

The recollections of one of Murray's daughters reveal a more fun-
loving side of his character with his own family members:

On winter evenings father would read to us [Robert] Moffat's book,
Rivers of Water in a Dry Place, and at the description of adventures
with lions, he would cause us great terror by imitating the roar of
these beasts of prey. Frequently our evening would end with a wild
romp on Tom Tiddler's ground. ...

On summer afternoons father and mother would sometimes
take us children for an outing up the hills, when we would be
regaled on cake and coffee, and father would then set up a bottle,
and teach us to throw at and hit it with stones. Occasionally he was
absent on long journeys from home, and great were the excitement
and the joy when he returned.[3]

Other early childhood recollections shared by that same daughter
centered around the family's interest in and support of missions:

We were early taught to forego our Sunday allowance of sugar, and
to place a threepenny bit in the mission-box as the witness to, if

2.   Du Plessis, *The Life of Andrew Murray*, pp. 199-200.
3.   ibid., p. 201.

not the result of, our act of self-denial. Many missionaries stayed with us from time to time, whose names I have for the most part forgotten. Dr Duff, the famous missionary from India, was one; also Fredoux, McKidd, Mr and Mrs Gonin and others. ... Right well do I remember the early start, on a foggy morning, of the wagon and horses which took father and the Gonins away to the Transvaal, Mr McKidd traveling, I believe, in another wagon.[4]

Alexander McKidd and Henry Gonin were the two individuals enlisted by Dr William Robertson in his recruitment trip to Europe to serve as DRC missionaries in the Transvaal. Murray accompanied McKidd and the Gonins to the Transvaal to assist them in gaining permission to establish mission works there and in deciding exactly where to locate. Leaving Worcester in April, 1862, the missionary party made its way the nearly 1,000 miles to Rustenburg, beside the Transvaal's Magaliesberg Range, arriving there near the middle of May. Murray proceeded to Pretoria where the government's Executive Council granted permission for the missionaries to settle in Transvaal, with the proviso that the consent of the indigenous chief of an intended district must also be gained before commencing a mission work there.

After returning to Rustenburg, Murray contacted Paul Kruger, whom he described in a 30 May letter to Emma as 'Boer Commandant, and great man of influence among the natives'. (Kruger later served four terms as President of the South African Republic [Transvaal].) Kruger instructed the missionary delegates to meet with Chief Magato at his kraal, which they did the final Tuesday and Thursday of May. Magato and some forty 'petty chiefs' rejected their proposal to begin a missionary work among them. 'They are so afraid of losing their many wives,' Murray wrote Emma of the polygamous tribesmen, '[as] this is almost all they have heard of the Gospel.'

From Rustenburg the missionary delegation traveled two days to Paul Kruger's home, arriving there on Thursday 5 June. Murray further related of Kruger in a letter to his children: 'He is a good,

---

4.   ibid.

pious man. ... Mr Kruger says that when God gave him a new heart, it was as if he wanted to tell everyone about Jesus' love, ... and so he could not bear that there should be any poor black people not knowing and loving the Savior whom he loved.'[5] Kruger invited a local chieftain, Ramkok, to come visit the missionaries at his house. After Murray had preached at morning and afternoon worship services there that Pentecost Sunday, Ramkok arrived with a dozen or so lesser chiefs. They, too, rejected the missionaries' overtures to establish a work in that region.

As things turned out, the better part of a year passed before McKidd received an invitation from a tribe in the Zoutpansberg Range vicinity to settle and minister among them. McKidd, in the meanwhile, had married Miss Hessie Bosman (Murray officiated at their wedding), and the young couple arrived at the Zoutpansberg in May, 1863. Though the McKidds, sadly, died of fever within two years of settling there, their foundation-laying ministry was not in vain. Their missionary successor, Stephanus Hofmeyr, ministered 'with great success' in that region for forty years.

The Gonins, who had remained in the Rustenburg area, spent nearly two years acquiring the local tribal language as they patiently waited for God to open a door of missionary service for them. At the end of that time, Gonin and the Bakhatla chief Gamajan jointly purchased Paul Kruger's farm. Gonin established a mission there which he, along with his wife, successfully carried out till his death forty-seven years later.

En route back to Worcester from Transvaal, Murray wrote Emma from Fauresmith at the end of June, 1862, casually stating: 'I have forgotten to mention that I am bringing you up another son, a boy of fourteen, from Mooi River, to study for the ministry. ... His name is Hermanus Bosman, and he is a relative of the Stellenbosch people of that same name.'[6]

---

5. ibid., p. 203.

6. ibid., p. 204. Bosman lived with the Murrays nine years. He went on to become the 'influential and highly respected' minister of the Dutch Reformed congregation at Pretoria.

That October the quinquennial Synod of Cape Colony's DRC convened in Cape Town. The esteem in which Murray, still a relatively young man at thirty-four years of age, was already held was manifested in his selection as the Synod's Moderator that year. The fact that he was chosen for that position just at that time is all the more significant in light of the fact that the Synod was then facing some deeply-concerning and potentially-divisive issues. That he was selected to lead the Synod through those challenging times indicates the high degree of confidence others placed in his leadership abilities. Indeed, the commencement of his Moderator duties at that time marked the beginning of eight years of extremely trying and taxing denominational leadership responsibilities for Murray.

The rationalistic or 'liberal' movement was still strong in Holland, and held sway over some of the young South African pastors who had received their theological training in the universities of the Netherlands. Liberal theological perspectives were also being promoted in a monthly journal and a portion of the public press of Cape Town. In addition, nineteen years earlier, in 1843, the Colony's Government had adopted a new 'Ordinance' intended to grant fuller self-governance to the congregations that made up the Established or State Church. Under the provisions of the Ordinance the Church could 'frame and enforce its own rules and regulations' without needing, as it formerly had, to first gain the Government's assent. Those provisions, however, were about to be called into question in a series of cases taken before the civil courts.

Over 100 ministers and elders, representing sixty-two congregations in the Colony and beyond, were in attendance at the 1862 Synod. When Andrew Murray, Sr, arose to speak in the Synod, he did so by first addressing the Moderator, his son, as 'Right Reverend Sir'. The son, in turn, as a token of respect for his father, immediately rose and remained standing until Murray, Sr, had finished speaking. Murray, Jr, repeated this pattern each time his father spoke throughout the Synod sessions that followed.

A number of delegates from the 'far east and north' regions of South Africa did not arrive until the Synod had been in session for several days. Du Plessis relates:

A considerable number of ministers and elders, all bound for the Synod in Cape Town, had embarked on board the steamship *Waldensian*, hoping thus to escape the long and wearisome journey by land. When in the neighborhood of Cape Agulhas, the most southerly point of the African continent, the vessel ran upon a shelf of rock, and threatened soon to become a total wreck. ... The steamer was crowded with passengers, and the whole night was spent in getting them ashore by boatloads. As dawn broke the last boatful, with the captain among its occupants, was landed without mishap. Not many minutes later a large wave was seen to strike the doomed vessel, which broke in two and immediately vanished from sight. When the rescued ministers and elders reached Cape Town and took their seats in the Synod, a wave of deep feeling passed over the assembly.

After one of the spared ministers provided a description of the incident to the Synod, 'prayer was made and devout thanksgiving rendered to Almighty God for this marvelous deliverance from the jaws of death'.[7]

But division in the Synod surfaced soon thereafter when Moderator Murray invited one of the newly-arrived ministers from Natal to present his credentials. An elder from a parish within Cape Colony instantly stood and protested the acceptance of delegates from congregations outside the Colony. A witness to the proceedings, Rev. F. Lion Cachet, afterward explained:

Hitherto it had been supposed that the Church was at liberty to extend itself beyond the Colony, and that extra-colonial congregations, although not under the political authority of the Colony, might yet remain under the spiritual authority of the Synod. But the ministers and elders from beyond the Orange River are almost all orthodox; wherefore the moderns and liberals in the Colony flatter themselves that they will count a considerable majority in the Synod, if they are able to drive back the extra-colonials beyond the border.[8]

---

7. ibid., p. 210.

8. ibid., p. 212.

Members of the liberal party insisted that the admission of delegates from outside Cape Colony proper was in conflict with the terms of the Ordinance of 1843, which defined the rights and duties of the Church situated solely within the Colony's boundaries. After giving due consideration to the protest, the Synod, by a large majority, refused to uphold it.

The liberals, unwilling to accept that judgment, promptly took their case to the civil courts. They introduced a test case in which they sought to have the decision of the Synod of 1852, to incorporate the congregations beyond the Vaal River in the Church of Cape Colony, declared null and void. Further, apparently in conjunction with that earlier Synod decision, they sought a ruling that the minister of the extra-colonial congregation of Fauresmith should be declared incapable of sitting, deliberating and voting in the Cape Colony Synod. Murray as Synod Moderator and Rev. A.A. Louw, minister at Fauresmith, were summoned before the Colony's Supreme Court to demonstrate why those rulings should not be granted.

On 26 November the court passed down its judgment in favor of the plaintiffs' second claim that Louw was not entitled to a seat in the Synod. That decision excluded from the Synod not only Louw but all ministers and elders from beyond the Orange River. In addition, the judgment cast grave doubts on the legality of the proceedings of the Synods of 1852, 1857 and 1862, since in each of those assemblies delegates had sat and voted who, according to the present court ruling, were unqualified to do so.

In announcing the court's ruling to the Synod, Murray verbalized the deep grief of the majority of the gathering over this decision that effectively severed the official ties they had heretofore had with their DRC brethren on the frontiers outside the Colony's borders. Before requesting them to withdraw, Murray commended them to God in fervent prayer, after which the delegates from Trans-Orangia took their leave.

The remaining assembly then deliberated the legality of its own proceedings at the present and two previous Synods. They concluded, 'the Synod views all its resolutions as legal, so long as their illegality is not proven'. But in order to have that question settled with greater certainty, the Synod decided to pursue the opinion of the Supreme Court on the issue. In light of the urgency and importance of the matter, the Supreme Court judges agreed to hear the case at a very early date. But the plaintiffs in the previous case objected to a more immediate hearing, stating their intention to present a case against the legality of the three Synods in question. The Synod was left with no other choice but to adjourn until such time as the court hearing was held and a judgment rendered.

The early adjournment of the Synod also left unresolved a pair of doctrinal conflicts that had surfaced involving two of Cape Colony's liberal ministers. Rev. J.J. Kotze, the pastor at Darling, was the acknowledged leader of the Colony's modernist party. Rev. T.F. Burgers, who ministered at Hanover, was 'more copious of speech than Kotze, but lacking the latter's dignity and learning'.

One of the three doctrinal formularies to which the DRC required its ministers to adhere was the Heidelberg Catechism. Cape Colony ministers were expected to provide an exposition of one of the Catechism's fifty-two sections each Sunday, thus preaching through the entire formulary every year. The exposition was to be a defense of each particular doctrine based on the authority of Scripture. At the 1862 Synod, Kotze protested against being compelled to defend the Catechism at every point. In particular, he objected to the answer to Question 60 which states that man is 'continually inclined to all evil'. Kotze asserted that such language was not fitting in the mouth of a heathen, far less of a Christian, and further stated his belief that 'the catechism is here in error.' He was invited both publicly and in private interview to retract or modify his statements. But he refused, and that is where the matter stood when the Synod had to adjourn.

Even before the 1862 Synod, Burgers was accused of being 'tainted with Rationalism' and of making statements that were contrary to the doctrines of the Church. Specifically, he was said, on certain occasions, to have denied the existence of a personal Devil, the sinlessness of Christ's human nature, the resurrection of the dead, and the personal existence of the soul after death. The examination of those charges had not been concluded when the Synod was adjourned.

Early the following year, 1863, the Supreme Court heard the case concerning the legality of the three contested Synods. In April the Court handed down its decision that the resolutions of those Synods were legal and binding in spite of the fact that delegates from consistories outside the Colony had participated in those assemblies. The Synod reassembled in the middle of October and again took up the cases involving J.J. Kotze and T.F. Burgers. Kotze still refused to make any retraction of his previous statements concerning the Heidelberg Catechism. Consequently the Synod voted by a 70 per cent majority to temporarily suspend him from his pastoral ministry. If Kotze did not submit a written retraction of his earlier statements to the Synodical Committee by the time of its next meeting the following April, he would be permanently deposed from his ministry.

During its October meeting, the reconvened Synod also appointed a committee to meet at Hanover to take written testimonies from the witnesses of T.F. Burgers's declarations that allegedly contradicted the historic doctrines of the Church. That committee subsequently collected those depositions and instructed Burgers to send his written plea in the case to the Clerk of the Synodical Committee before its April, 1864, meeting.

With Kotze under suspension, the responsibility fell to the regional Presbytery of Tulbagh to make provisions for the ministry of the Word and the sacraments to be carried out at Darling. Each minister of the Presbytery was assigned certain Sundays on which he was to minister at Darling. But the trustees of that congregation sent a letter to each of the presbyterial ministers, stating that if he came to Darling he would be refused access to the pulpit.

Despite receiving that letter himself, Andrew Murray, Jr, one of the ministers of the Tulbagh Presbytery, ventured to Darling on the first weekend assigned to him. He intended to remain in the parish for two weeks, not only preaching at the church but also making pastoral visits from farm to farm. When he arrived on 22 November, however, he found the church door locked to him. After efforts to obtain another hall in which to preach proved fruitless, Murray announced that he would hold a worship service at the house of his host, a Mr Basson. But when the appointed hour arrived, only the Basson family members, who were obligated to be there out of courtesy, and one other individual, Jacob Cloete, were present. Cloete informed Murray he was the only member of the Darling congregation who approved of the Synod's suspension of Kotze. Murray was forced to return to Worcester with his ministry intentions at Darling unfulfilled.

Kotze took his case to the Supreme Court, claiming that the Synod's action against him should be nullified. Months before that case could be heard by the Court, the Synodical Committee, chaired by Murray, met in Cape Town on 19 April, 1864. Since no retraction had been received from Kotze, the full sentence of the Synod was enforced and he was declared deposed from his ministerial office. Kotze chose to defy the Synod's decision by resuming his pastoral ministry at Darling on 1 May.

At the Synodical Committee's 19 April meeting it also gave further consideration to T.F. Burgers's case. After considering all the evidence, the committee 'demanded' of Burgers 'a clear statement of what he believed with reference to the doctrines specified in the four points of accusation'. Burgers declined to comply, declaring the committee's demand 'out of order and repugnant to acknowledged principles of justice'.

This difficult period was not without its blessings for the Murrays. Their fifth child and fourth daughter, Annie, was born on 25 October, 1863. That year and the next Murray had the joy of publishing his second and third books. Throughout his Worcester pastorate, Murray had established the custom of holding monthly baptismal services when he would preach directly to the parents on the subject of carefully raising their children for the Lord. His reflections on this subject led him, in 1863, to publish a book in Dutch entitled *Wat zal toch dit kindeken wezen?* (What manner of child shall this be?). Subtitled 'Meditations for believing parents on the birth and baptism of their children', the small duodecimo volume contained 230 pages divided into thirty-one chapters, a reading for each day of the month.[9]

The following year, 1864, Murray published another duodecimo volume in Dutch, *Blijf in Jezus* (Abide in Jesus).[10] A work of 221 pages in length, each of the thirty-one chapters, was intended to guide and encourage readers in some aspect of their Christian life. Murray's motivation in writing that book was to help establish Christians more firmly in their faith.

Another significant blessing came in May or June of 1864, when Alexander Duff, the celebrated Scottish missionary to India, visited the Murrays at Worcester. Duff had served in India for thirty-four years and was now returning to his homeland to promote the cause of foreign missions in the Free Church of Scotland. Despite his present physical weakness, Duff undertook a lengthy tour through South Africa, visiting mission stations in various parts of the country and giving advice in his area of expertise, the education of indigenous peoples. He sailed from Cape Town for Scotland on 20 June.

Whether or not Murray had any inkling of it at the time, a change in his own ministry setting lay not far off in the future.

---

9. Murray followed this same thirty-one chapter format in many of his subsequent books. A duodecimo or twelvemo volume contains small pages cut twelve from a single sheet of paper. Twenty-three years later, in 1886, an expanded English edition of this book was published under the title *The Children for Christ*.

10. It was published in English eighteen years later, in 1882, with the title *Abide in Christ*.

14

CAPE TOWN PASTORATE
1864–1867

Early in July 1864 Andrew Murray received a call to become one of three co-pastors of Cape Town's Dutch Reformed Church. The DRC constituency in the metropolis consisted of some 5,000 adherents and more than 3,000 communicant members. They met in two church buildings – the Groote Kerk (Great Church), with its 3,000 seats, and the Nieuwe Kerk (New Church), with a seating capacity for 1,000. Three ministers shared pastoral care of those congregations and preached in rotation at the two church buildings.

For Murray, now aged thirty-six, the opportunity to minister in such a prestigious and influential setting was doubtless extremely attractive. In addition, by relocating to Cape Town he could more conveniently carry out his responsibilities as Synod Moderator, especially given the ongoing struggles within the denomination. Of this new pastoral possibility Murray wrote his father:

> As far as my own impressions go, and the advice of friends outside of Worcester, everything appears to point to Cape Town, but it is difficult really to bring my mind to say *Yes*. So much is implied in that little answer, by which I venture to undertake such a great work. I shall be glad of your special prayers that I may be kept from going, unless it be with very special preparation from on high.[1]

When the Synodical Committee met again on 19 July it dismissed as unproven the charges against T.F. Burgers with regard to the resurrection of the dead and the personal existence of the soul after death. But it found him guilty of denying both the personality of the

---

1.   Du Plessis, *The Life of Andrew Murray*, p. 239.

Devil and the sinlessness of Christ's human nature'. As a result, the Synodical Committee voted to suspend Burgers from his pastoral ministry till the Committee's next meeting the following year. The Committee also stated its willingness to lift the suspension if Burgers provided an explanation of his views, a retraction of his errors, and an affirmation of his full assent to the doctrine of the DRC on the two points at issue. Burgers disregarded the suspension decision and, at the formal request of the Hanover Consistory, continued to serve as the congregation's minister.

Not knowing that Burgers would take that course of action, the Synodical Committee asked Andrew Murray, Sr, to preach at Hanover the first Sunday of August. Hanover was part of the Graaff-Reinet Presbytery. But when the seventy-year-old Murray arrived at Hanover, the Consistory, following Burgers's advice, refused him permission to preach or baptize.

Several days later, on 11 August, Murray, Jr, penned another letter to his father, this time sharing his decision concerning the Cape Town ministerial opportunity:

> Many thanks for your kind expressions of sympathy in the matter of the Cape Town call. You will have seen by the papers that I have accepted it. It is some comfort to me to think that I go in answer to many prayers, and that it may please God to use me as an instrument for the hearing of still more prayers, that are laid up before Him, for a blessing on that congregation. If God wills to bless, no instrument is too weak, and blessed it is to be the instrument which He condescends to use.[2]

J.J. Kotze's case was heard by the Supreme Court on Tuesday and Friday, 23 and 26 August.[3] The attorney who was to represent the Synod fell severely ill shortly before the trial and on very short notice Murray was called to present the Synod's defense himself. On Friday,

---

2. ibid., p. 240.

3. ibid., pp. 220-3 provides a summary of specific points presented by the plaintiff (Kotze) and the defendant (Murray), as well as rulings given by the Court.

with the courtroom 'crowded to the doors with interested auditors', Murray did so for four and a half hours. When Murray concluded, one of the Judges complimented his presentation: 'There can be but one opinion as to the ability and conscientiousness with which you have pleaded your cause. Few advocates could have done it equally well.'

One week later, however, the Court handed down its ruling in favor of Kotze. The Justices ruled that the Synod had not followed proper principles and procedures required to insure an impartial judicial examination. Furthermore, they affirmed Kotze's contention that his statements concerning the Heidelberg Catechism, when tested by the Word of God and other portions of the formularies, were not in conflict with the doctrines and formularies of the Church. As a result, the Synod's sentence against Kotze was overturned and he was reinstated in his rights and privileges as minister of Darling.

Murray concluded his pastoral ministry in Worcester, which had comprised nearly four and a half eventful years, in late October or early November. Emma wrote her mother of the painful final separation from their beloved congregation at Worcester as well as the misgivings she was having about their upcoming ministry in Cape Town:

> On Saturday and Sunday the church was overcrowded: a hundred carts, many horse wagons, whole families came to the farewell meetings. On the day we left many carts and wagons accompanied us out of the village. After half an hour's drive we all knelt in a circle, Andrew praying, after singing a Dutch hymn. Old men were weeping like children, and the leave takings were heartbreaking. I felt quite ill when I got to the farm near Wellington where we stayed. How I shall miss the dear Worcester people. They have been so kind and loving. And after all the wonderful times we have passed through together, I don't know how I shall get on in Cape Town. It will all be so stiff, not like our own dear homely people.[4]

The Murrays settled in a large house called Craig Cottage, located in an attractive setting on Kloof Street on 'the very outskirts of the city'. The front of the house looked out over Table Bay. The slope

---

4. Douglas, *Andrew Murray and His Message*, p. 99.

in front of the home had been leveled into a two-terrace garden in which a variety of fruit and ornamental trees grew. Behind the house a large green field sloped upwards to dense fir trees that covered the lower declines of the Lion's Head, a striking mountain that towered nearly 2,200 feet above the edge of the sea.

On Sunday afternoons the Murray family often enjoyed retreating up the hill behind their home. There Murray quizzed his children on the Bible lessons of the day or entertained them with stories of missionary heroism. Reportedly their family was the first to introduce the game of croquet into the Colony, and Emma Murray's sewing-machine was one of the earliest seen in Cape Town.

Murray began his Cape Town pastorate on 10 November. His pastoral colleagues in that charge were Dr Abraham Faure and Dr Heyns. Faure, who was sixty-eight years old and had served as a DRC minister for forty-two years, possessed 'the widest and most evangelical sympathies'. Heyns, with twenty-eight years of pastoral service to his credit, also served as professor of Dutch language and literature and tutor in Hebrew at the South African College.

Murray promptly plunged into a taxing round of varied ministry responsibilities. Besides regularly preaching in Dutch at the Great Church and the New Church, he also led a Sunday service in English, so often preached three times each Lord's Day. Many of the leading citizens of the city attended those services.

Murray actively ministered to Cape Town's underprivileged class as well. He held two weeknight services for fishermen and other poor individuals. They demonstrated their appreciation for his ministry by placing gifts of fish, eggs and similar commodities in the pulpit before the service started. Murray frequently spoke at one of the weekly services held at Cape Town's three DRC schools. Those schools, located in different parts of the city, ministered to more than 800 underprivileged children. Murray promoted active lay visitation in the poorer districts of town. He led by example in faithfully visiting the poor. During a severe smallpox epidemic that claimed many victims in the Cape Town area, he continued to visit the sick.

Murray also took an active interest in the spiritual and intellectual welfare of young men. He first participated in Cape Town's Mutual

Improvement Society, an association of young men who gathered to discuss public issues in the English language. Perceiving the need for an organization that could reach a larger number of young men and would have more definite spiritual aims, he helped establish a Cape Town chapter of the Young Men's Christian Association in August, 1865, and was elected as its first president.

T.F. Burgers, having seen the outcome of the J.J. Kotze case, similarly appealed to the Supreme Court to have the Synodical Committee's judgment against him rescinded. The Court considered Burgers's case on 26 May, 1865.[5] Murray again presented the formal defense, this time appealing to a provision in the Ordinance of 1843[6] that appeared to stipulate that a Church Court's ruling 'in the case of any scandal or offence which shall be brought before it and proved to its satisfaction' could not be prevented by 'any action, suit or proceeding at law'. But the Justices once more sided with the plaintiff, with the results that the Synodical Committee's sentence against Burgers was overruled and he was restored to his ministerial position and privileges at Hanover.

The Supreme Court rulings in favor of Kotze and Burgers, however, did not bring to an end the conflict within the DRC. Both the Tulbagh and Graaff-Reinet Presbyteries stated they could not officially recognize any authority other than the Synod which had decided to remove Kotze and Burgers from their ministerial office. When the Presbyteries met for their annual meetings in October, they refused to grant Kotze and Burgers permission to sit as the ministerial representative of their respective congregations. The two ministers then obtained interdicts from the Supreme Court, prohibiting the Presbyteries from refusing them their right to be seated as delegates. The Presbyteries subsequently decided to adjourn indefinitely, until the Synod itself could assemble and determine an appropriate course of action in these troubling circumstances. These disputes and developments in the Tulbagh

---

5. Du Plessis, *The Life of Andrew Murray*, pp. 225-6 summarizes the arguments presented by both sides in the trial as well as the Court's ruling.

6. The Ordinance of 1843 was referenced on pp. 153 of the present volume.

and Graaff-Reinet Presbyteries stretched out over the course of two years, from October of 1864 to October of 1866.

Meanwhile, in April, 1866, the Synodical Committee decided to appeal the earlier Burgers case (i.e., *Burgers vs. the Synodical Committee*, which had been tried by the Colony's Supreme Court in May, 1865) to the Privy Council in England. As Synod Moderator Murray was asked to proceed to England in order to communicate to counsel there pertinent information and advice. Accompanied by his wife and children, Murray embarked on 14 May, 1866 aboard the steamship *Roman*.

Less than a week after the Supreme Court's consideration of *Burgers vs. the Synodical Committee* Emma Murray had given birth to her fifth daughter, Isabella, on 31 May, 1865. Sadly, the infant died not quite eight months later on 28 January, 1866. Emma was expecting again, having completed the first trimester of her pregnancy, when the Murrays set sail for England.

One of the first letters Murray received from family back in South Africa upon reaching England brought the news of his esteemed father's death. After forty-three years of faithful pastoral ministry, all spent at Graaff-Reinet, Murray, Sr, had retired just a few months earlier due to his advancing age and declining strength. He died on 24 June at the age of seventy-two. From Tiverton, England, Murray, Jr, wrote to console his mother on 20 August:

The news of our dear father's departure has just reached me. And you will not think it strange if I say that I could not weep. I felt that there was too much cause for thanksgiving. How indeed can we thank God aright for such a father, who has left us such a precious legacy in a holy life, so full of love to us and of labor in his Master's work. May his example be doubly influential, now that we have him glorified with his Savior. For he is still ours. I cannot express what I felt yesterday in church – we received the tidings on Saturday evening – at the thought of what his meeting with his Master must have been, and what his joy in the perfect rest of His presence. It must be a joy passing knowledge, to find and see One of whom the soul has been thinking for fifty years, for whom it has longed and thirsted, grieved and prayed, spoken and labored

– all at once to find Him, and to find everything it has said or felt or tasted in its most blessed moments but as a shadow compared with the inexpressible reality. What a joy, what a worship, what a love that must be when, with the veil of the flesh torn away, the ransomed spirit recovers itself from its death-struggle at the feet of Jesus.

And I feel confident that my dearest mother has tasted in abundant measure the comfort and support which the Savior gives. Not but what there must be some dark and lonely hours; but they will make the Savior's presence more precious, and help the more to lift the heart heavenward in the prospect of the eternal reunion. We cannot but be specially grateful for the kind Providence which has arranged for Charles taking Papa's place, and keeping unchanged and sacred so many memories which otherwise would have been lost.[7]

When Murray, Sr, retired at the beginning of 1866, his namesake was invited to succeed him as the next minister at Graaff-Reinet. After Murray, Jr, declined that call, it was extended to his younger brother, Charles, who accepted it. Charles went on to serve that charge until his death thirty-eight years later.

The Judicial Committee of the Privy Council did not hear the Synodical Committee's appeal of the Burgers case until November 10 and 12. Advocate Neil Campbell of the Scottish Bar represented the Synodical Committee in the proceedings. An eye-witness of the opening day of the hearings reported:

Mr Murray was, of course, present. His appearance I found to be exceedingly prepossessing; and after having read his address to the Cape Supreme Court, I think he would have pleaded his cause better than Mr Campbell did. When the latter was half-way through his reply, Mr Murray left the court.[8]

The reason for Murray's sudden departure from the courtroom was that Emma gave birth to their second son that day, 10 November.

7. Du Plessis, *The Life of Andrew Murray*, pp. 241-2.
8. ibid., p. 243.

The newborn was named Andrew Haldane, receiving the first name of his father, grandfather and great-grandfather.

Relatively few specifics are known of Murray's family and ministry activities during that protracted stay in Britain. Doubtless Emma relished the opportunity to spend extended time with her mother and some other family members. Murray visited Holland and Scotland where he greatly enjoyed renewing old friendships from student days. In England and Scotland he had a number of opportunities to preach in various churches. In October he delivered a series of powerful sermons at a conference in Bath. Those addresses were promptly published in the November issue of *Evangelical Christendom*.

On Christmas Day Murray spoke in a prison to 200 thieves before they had their Christmas dinner. When he began to preach, the inmates started to cough him down. Taking out his watch, Murray responded good-naturedly: 'One at a time, gentlemen, one at a time. As the sailor said to the minister while the donkey brayed, either you or the donkey. So I will give you five minutes to cough and you will give me five minutes to preach.'[9] By the end of the five minutes the prisoners had become so interested in what he had to say that they did not think to cough again till after the service.

One of the London congregations at which Murray preached, the Marylebone Presbyterian Church, extended him a call to come as its minister after he had returned to South Africa. It appears a pastoral call from London's Regent Square Presbyterian Church was intimated to him as well. In 1868 Emma's mother wrote her daughter back in Cape Town: 'I am pretty much persuaded I shall see you all again. Several have an eye on Andrew. They are greatly at a loss for someone to take Mr Hamilton's place.' When Emma asked her husband if he would accept the call, he replied: 'No, my church needs me, my people need me, my country needs me. I must sacrifice myself for them.'[10]

---

9. Douglas, *Andrew Murray and His Message*, p. 102.

10. ibid., p. 104.

The Privy Council's Judicial Committee issued its long-awaited verdict in the Burgers case on 6 February, 1867. It, too, ruled in favor of Burgers. Immediately after that decision was handed down the Murrays sailed from England, arriving back in Cape Town on 14 March. They had been away exactly ten months. The following Sunday Murray preached to his own congregation from a fitting text, Exodus 18:7b: 'They asked each other of their welfare, and they came into the tent.' He soon discovered that in both the denomination and his own parish, he had returned to 'an atmosphere of heated, and sometimes acrimonious, controversy'.[11]

---

11.   Du Plessis, *The Life of Andrew Murray*, p. 244.

15

THE TRIUMPH OF CONSERVATISM
1867–1870

During Murray's absence in England Dr Abraham Faure had retired from his co-pastorate of the congregations under his charge in Cape Town. At the 18 February meeting of the combined Consistory that was held to discuss Faure's replacement, a petition was submitted signed by 527 of Cape Town's 3,000 DRC members. It formally requested that none other than Rev. J.J. Kotze be called as the church's next co-pastor! 'The choice of the minister mentioned,' the petition asserted, 'will greatly contribute towards removing the estrangement which has for some time existed between the Consistory and a large portion of the congregation.'[1] The request was not granted but the fact that it was made with the backing of fully one-sixth of the official membership shows the considerable strength liberalism had gained in Cape Town by that time. The congregation eventually called as its third minister Murray's cousin, Rev. G.W. Stegmann, Jr, 'a man of ability, great eloquence and wide culture'.

A young modernist minister, Rev. David P. Faure, had arrived at the Cape in 1866 while Murray was away in England. Having been raised in South Africa's DRC, Faure had recently completed his theological studies at the University of Leiden in Holland. His father was the first cousin of two of the Colony's conservative DRC ministers, Abraham Faure of Cape Town and Philip Faure of Wynberg. Years later David Faure revealed: "Even during the last years of my university life it had become abundantly clear to me

---

1. Du Plessis, *The Life of Andrew Murray*, p. 246.

that, if I succeeded in obtaining a congregation at the Cape that was willing to accept me as its minister, it would have to be one outside my Mother Church.'[2] Accordingly, he began holding Sunday services in Cape Town's Mutual Hall in which he expounded the doctrines of Unitarianism. He soon had a group of followers and they formed the Free Protestant Church (also called the Free Thought Church) of Cape Town.

Beginning in August, 1867 Faure held a series of lectures in which he addressed from a rationalistic perspective such subjects as human reason, the Old and New Testaments, miracles, Jesus Christ, the atonement and eternal punishment. Early in 1868 those lectures were published under the title *Modern Theology*. In response Murray delivered a series of thirteen Monday evening discourses in the Great Church. His topics, which addressed in detail the positions set forth by Faure, were human reason, divine revelation, the Old Testament, the New Testament, miracles, the resurrection, Jesus the Son of Man, Jesus Christ the Son of God, man, the atonement, eternal punishment, prophecy, truth and error.

Faure himself said of Murray's discourses, 'Both as regards matter and manner Mr Murray's lectures were far superior to those previously referred to, and they represent the only serious attempt made to meet argument with argument.'[3] Those discourses were delivered in Dutch and published in an octavo volume entitled *Het Moderne Ongeloof* (Modern Unbelief). For the benefit of those who did not understand Dutch, Murray also presented a related discourse in English in Cape Town's Commercial Exchange. That discourse was published under the title *A Lecture on Modern Theology*. That same year, 1868, Murray also wrote a short series of articles for *De Kerkbode* on the theme of 'God's Woord en de Dwaling' (God's Word and Error).

The way in which Murray and his church dealt with the secession of some of David Faure's relatives from the DRC during that same period is intriguing. Faure's mother, sister and two aunts notified

2. ibid., p. 232.
3. ibid., p. 246.

the Consistory of their plan to leave the church. In keeping with church 'law and custom', their names and intention were announced from the pulpit the Sunday after this notification was received by the church leaders. Murray employed Deuteronomy 13:1-18 as the Old Testament reading that morning and in his running comments on the passage emphasized the danger of being led astray by a false prophet or even by one's wayward family members and friends due to misplaced loyalty to them.

His sermon text for the morning was 1 John 2:18-23, and the words 'they went out from us but they were not of us' were applied explicitly to Faure's relatives and other followers who were leaving the church. He stated:

> We find some suddenly denying Christ who for forty or fifty years confessed and worshipped Him as the Son of God. We find some who formerly, when members of the consistory, led and edified the congregation, now laboring to secure a victory for unbelief. In spite of all this cry about deliverance from priestcraft, we find the teachings of a preacher accepted, solely because of attachment to his person, and by none as readily as by the so-called freethinkers. In spite of the boast of independence of inquiry, there are proofs in all parts of the country that members of the same family, merely because a man is a son or a relative, readily accept all his utterances.[4]

Murray's remarks may seem too pointed and heavy-handed to more irenic modern sensibilities. But these actions certainly point out the gravity with which the adverse influence of heresy was treated in that time and place.

When Cape Colony's DRC Synod was held in the latter part of 1867 it proved to be a short-lived gathering. Having fulfilled his term as Moderator, Murray was now elected as Actuarius, being 'entrusted with the special care of all legal and documentary matters pertaining to the Synod'. Dr Philip Faure of Wynberg was chosen as the next Moderator. But when J.J. Kotze and T.F. Burgers took their seats among the assembled delegates: 'The

---

4.   ibid., p. 247.

Synod found itself upon the horns of a serious dilemma. It was morally unable to rescind the sentences passed upon the two erring brethren, and it was conscientiously unwilling to set at defiance the judgments of the Civil Courts.'[5] Consequently the Synod decided to adjourn until the present unacceptable situation could be more satisfactorily redressed. As it turned out, that undesirable state of affairs dragged on three more years, in which time neither the Synod nor the Presbyteries of Tulbagh and Graaff-Reinet convened.

But during those years it became increasingly apparent that conservatism rather than liberalism was carrying the day in the Colony's DRC. This was due in part to a decision reached at the 1862 Synod with regard to a 'colloquium doctum' (learned colloquy) with the Board of Examiners at which all candidates seeking a ministerial license from the DRC needed to appear. Originally intended to measure the theological knowledge of a ministerial candidate, the Synod's 1862 decision had enlarged the colloquy's scope. Now the interviewing council was to make 'a special inquiry' about the ministerial candidate's perspectives on 'regeneration by the Holy Spirit' as well as his 'fidelity' to the other doctrines of the DRC. The Synod considered agreement on those key matters to be 'indispensable requirements' for all who were to be accepted as DRC ministers.

In addition, between 1862 and 1870 the orthodox Theological Seminary at Stellenbosch had trained upwards of forty DRC ministers. The majority of those were appointed to Colonial congregations while some went to serve parishes beyond the Orange and Vaal Rivers. Furthermore, David Faure's work tended to attract and hold those who were dissatisfied with the orthodox teachings of the DRC. As a result of all these factors, when the Synod reconvened in 1870 the liberal party had shrunk to a mere tenth of the more than 100 delegates assembled.

The primary concern of the 1870 Synod was resolving the ongoing impasse that had developed due to the conflicting judgments passed

5.   ibid., p. 229.

down by 'the Church Courts' and 'the Civil Courts' in the Kotze and Burgers cases. The delegates were divided along three main lines of opinion. The first and smallest group stated, in effect: 'Submit to the judgment of the Civil Power. You have acted irregularly and incurred censure. Accept the situation and pass on to the next question.' A second party, at the opposite extreme, believed the Church needed to steadfastly resist every infringement of its rights by the Civil Power; the sentences of the Church Courts against Kotze and Burgers should be upheld. A third group, seeking to promote a moderating position, suggested: 'Submit to the authority of the Civil Courts, but submit under protest. Rescind of your own accord the sentences passed against Kotze and Burgers, and grant them leave to sit and vote.'[6] In the end, after a great deal of debate and by a majority of only eight votes (fifty-two to forty-four), the Synod adopted the third party's compromise proposal.

The minority felt strongly that such a decision 'will have the effect of allowing the [Civil] Court to persist in the course it has adopted, permitting Unbelief to raise its head with greater boldness, and causing our testimony against error to lose much of its force'.[7] As a result, the minority submitted a formal written protest. Among the notable conservative ministers to sign the protest were Andrew, Charles and George Murray,[8] Nicolaas and Servaas Hofmeyr, J.H. Neethling and G.W. Stegmann, Jr.

As it turned out, the apprehensions of the conservatives did not materialize. After serving at Hanover only two more years, Burgers was elected President of Transvaal and severed his connection with the DRC. Kotze continued ministering at Darling until advancing age and infirmity compelled him to resign his pastoral charge. Some liberal pastors, finding themselves at odds with their fellow ministers and their own congregations, left the DRC. Others openly

---

6.   ibid., p. 233.

7.   ibid., p. 235.

8.   Murray's youngest brother George was then serving his first ministerial charge at the DRC of Willowmore in the Eastern Cape.

renounced their earlier liberalism or 'approximated gradually to the doctrines of the Church'.

At the 1870 Synod Kotze sought to turn the tables on Murray by accusing him of departing from the doctrine of predestination as taught in the Canons of the Synod of Dort. Kotze's purpose, of course, was not to defend one of the historic creeds of the Church. Rather, he was seeking to demonstrate that Andrew Murray, Synod Moderator and guardian of orthodoxy, was no different than the censured Kotze in that some of Murray's teachings diverged from the established doctrines of the Church. Murray answered those charges in successive issues of *De Volksvriend* (The People's Friend), a conservative Dutch newspaper.[9] The fallacy of Kotze's charges was readily demonstrated and the matter was dropped.

Despite Kotze's accusation against Murray and Murray's ending up in the minority on the Civil Court issue, his influence and the esteem given him at the 1870 Synod were considerable. Testimony to this was borne by an unlikely source. Writing anonymously, David Faure published a series of satirical sketches entitled 'Zakspiegeltjes' (Pocket Mirrors), which appeared in the liberal publication *Het Volksblad* during the Synodical meetings. Wrote Faure:

> First let me sketch the men of the ultra-orthodox party, who pose as watchmen on the walls of Zion. Under this category I begin with the Rev. A. Murray – a worthy leader. Eloquent, quick and talented, he has an acute mind and a clear judgment. He instantly divines the weak points of his opponents' arguments, and knows how to assail them. He carries the meeting with him; he is too clever for the most. He understands the art of making his ideas so attractive to the elders and the small minds among the ministers (who all look up with reverence to the Actuarius) that they very seldom venture to contradict Demosthenes, or, as another called him, Apollos. It would be sacrilege to raise a voice against the Right Reverend the Actuarius, Andrew Murray. There is no member of the assembly who possesses more influence than Andrew Murray,

---

9. Du Plessis, *The Life of Andrew Murray*, p. 249 summarizes Kotze's charges and Murray's responses to them.

and certainly there is no one among the conservatives who better deserves his influence. He is consistent, and consistency always demands respect.[10]

Two other children had been added to Andrew and Emma's family during their latter years in Cape Town. Their third son, John Neethling, was born on 7 November, 1868, while their sixth daughter, Frances Helen, was birthed on 30 March, 1870. Besides their own eight children the Murrays continued to have other young people living in their home as well. Hermanus Bosman, who had come with the Murrays from Worcester, continued to live with them throughout their years in Cape Town. Other youths who resided with the Murrays for differing lengths of time while pursuing their education in Cape Town included: Andrew Murray's younger sister Ellie; Willem Joubert, who later served pastorates at Uniondale and North Paarl; Frederick Kolbe, son of a highly-respected missionary with the Rhenish Society. Kolbe later bore this glowing testimony of his experience as part of the Murrays' household:

> I hope that Mr and Mrs Murray knew by instinct how I loved them, but I never could tell them. All I know is that if either of them had asked me to put my hand in the fire for them, I would have done it. That was the time I saw Andrew Murray at the closest possible quarters. I may have been shy, but I certainly was observant. He was a very highly strung man. His preaching was so enthusiastic, his gesticulation so unrestrained, that he was wearing himself out, and the doctor ordered him to sit while preaching. So he had a special stool made for Anreith's great pulpit[11] in order to obey the doctor without letting everybody know.
>
> Now, such an output of nervous energy (and he was a frequent preacher) might well mean some reaction at home – some irritation with his wife, some unevenness towards his children, some caprice towards the stranger within his gates. But no, I never saw him thrown off balance. His harmony with Mrs Murray was perhaps

---

10. ibid., p. 259.

11. The Groote Kerk's gigantic pulpit that was constructed and carved by sculptor Anton Anreith.

easy; she was such a gracious, wifely, motherly person, that not to be in harmony with her would itself be self-condemnation – but he never did condemn himself. He was solid gold all through.[12]

Kolbe's testimony of Murray's pleasantness even in the privacy of his own home is all the more impressive given the enormous ministerial problems and pressures Murray faced throughout those years. 'Why how is it you never get angry?' Murray was once asked. 'It takes too much trouble to recover your good temper,' was his sage reply.[13]

In addition to all his other work during those years of hyper-taxing ministry in Cape Town, Murray managed to carry out some further writing endeavors as well. He penned a series of thirty-one devotional studies on Psalm 51 which originally appeared in *De Kerkbode*. They were subsequently issued in book form in English, under the title *Be Merciful unto Me*, as a manual for spiritual seekers. Murray also printed a small tract entitled *Do You Believe This?* In 1869 serious illness forced Abraham Faure to discontinue his service as editor of *De Kerkbode*, a responsibility he had fulfilled for more than twenty-five years. Murray undertook that weighty duty and carried it out for several years. He even wrote some articles for a secular Dutch newspaper 'of a higher tone' which were intended to cultivate 'a sane and ideal political outlook' among the country's leaders.

---

12. Du Plessis, *The Life of Andrew Murray*, pp. 486-7. In adulthood Kolbe converted to Roman Catholicism and for many years served St Mary's Cathedral in Cape Town as the Rev. Dr Kolbe.

13. Douglas, *Andrew Murray and His Message*, p. 107.

16

WELLINGTON AND THE HUGUENOT SEMINARY
1871–1875

In July, 1871 Andrew Murray, then forty-three years of age, received a call to pastor the DRC in Wellington, a prosperous town of some 4,000 residents located forty-five miles northeast of Cape Town. Though many doubtless viewed such a prospect as a backward step professionally-speaking for Murray, he immediately began to give it serious, prayerful consideration. In responding to a letter from his brother John, Murray wrote on 21 July:

> Thanks for your kind note. It shows how each one must at last decide for himself. Just the things which you would think insufficient for a decision are those which weigh with me. The first attraction is the state of the Wellington congregation. The second, a sphere of labor where I can have people, old and young, under my continuous personal influence. Perhaps it is my idiosyncrasy, but the feeling of distraction and pointlessness in preaching and in other labor grows upon me as I flounder about without a church to preach in, a congregation to labor among systematically, or the opportunity for regular aggressive work at those who stay away from Sunday services simply because they have never been taught better. As to your arguments, I cannot see that either Cape Town or Wellington throws much into the scale of a possibly more prolonged life. And though the possession of fixed property here looks, and I thought might be, an important consideration, it somehow does not appear to weigh. If it be His will that I go, He will provide in this matter. Nor does Willie Stegmann's argument, Huet's 'ik ben onmisbaar' (I am indispensable) – the position of importance as representing the Church – appear to reach me. The whole thing is so very vague, and of course secondary. Your

179

first work, your calling, is to be a pastor, and where you can be happy in this work thither you feel yourself drawn.

I do think that I have honestly and in childlike simplicity said to the Father that if He would have me stay here I am ready and willing. I have waited on purpose to see if from the side of the congregation here there might be what would indicate His will. But as yet I cannot say I see it. Pray that He would not leave me to my own devices. I dare not think that He will.[1]

Many Cape Town residents made their way to Murray's home at Craig Cottage to urge him not to leave the metropolis. A deacon of his church who lived at the bottom of the street used to stop the people and reassure them: 'You need not bother. Andrew Murray will not leave us. He will soon be first Minister of Cape Town and that is a fine position, and he knows better than to leave.'[2]

Murray's Cape Town pastorate of nearly seven years had been extremely difficult and demanding, taxing both his strength and health. 'I am sure your dear father will kill himself,' Emma would sometimes worry to one of her daughters, 'see how exhausted he is.' Yearly in January or another hot month she tried to persuade her husband to retreat to some secluded seaside location for rest. His health was worn down enough that when one old Wellington farmer heard of a call being extended to Murray, he quipped, 'Why call him? In two years time we will have the expenses of another funeral.'

In the end, Murray did accept the call to Wellington. The family's move to its new ministry location may have been slightly delayed by the birth of Andrew and Emma's fourth son, William Stegmann, on 23 August. Murray's installation service at Wellington was held on Thursday 21 September. Professor Nicolaas Hofmeyr's sermon on that occasion, based on the words of Acts 14:1 – 'And it came to pass that they so spake that a great multitude believed' – proved prophetic of Murray's years of ministry there.

That Murray had properly ascertained God's will in going to Wellington is readily seen by the long and fruitful ministry he

---

1. Du Plessis, *The Life of Andrew Murray*, pp. 260-1.

2. Douglas, *Andrew Murray and His Message*, p. 110.

enjoyed there. He served as Wellington's minister for thirty-five years then continued to live in the town till the end of his life a little over a decade later. He came to be commonly referred to as 'Andrew Murray of Wellington'. From his supportive base in Wellington, Murray continued to provide influential leadership for his denomination and to promote visionary ministry schemes that greatly benefited Cape Colony and the regions beyond the Orange and Vaal Rivers. During his Wellington years Murray's speaking and writing ministries grew to international proportions, with Christians in various parts of the world gaining an acquaintance with and deep appreciation for his ministry.

Wellington was located in the scenic Berg River basin on the western side of the Drakenstein Range. The basin was known as the Wagonmaker's Valley owing to an early, enterprising settler who set up his prosperous manufacturing business in that location. Travelers between Cape Town and regions to the north and east commonly passed through that area. Both Wellington and the neighboring town of Paarl, seven miles to the south, manufactured large numbers of wagons and Cape carts for farmers in the interior. Wellington was the terminus of the railway from Cape Town between 1863 and 1875, after which the line was extended north and east to Ceres Road (modern Wolseley). One visitor described Wellington and the surrounding scenery as:

> Beauty in the lap of grandeur. On the south and east is a range of mountains whose rugged peaks present a panorama of ever varying delight to the eye, till the setting sun bathes them in exquisite rose and purple tints. Down the valleys, like broad green rivers, lie the vineyards, and on the hill slopes climb the orchards with their luxuriant foliage, blossoms and fruit.[3]

The numerous farms in the area, being primarily devoted to the cultivation of vineyards, were comparatively small.

The parsonage in which Murray and his family took up residence was a large two-storey house. It was located on Church Street, not far from the DRC. The parsonage was surrounded by its own

---

3. ibid., p. 112.

spacious grounds and gardens as well as outbuildings. Unfortunately, the home had no view of the surrounding mountains which were concealed behind leafy oaks and tall fir trees.

The Wellington congregation was largely composed of descendants of the Huguenots who had fled persecution in France and found a safe haven in South Africa. French names such as Le Roux, Malan and Rosseau were common in the congregation. These deeply religious people faithfully attended church services and observed Christian ordinances. The revival of 1860 had left its mark on the congregation, with a number in the church dating their conversion to that time.

Immediately after settling at Wellington Murray introduced the same visitation method he had employed at Cape Town by recruiting willing members of the congregation to carry out mission work in the different wards of the parish. The Paris Evangelical Mission had been established in the Wagonmaker's Valley in 1829 and still carried out a significant ministry among the descendants of former slaves. But a large number of mixed-race 'colored' people – day laborers, farm hands, household servants, herdsmen and others – remained untouched by those efforts. Murray took the lead in seeking to address the spiritual and social needs of that neglected class. An article in the 13 July, 1872 issue of *De Kerkbode* described the efforts he led and their success:

> As a result of the zealous labors of our minister, the number of colored people who attend the Sunday school in the Mission Hall on Sundays has now reached 120, with twelve teachers in rotation. And in the evening school, which was commenced only a month ago, the number has risen to 200, old and young, with only eight teachers. May many more hearts be moved to render assistance in this most useful institution. In the out-districts of the congregation, too, our minister has so advanced matters that Sabbath schools and evening schools for the colored folk are held in almost every ward. May the Lord command His blessing on these labors![4]

---

4. Du Plessis, *The Life of Andrew Murray*, pp. 265-6.

Another emphasis that Murray introduced early in his tenure at Wellington was the promotion of temperance principles. He did this despite the fact that most of the farmers in his congregation grew grapes and produced wine as their primary livelihood. Upon his arrival in Wellington, there were seven 'canteens' (taverns) in Church Street alone. Murray soon got four of those closed as well as a number of saloons on other streets. So successful were his efforts that for many years Wellington had only four bars, compared to the neighboring town which had forty.

Not everyone was supportive of Murray's efforts in that regard. 'Mr Murray,' one wine farmer in his church fumed, 'the congregation will be torn asunder by your temperance sentiments.'

'Never!' the pastor responded calmly but emphatically. 'We will, if necessary, take the scissors of love and cut it in two, having one section for temperance and the other not, but we will live together in love.'

Preaching to his congregation, which was unacquainted with temperance principles, Murray stated winsomely and confidently:

> When a farmer trains a young horse it will often shy at a stone or something else. The wise farmer will quietly lead the horse to the unfamiliar object and let him look at it and smell it till all fear passes, and it will not shy any more. So I will not force temperance upon you, but we will speak and preach about it till you are familiar with it and approve of it.[5]

But some of the townspeople were more threatening in their opposition to Murray's temperance measures. Years later one of his daughters reported:

> These people were very angry with him, and sought to burn down the parsonage. We had to be on the watch constantly, for rags soaked in paraffin were thrown in at the windows near the lace curtains, so as to cause them to burn. God, in His mercy, graciously protected us, but we exercised great care and watchfulness at this time.[6]

5. Douglas, *Andrew Murray and His Message*, p. 114.

6. ibid., pp. 114-15.

As had been the case in his earlier pastorates, so at Wellington Murray's preaching ministry continued to be fervent and searching. An old member of the congregation described the effect of Murray's preaching to one of Murray's children in these colorful terms:

> When your father arrived we felt ourselves worthy of the front seats in church. But soon we realized that for such sinners, a back seat was more becoming for us. He did not leave us there. We next felt unfit for any place but the doorkeeper's. But now he has cast us right out into the street and rolled us in the mire.[7]

The Murrays faced a combination of difficult family circumstances during 1872. On 22 January their infant son, Willie, died at five months of age. Two months later, owing to a dearth of suitable secondary schools for girls in South Africa, the Murrays carried out a painful decision to send their two oldest daughters – Emmie and Mary, ages fourteen and thirteen – to the Moravian Institution in Zeist, Holland.

Murray wrote regularly to his daughters during their stay of nearly two years in Europe. His letters were full of fatherly affection, concern, encouragement and guidance, as well as interest in their new circumstances. To Emmie on her fifteenth birthday on 20 April he wrote:

> How tenderly our hearts have been going out to you this morning, wondering where you are and what you are feeling as you think of home. We have almost daily been following you on your travels, imagining where you would most likely be. ... And now comes your birthday to remind you of home and of how we all will be thinking of you. Dearest child, we have been asking the Lord this morning, should you perhaps feel somewhat sad and desolate, to let you feel that He is near, and to give you a place near His own tender heart, so full of gentleness and love. May the blessed Lord Jesus indeed do it, and help you to begin the year with Him. ... How we shall be longing for your first letters from Zeist, to be able to form an idea of your mode of life. You must try and give us every

---

7.   ibid., pp. 116-17.

particular about how you spend your time from hour to hour. ...
How are you allowed to spend your [Saturday]? Are all your walks
in company, or may you go and wander in the woods alone? Tell us
too what people you know and like. ... Tell us particularly about
the children at the School, how many of them are English, and
what they are like; also about your Sundays – are the services all in
German, and do you profit by them? Tell us also what amount of
time is devoted to Dutch.[8]

Bereavement visited the Murray household a second time that year
when the youngest daughter, Frances, died early in October. She
was two and a half years old. Of her passing Murray wrote his
daughters in Holland:

My Darling Children – Your hearts will be very sad to hear the
news which this mail brings you. And yet, not sad alone, I trust.
For we had so much comfort in seeing our precious little Fanny go
from us, that we cannot but feel sure that He who has been with
us will be with you too, and will let you see the bow He has set in
the cloud – the bright light that our Precious Savior has caused to
shine even in the dark tomb.

Mama has written such a full account of all there is to tell about
our little darling, that I do not think there is anything more for
me to say. And I need not tell you how very beautiful and sweet is
every memory we have of her. Since you left us she has been so very
sweet, from early morning when she came tripping in to breakfast
to say good-morning to Papa, and all through the day. How often
she came to my room, just for a little play. Darling lamb, we shall
see her again; and, as Mama said, we cannot refuse her to Jesus.[9]

In 1872 three issues of *De Kerkbode* contained articles entitled 'Onze
Kinderen' (Our Children), which were written anonymously but
appear to have been penned by Murray. The articles, which were
afterwards circulated as tracts throughout the country, urged parents
to offer their own children for the service of Christ's Church so that

---

8.   Du Plessis, *The Life of Andrew Murray*, pp. 266-7.

9.   ibid., p. 270.

the ongoing pressing need for pastors, school teachers and other Christian workers might be adequately supplied. The Theological Seminary at Stellenbosch was producing only half the number of ministers needed to fill all the pulpit vacancies. The Colony's higher education was almost entirely in the hands of individuals who did not belong to the DRC or who made no Christian profession at all. Daughters, too, could be devoted to Christian service by nursing the sick, caring for the poor and especially (as Murray emphasized) being teachers of the country's children in its towns and on its farms.

During the family's seaside Christmas vacation at Kalk Bay, near Cape Town, that year, Murray read about the life and ministry of an influential American educationalist, Mary Lyon. In 1837 she had founded the Mount Holyoke Female Seminary in South Hadley, Massachusetts. That institution for the higher education of women was the first of its kind in the United States. Miss Lyon's educational motto was 'First the kingdom of God, but after that – and after that most certainly – all science and knowledge'.

Murray wrote another series of articles that were published in *De Kerkbode* during 1873 under the title 'Mary Lyon, and the Holyoke Girls' School'. He emphasized the foundational principles that had guided Miss Lyon in the establishment and operation of her school:

> (1) the Seminary [is] to be a strictly Christian institution, controlled by trustees who have in view the highest interests of the Church of Christ, and possessing as teachers women who are themselves inspired, and are able to inspire others, with a true missionary spirit; and (2) the domestic arrangements [are] to be neat but simple, the household tasks to be performed by the pupils themselves, and the fees for board and instruction to be so low that girls of the middle class (hitherto debarred by the expense from obtaining higher education) shall receive instruction of equal quality with their more favored sisters.[10]

Murray desired to see a similar school established in Wellington. He composed a pamphlet entitled 'The Huguenot School at

---

10.   ibid., p. 275.

Wellington' in which he set forth the reasons and plan for doing so. The members of the Wellington congregation were invited to a meeting at the church on 25 June to discuss his proposals.

The congregation enthusiastically followed his lead in these matters. The school would be open to local girls from the town and its surrounding farms as well as to girls from other districts of the Colony. It would provide girls with the opportunity not only to gain a quality education but also to become teachers themselves. An initial building would be needed that could house thirty to forty boarding students and that provided classrooms for them and the local students who would not live at the school.

To build such a facility would require at least 2,000 pounds. It was decided that after the congregation had raised the first half of that amount construction could begin on the building. Several months earlier Murray had written to the Mount Holyoke Female Seminary, requesting a lady teacher from there for the envisioned Wellington institution. He was now able to inform his congregation of the response just received, that two highly-qualified Holyoke graduates were willing to come. Before the congregational meeting ended the first 500 pounds were pledged and within four months 1,150 pounds had been contributed.

'Many were greatly averse to building in this expensive time,' Murray related in October, 'and the Committee therefore attempted to secure a suitable property by purchase.'[11] After some complications and delays, they were able to purchase a building and ground from a Mr Schoch at the cost of 1,600 pounds. Another 800 pounds would be necessary to remodel the building for its intended use. The building was 'large, airy and well-built'. The lower storey would be used as classrooms while the upper storey would provide bedrooms for a large number of boarding students.

The DRC Synod of 1873 was being held in Cape Town at that time. So great was the interest in the establishment of this school in Wellington that a special train was chartered to bring'a very large concourse of visitors, among whom were to be found almost all

---

11.   ibid., p. 278.

the members of the Synod' from the metropolis for the dedication of the newly-acquired property on 25 October. In addition, many other interested individuals came 'from all parts' of the country in their private carts and wagons to share in the celebration.

About three weeks later on Sunday 16 November, Emma, at age thirty-eight, gave birth to her eleventh and final child – a son who was named Charles. The Murrays were in Cape Town at the time, where Andrew Murray was still carrying out Synod business. From the Cape he wrote to share two pieces of very good news with Emmie and Mary:

> How glad you will be to hear that God has given us another little one in the place of our dear Fanny and Willie. A little boy was born yesterday morning – a fine little fellow – and both mother and babe are very well. Our hearts are filled with gratitude and love.
>
> We have still another blessing that has filled our hearts with gladness. On Saturday the two American ladies for our Huguenot School at Wellington arrived here. The impression they make is most favorable.[12]

Emmie and Mary were soon to leave Holland for Scotland. Concerning that change, Murray encouraged them:

> [B]ut as you are in Europe now, you must try and avail yourselves of the privileges Scotland may afford. May God implant deep in your hearts the desire to work for Him, and to seek the highest cultivation of all your powers with a view to being an instrument thoroughly furnished for God's blessed work. ...
>
> ... We are not without anxieties about your change from Holland to Scotland, but we desire to leave everything in God's hands. He has been so kind in other things that we do not doubt but that He will care for this too.[13]

By the time the Huguenot School (which came to be commonly called the Huguenot Seminary) officially opened on 19 January,

---

12.   ibid., p. 271. The two teachers were the Misses Ferguson and Bliss.

13.   ibid., pp. 271-2.

1874 no less than fifty-four boarding students had been accepted for admission. They came from more than fifteen different communities widely scattered throughout the Colony. As the existing building could accommodate only forty boarders, a new wing would need to be added immediately.

In order to promote the cause of Christian education and raise additional prayer and financial support for the seminary, Murray undertook an extensive tour of the Colony's Dutch Reformed congregations. Setting out on 16 February, over the course of the next four months he visited some thirty churches. He succeeded in raising 2,300 pounds for the Huguenot Seminary. Even more importantly to Murray, he discovered thirty young men and an even greater number of young women who expressed a ready desire to be trained as teachers of the rising generation. The reception Murray received from his congregation upon his return from that tour was truly remarkable. It was even recorded in *De Kerkbode*:

Our respected minister returned home on Friday last, after an absence of four months. Shortly after midday vehicles, numbering in all more than one hundred, began to roll from all quarters towards Bain's Kloof [Pass], and at half-past one a large crowd had already assembled. Precisely at two o'clock the reverend gentleman made his appearance, accompanied by some of the church wardens who had proceeded still further to meet him. As soon as Mr Murray had descended from the cart, the assemblage sang 'Dat's Heeren zegen op u daal' (God's blessing rest upon your head), after which the Rev. S.J. du Toit, the assistant minister, presented him with an extensively-signed address from his flock, and handed him a purse of 50 pounds on behalf of the sisters of the congregation. In replying to this address Mr Murray appeared to be much affected, and asked the friends to kneel down while Mr du Toit offered prayer, after which he himself poured out his heart in a most sincere and touching manner, thanking God for the protection, assistance and blessing which he had experienced on his journey. Two other addresses, from the scholars of the Blauw-vallei and Boven-vallei schools respectively, were also presented, upon which the cavalcade proceeded towards the village.

At the entrance to the parsonage an arch of honor had been erected, around which were grouped the young ladies of the

Huguenot Seminary and the pupils of the other local schools. The school children welcomed Mr Murray with a hymn, while the Seminary ladies offered an address, to which he replied in feeling terms. One of the young ladies carried a flag with the motto *Hosanna*, and the banner of another breathed the prayer *God bless our pastor*. Mr Murray's dwelling was decorated about the doors with garlands and flowers, and with the motto *Welcome home*, which was worked in orange blossoms and can only be described as exquisite. The cart and horses with which Mr Murray performed his journey were subsequently sold for 90 pounds, and this amount was also handed over to him as a mark of gratitude and esteem.[14]

The continued rapid growth of the number of Huguenot Seminary students soon necessitated not only the addition of a new wing but also the erection of an additional building. The foundation for the second edifice was laid in November of that year. Within a month or two, two more lady teachers from America, Misses Wells and Bailey, as well as a female instructor from Holland, Miss Spijker, arrived to join Misses Ferguson and Bliss as teachers at the seminary. Throughout the first half of the following year, 1875, the Murrays helped meet the pressing housing need by having sixteen students and a teacher board in their home! On 27 July, 1875 nearly 2,000 people gathered for a dedication ceremony of the new building. 'On my return from the opening of the new building,' Murray revealed, 'my mind was full of one thought, "He purposed doing it, He has done it!" [Isaiah 46:11].'[15]

Within three or four years of the founding of the Huguenot Seminary similar institutions for the education of young women and the training of lady teachers were established in Stellenbosch, Worcester, Paarl, Graaff-Reinet, Bloemfontein, Cradock and Somerset East.

---

14. ibid., pp. 281-2.

15. Douglas, *Andrew Murray and His Message*, p. 123.

17

Promoting Education and Evangelism
1876–1878

Early in 1876 Murray undertook a second tour to raise funds for the Huguenot Seminary. That tour, which lasted seven or eight weeks, was not as extensive or financially successful as his 1874 tour, but it underscored in his thinking the ongoing, pressing need for additional Christian workers throughout the Colony. Of that situation he wrote in part:

> In conversations with others on my journey I discovered that it is frequently the case that when families live forty-five or fifty miles away from the township, they seldom think of attending church more than once a quarter, at the communion season. And when we remember the hindrances that arise, owing to drought the one year and floods the next, as well as occasional sickness, we can understand how seldom the majority have the opportunity of listening to the preaching of the Word. ...
>
> And what shall I say of my experience with reference to teachers? This alone, that I have been convinced anew that all our toil for the benefit of the grownups will effect little, unless we win the hearts of the children for God's Word; and that the vast majority of the children of our land is not under the guidance of God-fearing teachers. May God lay this need heavy upon our hearts, and open our eyes to the heart-rending sight of children ... confided for years to the influence and the instruction of worldly teachers.[1]

Murray wrote to his wife of yet another ministry need he saw during that itineration, one he longed to help meet himself:

---

1. Du Plessis, *The Life of Andrew Murray*, pp. 290-1.

The more I travel the more I see the great need of our Church is Evangelists. And though I cannot in the least see it would be possible to give up Wellington, or to arrange for long absences, it does almost appear wrong not to undertake the work when one knows that there are hundreds ready to be brought in. It appears terrible to let them go on in darkness and indecision when they are willing to be helped. I have been much struck in reading the note on Exodus by the words of God to Pharaoh: 'Let My people go that they may serve Me.' He does hear the cry and sighing of the thousands of seeking ones and wants His servants to lead them out of bondage. And how can I help saying that if He will use me I shall only consider the honor too high. It is sad to preach one or two earnest Evangelistic sermons, to see the impression made and to go away feeling sure that if one could devote a little more time and individual attention to the work, souls would come to light and joy.[2]

Another missive related a threatening incident that had taken place while crossing a flooded river one Saturday morning. While attempting to cross at a ford, the cart wheels suddenly dropped into a hidden hole that the swollen river had recently washed out in the submerged road. The cart overturned, pitching its occupants into the river. 'A boy we had with us fell under the cart and was some time under water,' Murray reported, 'but God spared us what would have been a terrible blow, and he came out.' With difficulty, Murray and his companions were able to right the cart, and the horses pulled it from the river.

For more than a year Murray had been formulating a plan for the establishment of another school in Wellington, one where young men could be educated and trained as missionaries and missionary teachers. In February, 1876 he was able to announce that a suitable principal had been found for the proposed institution – George Ferguson, the brother of Miss Ferguson who superintended the Huguenot Seminary. He planned to come to South Africa the middle of the following year. Of the school's intended students and type of training Murray explained:

2. Douglas, *Andrew Murray and His Message*, pp. 123-4.

The objects we aim at in the establishment of this institution are these: there are young men who wish to engage in the work of the Lord, but who have no time, no aptitude or no strong desire to pay much attention to ancient languages or mathematics. For these there should be provided the opportunity to obtain a thorough Biblical and general training, so that they can take their places in the Church and in society both honorably and profitably. While we do not exclude the study of ancient languages, it will be our aim, without entering into competition with existing institutions, to afford young men who are no longer in their early youth the chance of obtaining a good general education through the medium of both English and Dutch. ...

We desire also to establish matters on so reasonable and simple a footing that youths in poor circumstances shall have access to all the privileges of a good boarding school. We also wish to offer to those who are already engaged in God's service – as ministers, missionaries or teachers – the opportunity of having their children educated for the same blessed service at the lowest possible price.[3]

Initially Murray thought a boarding school for forty or fifty male students would be necessary. He supposed the cost for such an undertaking would be between 4,000 and 5,000 pounds. But rather than delaying the start of the boys' training institute, Murray commenced it on a small scale. To one of his sisters he wrote:

As to our training school, we start the work with ten boarders -- five preparing for teachers and perhaps for mission work too – nice hopeful boys. And we have been led most kindly in regard to our teacher, Mr Weich, an assistant whom God has just provided too, and the domestic arrangements. God appears to be doing everything for us so that though there is at present no prospect of Mr Ferguson's coming, I am full of confidence that God is in His own way and time, step by step, going to unfold to us the blessings He has in store, and the kindness He is going to show us in the establishment of this institution.[4]

---

3. Du Plessis, *The Life of Andrew Murray*, p. 293.

4. Douglas, *Andrew Murray and His Message*, pp. 126-7.

Reports had been reaching South Africa in the past couple of years concerning the remarkable evangelistic campaigns of Americans Dwight Moody and Ira Sankey in Britain and the United States. Moody the zealous evangelist and Sankey his skilled song-leader lacked formal theological training and were little known outside the U.S. They went to the British Isles in June, 1873, intending to hold three months of evangelistic meetings. But the Spirit of God so mightily empowered and used their efforts that they remained in Britain for two years, holding 265 evangelistic meetings in England, Scotland and Ireland. 2,500,000 people attended those meetings and tens of thousands came to faith in Christ. After returning to the United States in August, 1875 Moody and Sankey began holding evangelistic crusades in some of America's large cities, beginning with Brooklyn, Philadelphia and New York late that year and early the next. There they continued to draw immense crowds and were used of the Lord to usher countless individuals into His Kingdom.

During 1874 and the years to follow, numerous articles in *De Kerkbode* were devoted to detailed consideration of the American evangelists, their meetings and methods as well as the extraordinary spiritual fruit that resulted from them. Various South African ministers who had recently visited Europe provided enthusiastic personal accounts of the spiritual revival they had seen and shared in there. These reports led many in Cape Colony to begin praying that God would again bring revival to their own communities and country. Professor Nicolaas Hofmyer toured several of the Colony's churches, telling of the dramatic spiritual revitalization taking place in Britain. Through these means, fresh stirrings occurred in Wellington, where Andrew Murray ministered, as well as at Cape Town, Montagu, Stellenbosch and Swellendam. A primary characteristic of these powerful movements of God's Spirit was the large number of young people who placed their faith in Christ.[5]

When the DRC Synod met in the closing months of 1876 it elected Murray, then forty-eight years of age, as its Moderator for

---

5. Nel, *South Africa's Forgotten Revival*, pp. 94-5 provides further detail concerning the revival in Montagu at this time.

the second time. The Synod gave considerable time and attention to the issue of promoting special evangelistic services in the Colony. A 'Committee for Special Gospel-preaching' was appointed and instructed to arrange for a series of evangelistic meetings in various congregations throughout the country. That committee, in turn, asked Murray and Servaas Hofmyer, minister of Montagu, to undertake special evangelistic campaigns. The committee further requested Murray and Hofmyer's respective consistories to release them from routine pastoral responsibilities for a period of months so they could carry out that vital ministry. But due to other pressing responsibilities, more than two years would elapse before Murray would be able to fulfill such an outreach mission.

The 1876 Synod also voted unanimously to establish a normal college for the training of teachers. There was considerable divergence of opinion over where the college should be located but in the end a narrow majority settled on Cape Town. Murray was appointed to the college's board of directors, a position he would fulfill until his retirement from active pastoral ministry nearly three decades later.

On 4 April, 1877 Murray sailed from Cape Town aboard the steamship *African* on the first leg of an intended tour to Europe and America. He was to serve as the official delegate of his denomination at the first ever Pan-Presbyterian Council of Churches when it met in Edinburgh, Scotland that July. He also intended to learn more about the state of education in the countries he visited and to recruit teachers to serve in South Africa. Further, he desired to investigate the spiritual life of the churches in the countries to be visited, especially in connection with Dwight Moody's evangelistic ministry as well as the popular Higher Life movement that had spread to South Africa in 1876.[6]

After arriving in London the last day of April, 1877 Murray promptly proceeded to Edinburgh where he visited various ministers about finding suitable professors for the new Normal

---

6. Consideration will be given to the Higher Life movement in the following chapter.

College in Cape Town. Returning to London, he was joined by his brother Charles, who had just arrived from South Africa. Together they embarked at Liverpool on the *Bothnia* on 12 May and reached New York ten days later. A few days after their arrival Charles reported in a letter to his sister:

> Last night ... a large company of gentlemen – professors, ministers, etc. – with their ladies, were invited to meet Andrew. He is Mr Murray. I introduced myself as the other Mr Murray. As two or three little coteries were in danger of monopolizing him, old Dr Bacon took a chair right opposite him and began catechizing him for the benefit of the whole company, on the political, social and religious condition of South Africa, and, of course, on the state and prospects of the Huguenot Seminary. I couldn't realize I was in North America when I felt how much at home we were.... Andrew is, in the circle in which we move, quite a lion. Such regrets that he cannot stay on to spend the Sabbath and preach. He is a precious brother and very convenient to travel with. On his back ... I get in anywhere.[7]

Charles also revealed, interestingly, of his older brother:

> You can't think how precious his conversation and society were on board [the ship], only he is awfully troubled on the point of first-style dress [and] manners. [For example], he had no peace till I had purchased a hateful high hat. Once he was horrified at seeing me eating an apple in the train, and made me swallow a mouthful unchewed when he noticed a known gentleman coming in.[8]

In addition to visiting the Mount Holyoke Female Seminary, the Murray brothers toured a number of other normal schools and colleges, where they received a hearty welcome and were invited to speak on the educational work in South Africa. 'We do not find half an hour unoccupied,' Charles related, 'and every day have new cause for regret that our time is so limited.' They received so many

---

7. Douglas, *Andrew Murray and His Message*, pp. 138-9.
8. ibid., p. 139.

speaking invitations that they needed to part company for a time in order to take advantage of more opportunities.

In Philadelphia they greatly enjoyed visiting the largest Sunday School in the country, Bethany Sabbath School, with its then 2,300 students.[9] In Boston the Murrays relished the opportunity to hear Dwight Moody and Ira Sankey who were then ministering there. Andrew and Charles assisted in counseling 'the anxious' in an 'inquiry meeting' after one of Moody's evangelistic services. Of their five-week visit in the United States Andrew Murray reported:

> Though we greatly regretted that our stay in that country was so brief, every day was full of pleasure and utility. The acquaintance which we made with the educational system, with the Sunday schools, with the religious life, and especially with the revival under Mr Moody's labor, and notably with the Dutch Reformed Church of America, have all yielded us much food for thought ...[10]

The Murray brothers left America late in June and arrived in Edinburgh in time for the commencement of the Pan-Presbyterian Council on 3 July. In attendance were 333 delegates, representing a total of 21,443 congregations from various Reformed denominations around the world. Throughout the eight-day conference an array of topics was addressed, including: Christian unity, the unanimity and authority of various Reformed confessions, the scriptural basis for and strengths of Presbyterian polity, world missions, evangelizing in an age of unbelief, helps and hindrances to the spiritual life and sanctification of the Christian Sabbath. A reporter summarized a presentation Murray made to the Council:

> Rev. Andrew Murray, Cape Town, addressed the Council on the training of the young, giving it as his opinion that the Lord had

---

9. Bethany Sabbath School had been started nearly two decades earlier in 1858 and for over fifty years was superintended by its founder, John Wanamaker, who also had the distinction of owning the 'largest clothing store in America'. That Sunday School reached its peak enrolment of nearly 6,100 pupils in 1897.

10. Du Plessis, *The Life of Andrew Murray*, p. 296.

Himself given to the children a place in the Church which it scarcely realized. The best pastors of the Church should give themselves to the work of the Christian training of the young and there should, moreover, be a link connecting together the home, the school, the Church; such a cord could not be broken.[11]

Murray provided a synopsis of those meetings, as well as his reflections on them, in a pair of long articles he penned for *De Kerkbode*.[12]

One week after the Edinburgh convention Murray spoke at a three-day conference in Inverness. Later that month he participated in an evangelistic conference at Perth. Before returning to Cape Colony, Murray managed to squeeze in a quick trip to Holland, Germany and Switzerland. He visited old acquaintances at Amsterdam and Utrecht, Holland, as well as the missionary training center at Elberfeld, Germany.

At the end of August Andrew and Charles sailed from Southampton, England for South Africa aboard the *Nyanza*. They were accompanied by fourteen lady teachers (twelve from America, one from Scotland and one from Holland) whom they had recruited to serve at girls' schools in Wellington, Stellenbosch, Worcester, Swellendam, Beaufort West, Graaff-Reinet and Pretoria. Also traveling with them was George Ferguson, the new principal of Wellington's Training Institute, along with his wife and five children. In addition they were joined by another teacher, a Mr Stucki, who was from Holland and who had authored a Dutch grammar book. While in Edinburgh for the Pan-Presbyterian Council, Andrew Murray was delighted to learn that a suitable rector, Mr J.D. Whitton, had been found for Cape Town's new Normal College. Since all the necessary building arrangements had not yet been made for the college it was agreed that Whitton would come to begin his service in South Africa the following January.

---

11. Douglas, *Andrew Murray and His Message*, p. 135.

12. A condensation of those articles is recorded in du Plessis, *The Life of Andrew Murray*, pp. 297-302.

At the outset of their voyage Murray suggested that they have a daily class for the study of Dutch, with himself and Mr Stucki serving as teachers on alternate days. This proposal was enthusiastically embraced by the delegation of teachers. Murray spent much of his time during the voyage reading in a quiet corner of the deck. But his fellow travelers quickly learned that he was quite willing to lay aside his book at any time in order to have a helpful chat with anyone who desired it.

Murray arrived back at Wellington on 24 September, after having been away five and a half months. A sizeable crowd met him at the train station, and 'a large number of vehicles' escorted him to the parsonage. There an arch of welcome, decorated with flowers and bunting, had been prepared. The students of the Huguenot Seminary and the local schools presented a special musical number, a member of the church Consistory made a brief speech and the congregation presented Murray with 'a well-filled purse' as a token of its appreciation for him. His sermon text the following Sunday was Romans 15:29-32, beginning with words that doubtless expressed the desire of his heart: 'And I am sure that, when I come unto you, I shall come in the fullness of the blessing of the gospel of Christ.'

For quite some time Murray and his ministerial colleagues in Cape Colony had received and discussed reports of Dwight Moody's evangelistic services and methods, including his use of 'after-meetings' to provide personalized spiritual council for individuals seeking salvation. There was considerable reserve on the part of South African ministers toward such after-meetings because they were viewed as a novel innovation. Murray reports how he first came to employ such meetings in ministering to his own congregation in the middle of 1878:

> As I traveled from one parsonage to another these things were the subjects of earnest conversation, and we often asked whether we ought not to venture on after-meetings. More than once we were just ready to begin when prudence held us back. In a wonderful way God loosed my bonds. In our Dutch Church it is customary to have daily prayer meetings during the ten days between Ascension

and Whit Sunday [Pentecost]. In my absence they had been held as usual at Wellington. At the first prayer meeting after Whit Sunday, the question was asked, 'We have prayed, why have we not received?' The answer was given: 'If we persevere we shall receive.' They resolved to begin again. The next week I arrived at home and joined them. We continued prayer for a week and then felt it [was] now time to work for the unsaved. This was done and the after-meetings during the next five weeks proved such a blessing that the fruit remains till this day.[13]

Murray's oldest daughter, Emma, who was twenty-one years old at the time of these events, later related of the dramatic converting movement of God's Spirit that then took place at Wellington:

> The first Whitsuntide after Father's return from England God granted him a wonderful ingathering of souls at Wellington. The elders requested him to preach on 'Hell' and he did so. Many a man and woman trembled under that sermon, but it was under the tender wooing of God's great love to us in the gift of Christ that they found peace. For three weeks he preached to a crowded church, which had sitting accommodation for over 1,000 people, night after night, on one text only: John 3:16 ... I can never forget his tender earnestness, as with simple but telling illustrations he brought the truth home to us personally. ... How anyone could withstand his pleadings and refuse to surrender to God used to puzzle me.

Often Mrs Murray and other workers were in the church till late at night, dealing with anxious inquirers. Mr Peter Stuart, whom Father called a 'Buttonhole Christian', assisted him greatly. He had the faculty of getting hold of people in the street or elsewhere and holding on to them while he presented the claims of Christ. Many were thus reached who would not have been led to Christ by the ordinary methods.[14]

---

13. Douglas, *Andrew Murray and His Message*, pp. 130-1.

14. ibid., pp. 131-2.

18

The Higher Life Movement
1877–1879

As early as the 1830s the American Holiness movement coalesced in the United States. Among the several proponents of the American Holiness movement to promote their beliefs to Britain was Presbyterian evangelist and holiness teacher William Boardman. In 1858 Boardman published a holiness book entitled *The Higher Christian Life*, and in the 1870s he held an evangelistic campaign in England to help spread the holiness message. He was accompanied by Robert Pearsall Smith and his wife Hannah Whitall Smith, author of what was destined to become a Christian classic, *The Christian's Secret of a Happy Life* (first published in 1875). Higher Life conferences were held at Broadlands and Oxford, England in 1874 and in Brighton and Keswick, England the following year.

Keswick (pronounced with a silent 'w'), England came to be the primary location for subsequent Higher Life conferences in years to follow, with the result that the movement also came to be known as the Keswick Movement. The Higher Life movement taught that subsequent to initial salvation the Christian should progress to experience a fuller work of God in his life. That fuller work is variously referred to as 'entire sanctification', 'the second blessing' or 'being filled with the Holy Spirit'. A believer who receives this additional blessing, it was claimed, could live a more holy and less sinful life. While some Higher Life proponents taught that a Christian could come to live a sinless life here on earth, the prevailing Keswick teaching came to be that every believer in this life is left with the natural tendency to sin and will do so without the counteracting influence of the Holy

ANDREW MURRAY

Spirit. Keswick teachers intentionally distanced themselves from the Wesleyan Methodist doctrine of eradication, the belief that original sin could be completely removed from the Christian's soul prior to death. Keswick teaching has been criticized in some Reformed circles as being a disguised form of 'perfectionism', a charge Keswick leaders denied. While embracing many Higher Life principles, Murray never taught any form of sinless perfection for the believer in earthly life. [1]

In 1876 Higher Life conferences were held in various South African towns including Cape Town, Tulbagh, Piquetberg, Adelaide and elsewhere. Andrew Murray was attracted to Higher Life teachings and sought to keep 'in close touch with the Spiritual movements of the world' by regularly reading a pair of holiness periodicals, *The Life of Faith* and *The Revival*.[2]

Nearly two decades later, at the 1895 Keswick Convention, Murray was pressed and rather reluctantly agreed to share his personal testimony of how he came to live by Higher Life principles. (His reluctance stemmed from his concern over drawing people's attention away 'from Christ to any experience'.) His testimony is quite enlightening concerning the inner spiritual struggles and growth he had experienced throughout his first quarter-century of pastoral ministry:

> The first ten years of my spiritual life were manifestly spent on the lower stage. I was a minister, I may say, as zealous and as earnest and as happy in my work as anyone, as far as love of the work was concerned. Yet, all the time, there was burning in my heart a dissatisfaction and restlessness inexpressible. What was the reason? I had never learnt with all my theology that [full] obedience was possible. My justification was clear as the noonday. I knew the hour in which I received from God the joy of pardon. [But] I remember in my little room in Bloemfontein how I used to sit and think, 'What is the matter? Here I am, knowing that God has justified

1. Douglas, *Andrew Murray and His Message*, p. 298, states: 'Andrew Murray ... held what is considered the orthodox teaching of a remaining sinful tendency, but also he held as quite compatible with this a freedom from actual sinning.'

2. Douglas, *Andrew Murray and His Message*, p. 158.

me in the blood of Christ, but I have no power for service.' My thoughts, my words, my actions, my unfaithfulness – everything troubled me. Though all around thought me one of the most earnest of men, my life was one of deep dissatisfaction. I struggled and prayed as best I could.

One day I was talking with a missionary. I do not think that he knew much of the power of sanctification himself – he would have admitted it. When we were talking and he saw my earnestness he said, 'Brother, remember that when God puts a desire into your heart, He will fulfill it.' That helped me; I thought of it a hundred times. ...

... So the Lord led me till in His great mercy I had been eleven or twelve years in Bloemfontein. Then He brought me to another congregation in Worcester, about the time when God's Holy Spirit was being poured out in America, Scotland and Ireland. In 1860, when I had been six months in the congregation, God poured out His Spirit there in connection with my preaching, especially as I was moving about in the country, and a very unspeakable blessing came to me. The first Dutch edition of my book *Abide in Christ* was written at that time [1864]. I would like you to understand that a minister or a Christian author may often be led to say more than he has experienced. I had not then experienced all that I wrote of; I cannot say that I experience it all perfectly even now.

Well, God helped me, and for seven or eight years I went on, always inquiring and seeking, and always getting. Then came, about 1870, the great Holiness Movement. The letters that appeared in *The Revival* ... touched my heart; and I was in close fellowship with what took place at Oxford and Brighton, and it all helped me. Perhaps if I were to talk of consecration I might tell you of an evening there in my own study in Cape Town. Yet I cannot say that that was deliverance, for I was still struggling. Later on, my mind became much exercised about the baptism of the Holy Spirit, and I gave myself to God as perfectly as I could to receive the baptism of the Spirit. Yet there was failure; God forgive it. It was somehow as if I could not get what I wanted. Through all these stumblings God led me, without any very special experience that I can point to. But as I look back I do believe now that He was giving me more and more of His blessed Spirit, had I but known it better.[3]

3.   Du Plessis, *The Life of Andrew Murray*, pp. 447-8.

In an article he wrote for *De Kerkbode* at the outset of his 1877 ministry tour to Europe and America, Murray referred favorably to the Higher Life emphasis that was developing in the Church at that time:

> There is ... another kind of labor [besides evangelistic] for which God has lately raised up chosen instruments. It consists not in the endeavor to bring in those who are without the fold, but in the endeavor to lead those who are within to a deeper comprehension of Christian truth and privilege. If there is one thing which the Church needs, it is labor directed to this end. The more we study as Christians the state of the Church of Christ on earth, the more is conviction strengthened that it does not answer to its holy calling. Hence the powerlessness of the Church against unbelief and semi-belief and superstition, against worldliness and sin and heathenism. The power of faith, the power of prayer, the power of the Holy Spirit, are all too greatly lacking. God's children in the first place require a revival – a new revelation by the Holy Spirit of what is the hope of their calling, of what God does indeed expect from them, and of the life and power of consecration, of joy and fruitfulness, which God has prepared for them in Christ.[4]

After visiting the United States and while en route to Scotland for the Pan-Presbyterian Council in July, 1877, Murray wrote one of his sisters, Ellen, from aboard the ship *City of Richmond*. The letter, dated 27 June, addressed a point of tension that Murray, Ellen and others who desired the so-called 'second blessing' of 'entire sanctification' or 'the baptism of the Spirit' were faced with: How were the many believers who longed for that fuller spiritual blessing, but who did not perceive that they had received it, to respond? Murray's letter recorded a number of conversations he had with Higher Life proponents in America that addressed that perplexing issue:

> I spoke to Mr Boardman on the point. Many feel as if the full baptism of the Spirit was wanting. His answers all ran in one direction. You must trust Jesus in the assurance that He will make everything right in due time. You really rest on Him for it. In

---

4. ibid., p. 295.

your desires for more blessing you must see that your joyful rest in Him as an all sufficient portion be not disturbed. ... I spoke with Mrs C. about it. She said we must remember the diversity of gifts and operations in different people and at different times. Mrs H[annah] W[hitall] S[mith] was still seeking for a baptism of the Spirit while everybody thought she had it remarkably – it might be we mistake in the idea we form of it. Experience, feeling, success were not given to all in the same degree.[5]

In New York City Murray visited with Dr Walter Palmer and his wife Phoebe, who had been prominent leaders in the American Holiness movement for nearly forty years. Without revealing to them that he was speaking of himself, Murray expressed a degree of 'discontent and dissatisfaction' over his present spiritual condition. 'It may be a temptation of Satan,' Dr Palmer responded. 'If this brother has truly surrendered everything, he must beware of being led off from his faith in Jesus by what he seeks in his experience.'

The three-day conference at which Murray spoke in Inverness, Scotland, one week after the Pan-Presbyterian Council in Edinburgh, included evangelistic and Christian-living emphases. Of that conference, Murray wrote to his wife:

It was a very good time. The attendance was not as large as I could have wished, but I think the Master was present. The subjects for the mornings, 'The New Creation', 'The New Service', 'The New Power', were quite in the line of the higher life, but the most of the speakers kept to the old elementary truths. Nevertheless the pervading spirit was good. In what I saw and heard and said myself I was much refreshed.[6]

In that same letter Murray revealed additional perspectives concerning spiritual conditions in Scotland at that time. He greatly rejoiced in the elevated spiritual tone and revitalized commitment to Christian service that had been brought about through God's remarkable blessing on Dwight Moody's ministry in that country

---

5. Douglas, *Andrew Murray and His Message*, p. 176.
6. Du Plessis, *The Life of Andrew Murray*, p. 303.

three years earlier. But Murray also longed to see Christians gain what he believed to be essential Higher Life principles:

> In the house in which I was staying (with an elder of the Free Church), and in intercourse with other laymen I could notice very distinctly the influence of Mr Moody's work. There is much more readiness to talk out, and much more warmth. I had noticed it in Edinburgh too, that the whole religious tone of Scotland has been lifted up and brightened most remarkably. I do praise God for it. Then, too, there is much earnest work being done, though I get the impression in many places that the activity and joy of work is regarded too much as the essence of religion. And I see that when I try to speak of the deeper and inner life, many are glad to listen, and confess to a want.[7]

Murray also stated the balance he thought needed to be struck between those two emphases:

> For myself I have learnt this lesson, that it will not do to press too much on the one side of holiness and communion with Jesus, without the other side of work. There is no joy like that over repentant sinners, no communion closer than 'Go into all the world and teach – and lo! I am with you' [Matt. 28:19-20]. And yet the joy of work and revival is not enough, God's children must be led into the secret of the possibility of unbroken communion with Jesus personally. But we may ask and trust Him who has visited Scotland so wonderfully in the one thing to lead His people on in the other. I cannot say how I have been impressed with the need of the union of these two matters: work and communion. Charles says it is what I have spoken on all along at the Cape, and yet it appears to me like something quite new.[8]

Murray noted that Christians in Scotland were 'terribly afraid of [Weslyan] perfectionism'. Back in South Africa he also encountered some reservation toward the Higher Life principles he sought to promote.

---

7.   ibid.
8.   ibid.

In 1879 he led a conference for ministers along those lines in Colesberg. That the conference was attended by sixteen ministers was seen as 'exceedingly encouraging' given the vast distances of sixty to a hundred miles that separated neighboring parishes and the fact that all travel was accomplished by horse and buggy. The focus of discussion at that conference concerned whether or not it was possible for believers to experience enduring, unbroken joy and peace in their Christian lives. Many of those present doubted that such an ideal could be realized this side of heaven due to their inevitable unfaithfulness (even when seeking to be completely faithful), which caused their consciences to accuse them, thus stealing away their joy. But Murray countered that it is possible instantly to confess such unfaithfulness, claim forgiveness through the power of Christ's atonement, and so immediately to recover the joy that had been lost.

Murray's Higher Life teachings were held up to close scrutiny and public evaluation. So also his congregation at Wellington was closely watched and evaluated to see if the Higher Life principles its pastor espoused were being lived out by his parishioners. More than once anonymous letters were published in *De Kerkbode* questioning Murray's teachings or his congregation's application of them. Murray's straightforward but non-defensive letters of response, which appeared in that same periodical, effectively corrected misunderstandings and promoted the principles he taught.[9]

In 1879 Murray was also finally able to conduct his first evangelistic tour of the Colony, in keeping with the Synod's request over two years earlier that he do so. As special evangelistic services were not common in the DRCs of that day, he wrote an article for *De Kerkbode* 'in order to remove all misunderstanding, secure the interest and cooperation of all true Christians, and encourage everybody to due expectation and preparation'.[10] Two members

---

9. Two such challenges and Murray's responses to them are recorded, ibid., pp. 315-21.

10. The full article is recorded in du Plessis, *The Life of Andrew Murray*, pp. 324-6.

of the Wellington Consistory accompanied Murray on the tour, which took place in August and September. He ministered to ten congregations, including those in Murraysburg, Hanover, Philipstown, Colesberg, Philippolis, Edenburg, Steynsburg, Middelburg, Adelaide and Graaff-Reinet. From Middelburg, sixty-five miles northeast of Graaff-Reinet, Murray wrote Emma on Friday 29 August:

> We arrived here an hour ago, and were glad to get our letters. ... At Edenburg [located about fifty miles southwest of Bloemfontein] our work was more difficult than it had been. I think worldly prospects, and the idea strongly adhered to, that assurance [of salvation] is not possible or else not needed, were the chief hindrances. But the Lord gave a blessing, and many who are not yet in the light got thoroughly aroused. ... We regularly take the first two days for the unconverted or anxious and the third day for believers.[11]

Murray's mother wrote a letter to family members on 27 September about the meetings at Graaff-Reinet:

> This last week has been a blessed time for this place. The services have been wonderfully blessed. ... It is a pity that there were not more workers here. There were so many anxious souls to be spoken to, and others that had found peace also wanted a word of counsel. The blessing has been great, and still is continuing. Charles says he cannot overtake nearly all of these cases. Mr Joubert, our elder, is very active in speaking to people.
> Andrew says that he was a wonder to himself that he was able to do all the speaking, since his throat was not all right. God's people were also stirred up.[12]

The reports various consistories made to their respective presbyteries toward the end of the year indicated the significant spiritual blessings that resulted from this ministry tour. Hanover reported 'a specially blessed work among the children and young people, not

11. ibid., p. 326.
12. Neethling, *Unto Children's Children*, p. 47.

merely in the village but in the [rural] wards of the congregation, and that the young men and young women of the town had commenced a weekly prayer meeting at which the greatest earnestness was manifested'. Colesberg testified: 'Believers have been quickened and strengthened. The indifferent have been aroused and, as we trust, brought to Christ. Youth and age rejoice together in a new-found salvation.' Graaff-Reinet related:

> The congregation was prepared for their coming and had prayed much for a rich blessing. The services lasted four days. The attendance was large beyond expectations, the interest sustained, the blessing distinct and glorious. The people of God have received a heavenly refreshment ... The language of complaint and doubt has made way for the grateful speech of assurance and faith. Even more noticeable is the blessing in the case of the many who have surrendered themselves to the Lord, and have had the glorious experience that He in no wise casts out those that come unto Him. Many have solemnly promised to confess Him with mouth and heart, and to thank Him unceasingly for the salvation He has wrought. Our God has proved again that He is the Hearer of prayer.[13]

Now fifty-one years of age, Andrew Murray had become likely the most prominent and respected leader of his denomination. Seemingly endless ministry opportunities and responsibilities lay before and upon him. Doubtless no one imagined that by year's end a development would come about that would largely curtail his public-speaking ministry for a period of years.

---

13. Du Plessis, *The Life of Andrew Murray*, pp. 328-9.

19

Seeking Divine Healing
1880–1882

Due to his voice being constantly taxed through relentless speaking responsibilities, toward the end of 1879 Andrew Murray began to suffer from a relaxed throat. (The condition, nicknamed 'clergyman's sore throat', commonly results in chronic throat pain and a perpetual cough.) The malady interrupted his regular ministries and led him into a period of enforced silence which, with only partial and periodic recoveries, stretched out for the better part of two years.

His ailment prevented him from participating in important conferences that were held in 1880 at Montagu and Worcester. Instead of fulfilling the invitations that were extended to him to speak at those conferences, Murray submitted written messages that were then read for him to the assemblies. When the Synod gathered in Cape Town that October Murray was unable to fulfill the accustomed responsibility, as the outgoing moderator, of officiating the opening ceremony. Nor could he actively participate verbally in the Synod's other proceedings that year.

The increased number of students preparing for vocational missionary service at Wellington's Training Institute necessitated the acquisition of another teacher, especially one to provide instruction in theological subjects. Rev. J.C. Pauw was hired to teach theology and Dutch in the Training Institute and to pastor Wellington's local mission congregation, ministering to the town's colored population.

Murray spent several weeks in the opening months of the following year, 1881, in the Karroo, where it was hoped that the dry climate and treatment by a doctor 'of special qualifications' would result in a cure. From Murraysburg, Murray wrote to his wife near the end of January:

> I have to see [the doctor] once every day to have the throat washed, and morning and evening I have to inhale for ten minutes the steam from boiling water, with something mixed into it. I am to take a regular walk in the morning before breakfast, and to speak as little as possible. This last injunction has been made known to all friends, so that I can keep quite quiet. I spend the greater part of the day alone, either in my room or in the garden. ...
>
> As I have brought no work with me I have begun making notes on the daily readings of our Union. Whether I ever use them or not, they are profitable to myself.[1]

The Union to which Murray here refers was an association he was then in the process of establishing to encourage Christians in regular Bible reading and prayer. The association became known as Bijbel en Bid Vereeniging (The Bible and Prayer Union). At this time Murray was composing some study notes to be used in the Bible readings from the Old Testament prophetic books.

While at Murraysburg Murray stayed in the home of his sister, Jemima, and her husband, A.A. Louw, who in more recent years had pastored the Murraysburg congregation, following his earlier ministry in Fauresmith. In mid-February Murray reflected in another letter to Emma:

> Mima [his sister] is very much concerned about my being so solitary in my room, but I enjoy the quiet and have not yet found time hanging heavy upon me. I have not done very much reading, but a good deal of study. For practical reading I have taken up again some old books, McCheyne's Life and Tersteegen[2] – both very beautiful and profitable. A letter in the former has led my thoughts a good deal to the question of God's purpose with this long silence. You know what I have said about the two views of affliction, the one always

---

1. Du Plessis, *The Life of Andrew Murray*, p. 331.

2. Gerhard Tersteegen (1697-1769) was a German Reformed pietist whose hymns and devotional writings have been translated into English.

seeing in it chastisement for sin, the other regarding it in the light of kindness and love. And you know what very great kindness I have felt it, to have such a time for the renewal of bodily strength, and of mental quiet and refreshment for the work before me. The thought has come whether I might not be in danger of overlooking the former aspect. I have been asking the Lord to show me what specially there is that He wants changed. The general answer is a very easy one, and yet it is difficult to realize at once distinctly where and how the change is to come. What is needed is a more spiritual life, more of the power of the Holy Ghost, in the life first and then in the preaching. And yet it looks as if one's life is very much a settled thing, and as if there is not much prospect of one's being lifted to a different platform. If the Holy Spirit were to come in great power to search out and expose either individual failings or the general low state of devotion in the soul, this would be the first step towards forsaking what is behind. Let us pray earnestly that our gracious God would search and try us and see whether there be any evil way in us.[3]

Murray greatly enjoyed a brief visit to some of his family members at his boyhood home in Graaff-Reinet. His brother Charles innocently related to *De Christen*[4]: 'The minister of Wellington is at Graaff-Reinet at present. The condition of his throat shows no improvement. He speaks as little as possible and that little as softly as possible.' That unfavorable report caused 'considerable uneasiness and anxiety' to Murray's wife and congregation back in Wellington. Learning of this back in Murraysburg, Murray wrote Emma on 12 March: 'I am so sorry that you should have been troubled by Charles' notice in *De Christen*. I cannot say that it struck me, for it just said what is the fact. ... Be restful, whatever you hear; and be sure I write you all there is to say.'[5]

The following day he related of his writing projects at that time:

I am enjoying my time for writing. I think I told you of a little book I am engaged on, concerning following Christ, and in between another tract for our Scripture Union. ... The former subject

3. Du Plessis, *The Life of Andrew Murray*, p. 332.

4. For a brief period of years, 1879-1883, *De Kerkbode* was entitled *De Christen*.

5. Du Plessis, *The Life of Andrew Murray*, pp. 332-3.

interests me deeply. May God give me the right words, 'words which the Holy Ghost teacheth' [1 Cor. 2:13], to set forth as a living picture the Christ we are to be like. If we could only study it as we study the pictures of the Masters, until we see the beauty of every trait of His character! This would make us long to be like Him.[6]

Just three days later he was unexpectedly able to report of his throat treatment:

When I saw the doctor today, I was a little bit surprised to hear him say that by the end of next week the treatment would be at an end. It would not be advisable, he said, to continue the application of the silver nitrate, and after that there was nothing needed but care and the gentle and gradual exercise of the voice. I almost feel as if I would prefer waiting a couple of months longer to have a complete cure before beginning again. But he does not appear to encourage this idea. He says I must begin preaching by reading or speaking aloud in a room, and so go on to short addresses slowly uttered. All the same I want very much to stay here a week or two longer, to see how the throat gets on when I begin to speak.[7]

Another matter of marked concern had been weighing on Andrew and Emma's minds throughout his stay in Murraysburg. The First Anglo-Boer War, also known as the Transvaal War of Independence, had erupted on 20 December of the previous year. Three years earlier, in 1877, Britain had annexed the Transvaal, which Boers bitterly protested was a violation of both the Sand River Convention of 1852 and the Bloemfontein Convention of 1854.

Especially concerning to the Murrays was the safety of some of their own family members who were living in the Transvaal at that time. Their oldest daughter Emmie was teaching in Pretoria, where the British had a fort which came under siege by the Boers. Murray's brother-in-law and sister, Rev. Hendrik and Eliza Neethling, were ministering within thirty miles of where most of the major fighting

---

6. ibid., p. 333.
7. ibid.

was taking place. Murray's younger brother James also lived in that vicinity and, in fact, fought on the Boers' side in the final, decisive battle at Majuba Hill (near present-day Volksrust) on 27 February, 1881. James Murray laid a handkerchief over the dead face of the commander of the British forces who perished in that conflict, Major-General Sir George Pomeroy Colley.[8]

Hostilities continued till 6 March when a truce was declared. Ten days later, in the same letter in which he informed Emma that his throat treatments would be ending the following week, Murray wrote:

> We are longing for confirmation of the news of peace. The Lord grant it may be true and a sure peace. I have offered myself to Him if ever He sees fit to use me for the Transvaal (once they have quieted down), to take them the special message of His saving love. But that cannot be soon, both for their sakes and mine.[9]

A formal peace treaty was signed on 23 March. Three days afterward Murray wrote his wife:

> We have just received the tidings of peace. I do bless God for it. I had begun to fear it would be difficult to agree on terms which both parties would think would satisfy their honor. I do pray God the arrangements may be permanent. Now of course Emmie can come away. But there will be the new difficulty of whether they will be willing to leave just as they can commence their work again. ... At all events, there is every prospect of our hearing soon now. Dear child! I long to know what this three months' imprisonment and inactivity will have been to her.[10]

Before long Murray learned that Emmie was quite well and had suffered no serious privations during her recent incarceration at the fort in Pretoria. So strong was Murray's sense of fulfilling one's duty that he wrote to encourage Emmie to continue on in

---

8. Colley was also the British Governor of Natal and Transvaal as well as High Commissioner of Southeast Africa.

9. Du Plessis, *The Life of Andrew Murray*, p. 333.

10. ibid., p. 334.

her teaching responsibility in Pretoria rather than returning home to Wellington:

> We were delighted to hear from you from Heilbron.[11] Do send us your journals at once – we surely can pay the postage – we are longing to know all about your long confinement. Now that peace is arranged and school has begun again, I think it far best you should return at once [to Pretoria]. We are deeply grateful to hear you are so well, and hope you may still long feel the benefit of the enforced holiday. ...
>
> From your last I see that your heart begins to long for home, and that you find it difficult, amid all the rumors that surround you, to look brightly towards your work at Pretoria. As far as I can see, you need not trouble yourself about the rumors. I have a strong hope that the God who so unexpectedly intervened to give peace will perfect what He has begun and give a lasting settlement of what now appears so difficult.[12] ... Do not be too much disturbed by the rumors, and if the school be really going on, go back to it by all means at the earliest opportunity that can be found. The place of our work is to us the safest and the best. And if once you could get back to that, I think you would find it more easy to forego the pleasant thoughts of visiting home again.[13]

On 12 April Murray was able to write his wife with good news concerning his partial recovery:

> I preached yesterday for twenty-five minutes, and the doctor says it has done me no harm. There is still a huskiness about the throat,

---

11.   Heilbron was about 120 miles south of Pretoria.

12.   As circumstances worked out, peace was re-established between the British and the Boers for the better part of two decades. The final peace treaty, the Pretoria Convention, was signed on 3 August, 1881, and ratified by the Transvaal Volksraad on 25 October of that same year. Under the terms of that agreement the Boers were granted complete self-government in the Transvaal under British suzerainty. The Boers, in turn, accepted the Queen's nominal rule as well as British control over foreign relations, African affairs and native districts relating to the Transvaal.

13.   Du Plessis, *The Life of Andrew Murray*, p. 335.

which he says will wear off with the use of the voice. My text was 1 John 2:6, 'Abiding in Him, walking like Him'. Let us bless the Lord for again permitting me to preach Christ, and pray that it may henceforth be in the power of the Holy Ghost.[14]

After an absence of three months Murray was able to return to Wellington near the end of April. During Pentecost services that followed not long thereafter he emphasized the cause of missions. The Wellington congregation, as a token of its gratitude for the restoration of Murray as well as the end of the Transvaal War and the breaking up of a prolonged drought, held a special thanksgiving service and determined to raise funds for a building for the missionary Training Institute. Within a few months 2,000 pounds were collected for that purpose.

The latter half of that year the condition of Murray's throat seemed to continue to improve. He preached regularly and his sermons did not need to be abbreviated. During that same period he also completed the book he had started at Murraysburg, *Gelijk Jezus* (Like Jesus). In addition, he produced his first work in English: *Abide in Christ*.[15]

Murray's fifty-five-year-old brother John spent several months in Europe that year in an effort to restore his health which had been in decline for some time. When Professor Murray and his family returned to Cape Town early the following year, 1882, the steamer on which they traveled was found to have smallpox on board. So it was sent under quarantine to Saldanha Bay, about sixty-five miles northwest of Cape Town. Andrew Murray wrote to his brother there:

Welcome back! And though the reception the Cape has given you has not been a very friendly one, the delay will make your restoration to us all the more acceptable when it does come. And the stay at Saldanha Bay may possibly be what was needed to give you a little

14. ibid., p. 334.

15. Three years later *Gelijk Jezus* was issued as a 256-page volume in English under the title *Like Christ*. *Abide in Christ*, 223 pages in length, had originally been published in Dutch in 1864 with the title *Blijf in Jezus*.

more rest before beginning your work again. I trust the heat will not be such as it is here, and that the visit may have so much of a pleasant picnic life as not to be quite unbearable.

My throat was improving, but got put back, partly by a cold taken at Moorreesburg on the occasion of the induction of Retief,[16] and partly owing to the strain of the New Year and prayer week services.

Thanks for your hints on my English style in *Abide in Christ*, of which I have now received a parcel from Nisbets [the London publisher]. There are a good many misprints still – e.g., *strangulation* for *stagnation* – but this cannot now be helped. I feel a little nervous about my *debut* in English.[17]

In *Abide in Christ* Murray had modestly identified himself only as 'A.M.' A prominent Presbyterian journal soon divulged: 'This excellent work is by a well-known and esteemed minister at the Cape.'[18] As it turned out, Murray need not have doubted the appeal of his first English volume. It was an immediate success, with more than 40,000 copies selling in its first four years of circulation.

The relapse in Murray's throat condition was so serious that his Consistory recommended he go to Europe for 'a complete change of air and scene' and in order to seek the best medical advice. Arrangements were made for Murray and Emma to sail from the Cape in May and for their younger children to remain in South Africa under the care of a long-time friend of the family, Miss McGill.

Just days before the Murrays' departure a special ceremony was held in Wellington for the laying of the foundation stone of the new Training Institute. Professor Hofmeyr delivered the public address for that special occasion. Due to his weakened health, Murray's part in the proceedings was 'little more than formal'.

After Murray had been in Europe for a number of weeks he wrote his congregation at Wellington a pair of letters in which he

16.   Rev. J.D. Retief; Moorreesburg was around sixty miles north of Cape Town.

17.   Du Plessis, *The Life of Andrew Murray*, p. 337.

18.   ibid., p. 462.

chronicled what he believed to be the Lord's leading of him to seek healing on the basis of faith rather than through traditional medical treatment. The first letter, dated 20 September, stated in part:

> At the Cape I had already frequently given thought to James 5:14-16 – 'the prayer of faith shall heal the sick' – and in union with others I had already made this matter of faith healing a subject of intercession. What I had read concerning the work of Dorothea Trudel and Dr [Charles] Cullis[19] had removed from my mind all doubts but that the Lord even yet bestows healing on the prayer of faith. And yet it was as though I could not reach that faith. When I resolved upon the trip to Europe I felt that it would be a serious question for me whether I should place myself under the treatment of a physician, or should turn to those who appear to have received this gift of healing from the Lord. ...
>
> How it happened I do not know, but on the voyage my attention was not directed to the matter in any especial degree: I could only beseech the Lord to guide me. The man whom I desired particularly to see was Pastor Stockmaier, whom I had learnt to know in Switzerland five years earlier as a truly spiritual man, of strong faith, and who now stood at the head of an institute for faith healing. But I did not expect to meet him before I got to Switzerland. And so it happened that, having received no clear guidance, I placed myself the day after my arrival in the hands of a famous London physician, Dr Kidd. He prescribed a few medicines for me to use and sent me to a cold-water establishment in the vicinity of London, with directions that I should call on him from time to time. The following week was appointed for the Mildmay Conference, which was to last for three days, and I obtained permission to attend it.
>
> At this conference, just a week after our arrival in London, I heard that Mr Stockmaier was also present. I called on him

---

19. Trudel had a highly acclaimed faith-healing ministry in Mannedorf, Switzerland, until her death in 1862. Cullis, a medical doctor, carried out extensive faith-healing ministries in the north-eastern United States in the 1870s and 1880s. His teachings had a strong influence on the faith-healing perspectives of A.B. Simpson and the Christian and Missionary Alliance denomination that Simpson founded.

and discussed my throat trouble with him. In the course of our discussion I said that I, too, had wanted to make use of James 5:14, but that it seemed to me that I could not reach that faith. Perhaps that was due to the secret doubt I cherished that it was certainly God's will that I should be healed. ... Surely suffering and trial are means of grace which God employs to sanctify His people. Mr Stockmaier replied: 'You are still fettered by the customary views of Christians about suffering. Observe how carefully James distinguishes in verses 13 and 14 between suffering and disease. Of suffering he says, "Is any among you *afflicted* (or *suffering*), let him pray" – for patience (James 1:2-5, 12). But then again, "Is any *sick* among you ... the prayer of faith shall save the sick." There is no unconditional promise that suffering, arising from the many temptations and trials of life, will be taken away; but there is such a promise in the case of sickness.' ...

Mr Stockmaier invited me to attend in the course of the following week the meetings of Dr [William] Boardman, writer of *The Higher Christian Life*, on the subject of faith healing. Shortly before my departure from the Cape I had perused Dr Boardman's other work *The Lord thy Healer*, but it left no special impression upon me, perhaps because in my opinion he built too exclusively upon the Old Testament. I now learnt that only a few months before an institute for faith healing had been opened in London under his supervision. This institute [the Bethshan Home for Healing] I visited in the following week, when everything became clearer to me and I decided to ask if I could not be received as an inmate. The reply was that there would be a vacancy in the course of a few days, when I would be welcome.

I entered the institute three weeks after our arrival in London and remained in it for another three weeks. It would be difficult to describe how much instruction and blessing I obtained during those weeks. ... Morning by morning the sixteen or eighteen inmates were assembled around the Word of God and instructed as to what there still remained in themselves to prevent them from appropriating the promise, and what there was in Scripture to encourage them to faith and to complete surrender. I cannot remember that I have ever listened to expositions of the Word of God in which greater simplicity and a more glorious spirit of faith were revealed, combined with heart-searching application of God's demand to surrender everything to Him. ...

When Mr Stockmaier prayed with me the first time he made use of the expression which occurs in 1 Corinthians 11:31, 32, saying, 'Lord, teach him to judge himself, that he may no longer be judged or chastened.' In that whole passage we find the main thoughts concerning sickness and cure. Disease is a chastisement, because God judges us in love so that we may not be condemned with the world. If we judge ourselves in such manner as to discover the reason for which we are being chastised, then, so soon as the reason for chastisement is removed, the chastisement itself is no longer necessary. The disease was designed to bring us to complete severance from what God disapproved of in our life, and when the Lord has attained this purpose the disease itself may be removed. It is not necessary for me to say that God judges us sometimes (though not always) for some definite sin. This may be lack of complete consecration, the assertion of one's own will, confidence in one's own strength in performing the Lord's work, a forsaking of the first love and tenderness in the walk with God, or the absence of that gentleness which desires to follow only the leading of the Spirit of God.[20]

In his subsequent correspondence to his congregation Murray shared further perspectives he had come to have:

One of the first things that struck me as being in conflict with my expectations was that in most cases slow progress is made with the healing process. I thought, and others have expressed the same opinion, that if healing is an act of God's almighty power there can be no reason why it should not be perfected at once. This point I discussed with Dr Boardman and others, whose reply was somewhat as follows: 'First of all, experience has taught that at the present time most cases of healing are subject to this rule; so that, even though we cannot understand why it should be so, we have merely to observe what God actually does. Then, too, we have to notice that this gradual recovery stands in close connection with learning to trust in the Lord and to continue in constant dependence upon Him. It is as though the Lord, by this slow and gradual process, is educating His child to the increasing exercise of faith, and to a continuance in communion with Himself.' …

---

20.   Du Plessis, *The Life of Andrew Murray*, pp. 339-41.

At first I could not entirely assent to this view of the matter. I asked Dr Boardman if it would not be a much more powerful proof, both for His children and for the world at large, that God hears and answers prayer, if the cure of disease were instantaneous and complete. I said that if I could write to my congregation that I had wholly recovered my voice as at the first, the thanksgiving would be more abundant to the glory of God. Would it not also be for the greater glory of God if I desired of Him this instantaneous restoration? His answer was, 'The Lord knows better than you or your congregation what is for His greater glory. Leave it to Him to care for His own glory. Your duty is to hold fast to Him as your Healer, in whom you already have the healing of your malady, and He will enable you, in such manner as He sees fit, to perform all your work.' In this point of view I was able, ultimately, wholly to acquiesce.[21]

The Murrays sailed for South Africa on 19 October. Upon their arrival there they found Miss McGill, who had been caring for their younger children in their absence, seriously ill. She greeted Murray and Emma with the sober declaration, 'I have lived just long enough to deliver up my charge to you again.'

'By no means,' Murray promptly responded. 'Though doctors despair, there is hope and recovery in the Lord who heals us.' He then explained to her the principles of faith-healing and prayed earnestly for her restoration. Miss McGill soon regained her strength and health and went on to faithfully serve the Lord for many years in connection with the Young Women's Christian Association in Cape Town.

Before 1882 came to an end, however, Murray's beloved older brother John passed away rather suddenly. After speaking at a Christmas Eve service on 'a little child shall lead them' [Isa. 11:6], John returned home feeling tired and ill. Christmas Day he did not rise but rested quietly. Two days later, 'with hardly a farewell', he passed to his eternal rest.[22] He was only fifty-six years old at the time of his death.

---

21. ibid., pp. 342-3. Murray also revealed in that letter that he was contemplating whether or not he might have the requisite gifting to devote himself 'for a time at least' to the ministry of faith-healing. While he did go on to do some teaching and writing on the subject of divine healing, he was not led into a faith-healing ministry.

22. Neethling, *Unto Children's Children*, p. 86.

20

RESTORED TO ACTIVE MINISTRY AND LEADERSHIP
1883

Andrew Murray's extended enforced hiatus from active ministry resulted not only in his physical restoration but also in his spiritual transformation. Many years later, after his death, a long-time friend of the family wrote to Murray's daughter Mary of that transformation:

> Do you remember the time when he was not allowed to preach? A great change came into his life after that. He used to be rather stern and very decided in his judgment of things – after that year he was all love. His great humility also struck me very forcibly at that time. I remember his coming home one day from a walk with his face beaming; he had conversed with an old colored woman on the road and had learnt so much of God's love from her.[1]

Murray's oldest daughter similarly testified:

> It was after the 'time of silence' when God came so near to Father and he saw more clearly the meaning of a life of full surrender and simple faith, that he began to show in all relationships that constant tenderness and unruffled lovingkindness and unselfish thought for others which increasingly characterized his life from that point. At the same time he lost nothing of his strength and determination.[2]

---

1. Douglas, *Andrew Murray and His Message*, pp. 255-6.
2. Leona Choy, *Andrew Murray, Apostle of Abiding Love* (Fort Washington, PA: Christian Literature Crusade, 1978), p. 148.

Murray continued to devote considerable attention to the issue of faith-healing following his return to South Africa in 1882. Two years later he published a small duodecimo volume of 183 pages in Dutch, entitled *Jezus de Geneesheer der Kranken* (Jesus the Physician of the Sick).[3] He presented his book as 'a personal testimony of my faith' and related that, after more than two years of not being able to carry out his ordinary duties, he had been healed through divine mercy in answer to the prayers of those who recognized God as the healer of His people.[4]

Even with his strong convictions about faith-healing Murray came to see that God remained sovereign over whether such healing would or would not be granted. Du Plessis records two of 'several cases' Murray observed 'in which faith was exercised and all the conditions of healing seemed to be completely fulfilled', yet prayers for healing were not granted and the sick individual died. The first such instance occurred in the opening months of 1883, the year before Murray's book on faith-healing was originally published.

Rev. Pieter Hugo, who was married to a niece of Murray, developed symptoms of tuberculosis that forced him to suspend his pastoral labors and threatened to end his life. Leaving his congregation in the Colony's Eastern Province, he went to rest in his mother's home in Paarl, seven miles south of Wellington. For a time Hugo, 'a truly pious and devoted man', appeared to be improving, and he firmly believed he would recover. In mid-April, acting on the principle of considering himself as already healed, he undertook a long journey to Middelburg in the Central Karroo to attend a ministerial conference in which Murray also participated.

Murray's reports on the condition of Hugo's health reveal that he was watching the case closely:

---

3. In 1900 a 217-page English edition was published in America under the title *Divine Healing*.

4. Du Plessis, *The Life of Andrew Murray*, pp. 346-8 and Douglas, *Andrew Murray and His Message*, pp. 193-7 cite from the book's introductory chapter Murray's nine 'chief reasons why we believe in Jesus as the Physician of the sick' and his eight 'main conditions upon which a sick person may obtain health from the Lord'. Murray called the latter 'The Rules for Faith Healing'.

P. Hugo did not cough as much as at home, so he says, and was not overtired.

P.H. is still wonderfully well, considering the distance traveled. The Lord be praised.

P. Hugo stood the two days' hard driving – over ten hours [sixty miles] yesterday – better than I thought, as far as fatigue is concerned. He slept very well the last two nights, though he coughs a good deal. I think this may be owing to the dust in traveling.[5]

But two days after Hugo's return to Paarl he began to weaken rapidly. One evening he complained of a feeling of utter weakness and retired to his room, where he passed away a short while later. His death was a sharp blow to Murray who had confidently expected his nephew to recover.[6]

Du Plessis provides an enlightening and balanced summary of Murray's practices and perspectives relative to physical healing as he continued through life:

In the case of his own bodily health Mr Murray continued for many years to follow the principles of faith healing. In 1893, when traveling in Natal on one of his evangelistic tours, the cart in which he was journeying was upset, and he sustained severe injuries to his arm and his back. But in spite of this accident he determined to carry out his program, and in this determination he succeeded, though at first he had to be assisted into the pulpit. On these prolonged tours his throat still caused him occasional trouble, but he insisted on fulfilling all his engagements, 'looking to the Lord for healing', and when he reached home his throat was generally better rather than worse. When peace was declared at the close of the Anglo-Boer War in 1902 he found himself very much in need

---

5.   Du Plessis, *The Life of Andrew Murray*, p. 349.

6.   ibid., p. 350 relates another such instance, more than twenty years later, when 'an exceedingly earnest and capable young missionary, Rev. Pieter Stofberg' died of illness though he, Murray and many others prayed in great faith and fervency for God to heal him.

of rest after the continuous strain of three years of toil and anxiety, and undertook another trip to Europe where he consulted medical men both in London and in Switzerland. After the death of Mrs Murray, who was like himself strongly convinced of the truth of faith healing, he regularly consulted a doctor, mainly in order to please his children; and when confined, as he sometimes was, to a sick-bed, no patient could be more obedient to instructions, more cheerful in demeanor, or more grateful for the least attention.

These facts prove clearly that towards the end of his life Mr Murray did not give the same prominence to faith healing as in the years immediately following his stay at the Bethshan Institute of Healing. It cannot be said that he relinquished the views he held in 1883, but he came to acknowledge that faith healing was not for everyone ... Some of the views set forth on this question of faith healing, as for example the assertion that suffering, even in the believer, is [always] due to some special sin, can hardly be regarded as true to Scripture or to experience, and were probably not insisted on by Mr Murray in later years. In the fervency with which he both preached and practiced the doctrines of healing by faith, we have an instance of that intensity of conviction which characterized him, and led him at times to lay such exclusive stress on certain aspects of the truth as almost to overbear, without removing, the doubts which other minds expressed and the difficulties which weaker wills encountered.[7]

Douglas further relates:

Although Mr Murray never ceased to trust God for his bodily as well as his spiritual health, yet for the sake of easing the minds of relatives and friends he did not refuse, as a rule, to see the doctor if they so desired. But this was not always so. As recently as [1904?][8] he suffered from a severe attack of influenza and it seemed as though he was likely to be carried off by it. Miss Murray [Annie] says: 'Father was very ill and my Mother was quite brokenhearted and asked me, "What am I to do?" I went in to Father and said,

7. ibid., pp. 351-2.

8. Douglas incorrectly dates this incident as having occurred in 1907. Emma Murray, who was still living at the time of this event, died on 2 January, 1905.

"Father dear, which will you do? Will you have the doctor or will you have someone to anoint you and pray with you?" He said, "Neither, my child. I will have neither. You can hold as many prayer meetings as you like but I WILL TRUST IN GOD." I went out and arranged for three different meetings for prayer to ask for his restoration to health. To the praise of God it is said he preached the next Sunday, a most remarkable sermon on the text, "They limited the Holy One of Israel" (Ps. 78:41). Once more he proved the faithfulness of God.[9]

The same day Pieter Hugo died in Paarl – 14 May, 1883 – Wellington's spacious new building for the missionary Training Institute was opened 'with great acclaim'. Total cost for the ground and the building, which included classrooms and boarding rooms, totaled 4,500 pounds. Of that amount the Wellington congregation had already contributed 2,700 pounds, and by year's end the debt was reduced by another 300 pounds.

The Bible and Prayer Union first envisioned by Murray more than two years earlier while seeking treatment for his throat in Murraysburg was formally inaugurated in 1883. An almanac was issued that included daily Scripture-reading portions as well as suggested prayer subjects for each day. By 1885 Murray found it necessary to turn over the directorship of the Union to Rev. J.J.T. Marquard, under whose capable leadership the association grew to over 20,000 members. For more than forty years Murray would serve as editor of the Union's daily devotional guide, *Uit de Beek* (Out of the Spring).[10]

When the Colony's DRC Synod convened in October of 1883 Murray, now fifty-five years old and once again in restored health, was elected as Moderator for the third time. He wrote of this to his wife on 9 October : 'To my utter amazement I am Moderator again. How or why, I know not. May the Lord give me grace to act so that any influence I have to exert may be for His glory, and to

9. Douglas, *Andrew Murray and His Message*, p. 199.

10. Du Plessis, *The Life of Andrew Murray*, p. 359; Choy, *Andrew Murray*, p. 111.

testify for a religion that is higher than organization and work.'[11] Du Plessis describes Murray's capable and commendable characteristics as Moderator:

> He possessed firmness without obstinacy, tolerance without compliancy, and impartiality without indecision. While resolute to uphold the dignity of the chair, he was courteous and tactful in public and readily accessible in private. Among his most outstanding qualifications for the office he was called to fulfill were his remarkable insight into the true bearing of the subject under discussion and his rapid decision as to the best course to pursue. ...
>
> ... Mr Murray displayed great tact in guiding the discussions ... which took place in the Assembly. His knowledge of human nature was unsurpassed ... He knew how to intervene in a debate at the [appropriate] psychological moment, and to suggest that a matter which was exciting strong feelings, or which needed to have more light cast upon it, should be referred to a committee for consideration and report. In the appointment of committees he exercised great wisdom and the strictest impartiality. It was seldom indeed that a ruling given by him as chairman, or an appointment made, was challenged by any member of the Synod. His personality and lofty Christian character inspired at all times the utmost regard and confidence.[12]

At one Synod a matter was introduced that affected a difficult point of Church law. The Synod appointed a small committee, of which Murray was a member, to come up with a feasible solution to the complex situation and to present its proposal when the assembly reconvened that afternoon. The committee agreed to meet an hour before the afternoon session but at the appointed time only one committee member had arrived. Several minutes later one or two others arrived and started a desultory discussion of the issue they were to consider. Finally just twelve minutes before the Synod was to reassemble, Murray hurried in and stated apologetically, 'I am

---

11.   Du Plessis, *The Life of Andrew Murray*, p. 354.

12.   ibid., pp. 355-6.

sorry, brethren, that I could not be here sooner. But I hope you have the report ready for me to sign.'

'No,' came the response, 'We have been waiting for your arrival. However, as there is no time to discuss the question now, we shall have to request the Synod to postpone the consideration of our report.'

'Not at all,' rejoined Murray. 'There are still twelve minutes, which are all that we require.' Turning to the youngest committee member, he asked, 'Can you write quickly? Then take a pen and write to my dictation.'

He then proceeded to dictate a 'luminous' report, clarifying the nature of the issues involved and recommending the procedure that should be followed. His fellow committee members agreed that the report could not be improved, and the Synod adopted it as providing a completely satisfactory solution.

Du Plessis bears further testimony of Murray's superlative leadership abilities:

> Andrew Murray was not merely a capable Moderator of Synod. He was a great Church statesman. He possessed all the qualifications for true and effective leadership. He recognized both the strength and the weakness of the Church which he served. He divined with infallible precision the ailments from which it suffered, and labored to remove or ameliorate them. He knew also what the Church was capable of, and strove to call forth and strengthen the powers which still slumbered unutilized. In almost all new developments he not merely took the initiative but also supplied the driving force. He was the acknowledged leader in any committee on which he sat, being possessed of a mind which firmly grasped the largest issues without neglecting the smallest minutiae. His knowledge of details was truly marvelous, and the writer of these lines, who was associated with him on more than one board, had frequent cause to remark that Mr Murray's acquaintance with any given subject under consideration was equal to that of all the other members combined.[13]

---

13. ibid., pp. 356-7.

A temperance controversy that had been simmering in Cape Colony's DRC for several years boiled to the surface during the 1883 Synod. From the early years of his Wellington pastorate, beginning in the early 1870s, Murray had promoted temperance principles there. In 1877 Murray spoke at the dedication ceremony of a new building for the Stellenbosch Young Men's Christian Association. He reported that in America the temperance movement was making great progress and the use of alcoholic beverages was gradually disappearing in Christian circles. American YMCAs were exerting great efforts to combat 'the drink evil' and to promote the cause of total abstinence. Murray concluded that such should be the endeavor of societies of Christian young men everywhere.

Professor Hofmeyr took to heart Murray's challenge on that occasion and subsequently established a Total Abstinence Society. Hofmeyr pleaded the matter from many pulpits and published numerous pamphlets and letters in the press on the issue. He maintained that it was the duty of every Christian to abstain from drinking alcohol or any other practice that would offend a weaker brother or cause him to stumble. He even went so far as to declare that 'alcohol is a poison, and ... therefore, according to the will of God, its use is forbidden to the healthy human being'.[14] Though Murray was a strong proponent of abstinence he did not agree in all points with Hofmeyr's position. Murray believed that Hofmeyr's efforts to prove that the Bible commands abstinence went beyond the letter of Scripture.

Hofmeyr's teachings and activities stirred up a storm of protest from the Stellenbosch farmers, nearly all of whom were wine producers. They pointed out that wine production was introduced in South Africa by pious Huguenots. They insisted that the country's wine farmers as a class were earnest, God-fearing men who staunchly upheld the Church of their fathers and generously supported both foreign missions and 'home philanthropies'. Beyond asserting that Stellenbosch's Theological Seminary (where Hofmeyr served as senior professor) was originally erected

---

14.   ibid., p. 362.

and presently maintained largely by the contributions of wine producers, they threatened to withdraw further support if all abstinence propaganda were not relinquished. When Hofmeyr stood firm, many stayed away from church services when it was known that he would occupy the pulpit.

When the issue of abstinence was taken up for discussion at the 1883 and 1886 Synods 'Interest was at fever heat. Questions, petitions, proposals, overtures covered the Moderator's table.'[15] While Murray strongly favored abstinence, as Moderator he was bound to exercise strict impartiality and to moderate between conflicting perspectives. In addition, he needed to exercise care in his position as minister of Wellington and representative of that congregation in the assembly. As was the case at Stellenbosch, so at Wellington the most faithful members and the strongest financial backers of the church and its various ministries were predominantly the wine farmers. For Murray to condemn their livelihood would be to harm or even destroy the trust and influence he had with them.

As it turned out, the 1883 Synod reached a compromise position in a public statement it issued on the temperance issue. Murray acquiesced in this decision, though he wished the statement would have been more strongly worded. The statement, which was published in *De Kerkbode*, read:

1. Wine is a good gift of God, to be received with gratitude and to be used to His glory.

2. Scripture nevertheless teaches us that the Christian is at liberty to refrain from the use of such gifts, where such self-denial is exercised in the spirit of holiness, out of love to others, or to protect oneself against temptation to sin.

3. Experience has taught us that for those who are enslaved to drink, or are in danger of becoming so enslaved, total abstinence is one of the most powerful means of protection; and for this reason such persons should be encouraged to undertake it.

---

15. ibid.

4. For those who think that by their abstinence they can encourage and strengthen the weak it is permissible voluntarily to bind themselves to help such weaker brethren by their example and in the fellowship of love.

5. It must be emphasized that, as there is no salvation without faith in the Lord Jesus, so, too, Biblical Temperance Societies only possess value for eternity in so far as they seek to pave the way for the preaching of the Gospel, and aim at leading their members not merely to a temperate but to a truly godly life.

6. For this purpose it is permissible to enter into a mutual undertaking to abstain, with God's help, from the use of all intoxicating drinks, and to put forth every endeavor to oppose the abuse of strong drink on the part of others.[16]

---

16. ibid., p. 363.

21

Blossoming Ministry Opportunities
1884–1889

Throughout 1884 and 1885 Murray devoted much attention to the topic of prayer. At the 1884 installation service of a young minister, Rev. G.F. Marais, Murray delivered the charge, taking as his theme 'The Pastor as Man of Prayer'. At a ministerial conference held at George that same year the focus was again on prayer. Murray preached a powerful sermon on 'The Priestly Prayer Life', employing Isaiah 61:6 as his text, 'But ye shall be named the Priests of the Lord: men shall call you the Ministers of our God'.

That same year Murray published a 253-page volume entitled *De School des Bebeds* (The School of Prayer). Of it, a fellow minister effused: 'Oh, why did not the author give us this book twenty-five years ago? ... *The School of Prayer* is a perfect treasury, and had the honored writer published nothing else, our country would have owed him a great debt of gratitude.'[1] The following year, 1885, the volume was released as a 274-page work in English under the title *With Christ in the School of Prayer*. It enjoyed a wide circulation, especially in America, and went on to become one of Murray's best-known works and an enduring classic on prayer. After reading the book while on a spiritual retreat away from his parish, Alexander Whyte, the esteemed minister of Free St George's Church in Edinburgh, wrote to Murray:

> I have read a good deal during last week, but nothing half so good as your *With Christ*. ... [Y]our book goes to the joints and the

---

1. Du Plessis, *The Life of Andrew Murray*, p. 463.

marrow of things. You are a much honored man: how much only the day will declare. The other books I have been reading are all able and good in their way; but they are spent on the surface of things. Happy man! – you have been chosen and ordained of God to go to the heart of things. I have been sorely rebuked, but also much directed and encouraged by your *With Christ*. Thank you devoutly and warmly this Sabbath afternoon. I am to send your book to some of my friends on my return to town tomorrow.[2]

1884 also brought the publication of Murray's *Like Christ*, the English counterpart to his *Gelijk Jezus* which had been produced three years earlier. Considered the companion volume and sequel to his popular *Abide in Christ*, the 256-page *Like Christ* sold some 19,000 copies in its first two years of circulation. In 1885 Murray also published a 246-page volume, *Het Nieuwe Leven*, which six years later was issued in English under the title *The New Life*. Du Plessis states of Murray's blossoming writing ministry at that time:

> Mr Murray was now finally embarked upon his career as a devotional writer. His name was widely known, and new books from his pen were awaited with eagerness. The next book in English was *The Children for Christ*[3] ... In the years 1887 and 1888 he wrote *Holy in Christ* and *The Spirit of Christ*, books which give evidence of close theological study as well as of warm evangelical fervor.[4]

Abide in Christ, his first English venture, appeared in 1882 and in 1888 were published *Holy in Christ* and *The Spirit of Christ*, which

---

2. ibid., p. 478.

3. Published in 1886, it was an expanded version of a Dutch work Murray had originally produced twenty-three years earlier, *Wat zal toch dit kindeken wezen?* (What manner of child shall this be?). While the original Dutch edition contained 230 pages divided into thirty-one chapters, the expanded English version had 448 pages comprising fifty-two chapters, thus providing a reading for each week in the year.

4. Du Plessis, *The Life of Andrew Murray*, p. 463. *Holy in Christ* was 302 pages long. *The Spirit of Christ*, 394 pages in length, was also published in Dutch as *De Geest van Christus* that same year, 1888.

(together with *The Holiest of All*) represent the high-water mark of his literary and theological achievements. Between the above-mentioned dates he had found his audience, for when *The Spirit of Christ* was issued his first work had already reached its fifty-third thousand. His readers, counted by tens of thousands, were scattered all over the globe.[5]

At the encouragement of the DRC Synod and with the blessing of his Wellington congregation Murray had conducted his first evangelistic tour to ten South African communities in 1879. In late 1884 and early 1885 he carried out a second evangelistic tour, this one to a number of churches and towns in the Colony's eastern districts, Orange Free State and Transvaal. In five of the six years that immediately followed he conducted further evangelistic trips:

1886 – third evangelistic tour, to the Colony's
       southwestern districts

1887 – fourth evangelistic tour, to Natal, Transvaal,
       Orange Free State

1888 – fifth evangelistic tour, to the Colony's eastern
       districts

1890 – sixth evangelistic tour, to Namaqualand (north of
       the Western Cape)

1891 – seventh evangelistic tour, to the Colony's
       northeastern districts[6]

Those tours ranged in length from a few weeks to several months. Murray's Consistory and congregation at Wellington, realizing the urgent need of the broader Church for this type of ministry and the special gifting of their pastor to help provide it, willingly granted him extended leaves of absence to carry it

---

5. ibid., p. 442. *The Holiest of All*, mentioned here, was published in 1894.

6. This list is compiled from ibid., p. 522.

out. Unfortunately, relatively little detail has been preserved about most of the trips.

Of the preparations for and responses to these evangelistic meetings, Du Plessis reveals:

> Mr Murray was accustomed to insist strongly on the previous preparation of the soil. He instructed the minister of the congregation he was about to visit how best to kindle large expectations, and so to provide an audience that was both psychologically and spiritually ripe for the reception of Divine Truth. Christians were urged to continuous and believing prayer for an individual and a general blessing. The Church at large was invited to join in fervent supplication that it might please God to grant a rich harvest of souls. ... Wherever he journeyed there were prejudices to be removed, difficulties to be smoothed away, ignorance to be dispelled, and coldness and diffidence to be overcome. He had to do frequently with ministers who were not averse to 'special services', but feared that the 'after meetings' formed an undesirable feature. 'I tell them,' wrote Mr Murray, 'that it would be breaking off the point of the arrow. Imagine a Salvation Army meeting without a penitent form!' In spite, however, of superficial differences, his fellow ministers, in almost every case, received him gladly and accorded him the heartiest sympathy and cooperation; while the audiences, if sometimes unenlightened, listened always with the most respectful and earnest attention.[7]

While Murray, accompanied by Emma, was ministering in Transvaal early in 1885, their oldest son, Howson, suddenly and unexpectedly became gravely ill and died. Howson possessed 'staunch Christian principles' but not robust physical health. Instead of pursuing higher education he entered the business of his uncle, Frederic Rutherfoord, in Cape Town. Howson was residing there when he passed away at just twenty-three years of age. Murray and Emma, doubtless accompanied by supportive Christian acquaintances, had a memorial service for Howson at the very hour their children were

---

7. ibid., pp. 436-7.

attending his funeral service. Just before those services, Murray wrote his surviving children:

> Here we are all ready to start for Middelburg and Lydenburg, but just waiting to have a funeral service from 4 to 5, at the same time as you. Dear Howson! He was not a man of strong mind or will, and yet he did amid all failure cling to his Savior. He did seek to know his own weakness: how often he has, with a most childlike simplicity, told me his faults; and his very last letter to Mary expressed his desire to be humble and Christlike. And now – we do bless the Lord for the hope that he is in His presence, without fault before the throne. We gave him to his God in the covenant once, and gave him a thousand times since that, and now we do lovingly give him up to Him who will keep him for Himself and for us too. ... And let his going be a new bond of love to make us all gentle and very loving as if we were going to part very soon. ... The Lord bless you, the Lord comfort you, the Lord keep you.[8]

The following year, 1886, witnessed the completion and formal dedication of a new building for Wellington's Huguenot Seminary. Named Goodnow Hall after the American benefactor who had supplied the majority of the funding, the structure contained a spacious hall for meetings as well as a number of classrooms.

Murray was elected to a fourth term of service as Moderator when the DRC Synod met in the closing months of that year. Concern over the total abstinence issue was just as great as, if not greater than, it had been at the Synod three years earlier. As a result three days of discussion were devoted to the issue at the 1886 assembly.

The abstinence question continued to be hotly debated in the public press for a number of years. Eventually the controversy died down and both sides assumed a more tolerant attitude. Christian wine producers acknowledged that temperance advocates were not motivated by hostility toward themselves personally but by a strong conviction that the evils of alcohol abuse needed to be opposed with

---

8. Douglas, *Andrew Murray and His Message*, pp. 213-14.

more than mere words. Abstainers made allowances for Christian men who viewed wine farming as a legitimate industry and who pointed out, with a degree of truth, that if they stopped producing wine they could not subsist on their small farms. Over the years, the DRC Synod 'made its voice heard with increasing urgency on the side of temperance'.[9]

The year 1886 also saw a 'remarkable increase' of interest in foreign missions on the part of the Colony's DRC ministers.[10] After four years of service as the 'devoted and beloved' pastor of Britstown, Rev. Samuel Helm resigned his charge to go as a missionary to the Zoutpansberg. In addition, Murray's nephew, Andrew C. Murray (son of Charles), having just graduated from the Stellenbosch Theological Seminary, announced his desire to serve as a missionary, preferably in 'a distant and unoccupied field'.

At the suggestion of a young minister, Rev. H.C. de Wet, and with Murray's active involvement and guidance, the Ministers' Mission Union (Predikanten Zending Vereeniging) was established on 11 November of that year. Individual members made annual pledges, ranging between five and twenty pounds, from their personal income in support of missions. The original forty members collectively pledged 300 pounds in annual contributions. Murray would go on to serve as the lifelong chairman of this Union.[11]

The Ministers' Mission Union (MMU) approved A.C. Murray for service and, after completing a brief course of medicine at Edinburgh University, he was ready to go to the field in 1888. The MMU Executive Committee met at Wellington on Tuesday

---

9. Du Plessis, *The Life of Andrew Murray*, p. 365.

10. 'The Home Mission consists of work among the colored and black races *within* the confines of the Cape Colony, and the Foreign Mission of work among those living *beyond* the Colonial frontiers' (ibid., p. 374).

11. When Murray retired on a pension he continued to contribute twenty-five pounds per year to the Ministers' Mission Union. Once when he forwarded his annual contribution the MMU Secretary returned the donation, saying it must surely be a mistake as it was too much. But Murray sent back the donation with a note stating there was no mistake (Douglas, *Andrew Murray and His Message*, p. 228).

19 July, of that year, to consider whether he should serve in Transvaal or at Bandawe on the west coast of Lake Nyasa.[12] The Free Church of Scotland had invited A.C. Murray, as a South African DRC missionary, to serve alongside its missionaries, headquartered at the Scottish mission station at Bandawe. Given the fact that the closest mission station west of Bandawe was some 550 miles away at Makuru, the MMU Executive Committee recommended that A.C. Murray should be sent to minister in that vast unreached region. The Ministers' Mission Union affirmed that recommendation and A.C. Murray sailed to his appointed place of service in the course of 1888. After he was joined there the following year by T.C.B. Vlok they founded the Nyasa Mission of the DRC at a location called Mvera on Lake Nyasa's western coast.

Another issue to which Murray devoted some time and attention in 1888 was the dearth of schools for children in extensive, sparsely-populated regions of Cape Colony. Many poor farmers were not only uneducated themselves but also had little ability or desire to secure education for their children. Dr Langham Dale, Superintendent-General of Education for the Colony, was greatly concerned over that state of affairs and promoted a system of Circuit Schools by which the problem could be addressed. Dale persuaded Parliament to provide the annual salary of traveling teachers who would offer instruction at two or three farms during the course of a year. Parents of the children needed to supply only an adequate schoolroom and the teacher's lodging. It was thought that each school would consist of at least twenty students.

Through his wide-ranging travels Murray had become well aware of the lack of adequate educational opportunities for many children in various rural districts of the Colony. He definitely shared Dr Dale's deep concerns over the situation. So in June of 1888 Murray wrote an article for *De Kerkbode* explaining and promoting Dale's proposal. In part Murray stated:

---

12. Lake Nyasa (modern Lake Malawi) is an African Great Lake located between the present-day countries of Malawi, Mozambique and Tanzania.

What Dr Dale now asks is that ministers who believe that there is an opening for such schools in their congregations will advise him of the fact as speedily as possible. He will be glad, too, to receive any suggestions as to the modification of his scheme, in the direction, it may be, of a reduced [government] grant in the case of a smaller number of pupils. I am convinced that there are districts where larger numbers of poor children can by these means be assisted to the education which they so much need, and I have no doubt that there will be many applications for circuit schools ...[13]

This system was soon adopted and had considerable success, especially in the northwestern region of Cape Colony. The designation 'circuit school' was soon changed to 'poor school' because it proved more practical for teachers to offer instruction in fixed locations rather than moving from one farm to another during the course of a year.

While seeking the restoration of his health in England in 1882 Murray had met at Keswick twenty-three-year-old W. Spencer Walton, who revealed that he was seriously considering devoting his life to mission work in South Africa. Murray assured him that if he were led of the Lord to do so he would receive a hearty welcome from Cape Colony Christians. Five years later a Mrs Osborne, who was involved in Christian ministry to soldiers and sailors in South Africa, heard Walton speak at a convention in Leamington, England. Acting on 'a sudden inspiration', she penned Walton a letter, inviting him to come on a speaking mission to the Cape. After consulting with several evangelical leaders Walton accepted the invitation and in 1888 sailed for Cape Town. He was accompanied on the voyage by Murray's son, Haldane, who had just completed a course of study at Christ's College, Cambridge.

Walton was warmly welcomed not only by Murray and Mrs Osborne but also by 'a large number of evangelical ministers and Christian friends'. A series of meetings were held in Cape Town, for which Murray and other earnest Christians had made long and prayerful preparation. First the YMCA Hall then the Metropolitan Wesleyan Church proved inadequate to accommodate the growing

13.   Du Plessis, *The Life of Andrew Murray*, p. 404.

crowds that gathered for the meetings. When the Exhibition Building with its 2,000-seat capacity was procured for use, it was crowded to overflowing many successive nights. The entire city was 'greatly stirred' and many individuals were led to saving faith in Christ through those meetings. Christians of all denominations were strengthened in their faith and motivated to fuller consecration in their service of Christ.

Walton returned to England toward the end of that year, fully assured that God was calling him to serve in South Africa, and immediately began making plans to establish an organized mission in Cape Colony. Within a few months, in March, 1889, the Cape General Mission (CGM) was established, with a managing Council in London and Walton to serve as Director in South Africa. The following August the first party of six CGM workers left England for the Colony. Not many months after their arrival, the foundation stone of a suitable meeting hall for the new mission was laid in Cape Town, with Murray officiating that ceremony. Murray was chosen as President of the CGM's South African Council, an office he would fill to the end of his life.

In time the Cape General Mission developed three primary objectives: to encourage believers to pursue 'a more exalted standard of Christian life'; to carry out evangelistic work among neglected, largely-irreligious classes of white people in larger towns; to undertake foreign mission work among native groups in regions that were 'unentered or insufficiently occupied'. As part of fulfilling the first objective, the CGM organized a number of 'Holiness Conventions', one of which was held at Johannesburg in the early days of the mission's existence. Murray led and was the most prominent speaker at that convention. One of his co-laborers at those meetings reported, 'crowded audiences not only listened to addresses on consecration, but many transacted the Solemn Deed and Covenant by dedicating their all to God'.[14]

Walton and Murray soon inaugurated an annual convention at Wellington that afterward became known as the 'South African

---

14. ibid., p. 385.

Keswick'. Of Walton's key role in founding this convention, Murray testified:

> At the commencement it was specially in conventions that he [Walton] was used of God to help many Christians to see what a true life of consecration ought to be, and to understand how it could be received through simple faith with a whole-hearted consecration. We owe it specially to him that the S. A. Keswick at Wellington was commenced, and that all the powers of the workers by whom he was surrounded were concentrated on the work that was done there. Eternity alone can reveal what we owe, in our [Wellington] schools too, to the blessed truth of a life of full devotion to Jesus Christ.[15]

Murray was chosen as President and Chairman of South African Keswick, another ministry position he fulfilled throughout the remainder of his earthly life. Douglas testifies:

> Those who were privileged to be present at the early conventions will never forget the powerful messages given by our beloved President, and the sacred sense of the nearness of God throughout the week spent together in His presence. Most of those who attended these meetings were led to a new place of surrender to Christ and to fellowship with God. The far-reaching results of the convention held in [the Huguenot Seminary's] Goodnow Hall upon the Church of Christ in South Africa will never be fully known. But let it be said that many of the outstanding workers of today in the different churches and missions, ministers and laymen who have been used mightily of God, received their inspiration and equipment in these gatherings ...[16]

In fulfilling its second ministry objective the Cape General Mission carried out abundant labors to soldiers, sailors, railway employees, the poor, the morally 'lapsed' and 'the outcast generally'. Aided by Murray's ongoing support, guidance and encouragement, the CGM would before long begin to realize the accomplishment of its third

---

15. ibid., pp. 385-6.

16. Douglas, *Andrew Murray and His Message*, p. 171.

major objective of carrying out foreign missionary work among unreached native people groups.

The year 1889 was also one of expanded ministry and influence for Wellington's Huguenot Seminary. That year the founders of a popular girls' academy at neighboring Paarl approached the Trustees of the Huguenot Seminary about taking over the Paarl institution and running it as a branch school. With Murray's encouragement the proposal was accepted and teachers were sent from the Seminary to assume that new responsibility. Not long after, the Huguenot Seminary was invited to open two other branch seminaries, one at Bethlehem in the Orange Free State and the other at Greytown in Natal.

One other significant event in Murray's life in 1889 was the death of his beloved mother at eighty years of age. She had faithfully served with her husband in Graaff-Reinet for some four decades. Following his death in 1866 she was able to continue living in the Graaff-Reinet parsonage for another twenty-three years, as her son Charles had succeeded his father as minister of that parish. Maria Neethling revealed of the closing years of her mother's life:

> Four times during her widowhood she took the long journey to Cape Town during Synod time remaining from October to April, and spending some weeks in the homes of William at Worcester, John and Maria at Stellenbosch, Jemima at the Paarl and Andrew at Wellington. As Stellenbosch was the most central, more than one delightful family gathering was held there in the drawing room of the Parsonage. Brother Andrew was the convener, and everyone made an effort to be present. Then in that large circle of brothers and sisters, one after another would testify of the lovingkindness of our Covenant-keeping God. And many heartfelt prayers went up to the 'God of our fathers', asking Him to 'be the God of their succeeding race'.[17]

Toward the end of August, 1889 the senior Mrs Murray became very weak and congestion developed in her left lung. Charles wrote

---

17. Neethling, *Unto Children's Children*, p. 76.

to family members just hours after the passing of their dear mother and grandmother:

> There was no pain, no effort; her breathing stopped so gently, that we could hardly realize that she was really gone. ... During the last days her mind had been in a state of most perfect peacefulness. Even to the close of her present life she did not seem to realize that she was really going; this must have become clear to her only when she awoke in the likeness of God.[18]

---

18. ibid., p. 78.

22

Addressing Spiritual and Social Needs
1890–1894

The town of Wellington celebrated its fiftieth anniversary in 1890. In honor of the occasion Murray's church desired to take up an offering for some special cause but a difference of opinion developed over exactly what that should be. Murray was among those who desired to help some missionary undertaking, while others wished the special funds to be used in the construction of a church tower. Not a few considered the latter suggestion a less spiritual, even worldly use of funds.

So everyone was surprised to discover, when a list of donors toward the church tower was circulated, that it was headed by a generous donation from Murray himself. When one of his conservative Christian friends remonstrated, Murray replied, 'Let us draw them into the Church by love.' Such proved to be the case. The new structure was spoken of as 'the tower of love' and 'many' of Murray's former opponents became his supportive friends.

One of Murray's daughters described the inspiring communion services that took place at Wellington during those years:

> Can one ever forget the communion seasons at this time? There, gathered round the Lord's Table, 500 or 600 communicants, and a holy influence permeated the church. Can we forget the holy awe, the deep reverence, the joy and often the rapture written on father's face? The holy joy that filled heart and soul at these never-to-be-forgotten seasons of communion, when 'Heaven came down our souls to meet!' …
>
> We left the table feeling that we had indeed been fed on heavenly manna, and we rose with a deeper love and fuller determination to

do and dare all for our adorable Lord and Master. ... After one of these refreshing times I remember a farmer coming to father with fifty pounds for the mission cause or for the cause of education.[1]

In 1890 Murray carried out his sixth evangelistic tour, this one to Namaqualand, the region north of the Western Cape. He was also elected for the fifth time to serve as Moderator of the DRC Synod when it convened later in the year. A primary issue the Synod took up that session concerned promoting an increased emphasis on the study and use of the Dutch language in Cape Colony's educational system. Theoretically, school boards were free to choose their own language medium for instruction. But practically, English was the only language employed. 'There were very few teachers who were able to impart instruction in both languages [Dutch and English], the normal training of teachers at the recognized institutions was confined to English, school inspectors performed their work in English, and [there was a] lack of suitable schoolbooks in any other language than English.'[2] As a result, interest in the Dutch language and literature had languished. All this was the case despite the fact that Dutch was the native language of the large majority of the Colony's European population. The 1890 Synod appointed a committee to study the issue and make recommendations of how best to address the problem. That was the DRC's first practical step in a protracted, society-wide process which would prove highly successful in the end.

In April of the following year, 1891, Murray participated in a ministers' conference at Somerset East, around eighty miles southeast of Graaff-Reinet. From Somerset East he wrote his wife: 'Our conference began well – twenty-two ministers, some very earnest. This morning we had the second chapter [of Hebrews]: He calls us brethren. The place and weather are very beautiful.'[3]

Continuing on from there Murray set out on his seventh evangelistic tour, this time through the Colony's northeastern

---

1. ibid., pp. 117-18.

2. Du Plessis, *The Life of Andrew Murray*, p. 407.

3. ibid., p. 437.

districts. After ministry stops at Cradock and Tarkastad along the way, he reached Dordrecht (nearly 200 miles northeast of Somerset East) on Friday 1 May. The next day he related in a letter to Emma:

> We left Cradock on Thursday morning and were here on Friday at 5 p.m. after a rattling drive of twenty hours. Our first meeting last night was very good, and both P.D.R. and I feel a great difference between Tarkastad and this. The shaking there has been very real, but at first we felt like [we were] speaking against a dead wall. Here there appears much more openness. We are expecting large blessing.[4]

Two days later, still at Dordrecht, Murray wrote: 'Our services here are over. Deep feeling with many, and open confession with some. We praise God. At the conference at Somerset East I had hard work, doing most of the talking, but the change here has so set me up that I hardly feel tired. He gives strength.'[5]

After ministering at Barkly East, sixty miles northeast of Dordrecht, Murray traveled forty-five miles northwest to Lady Grey, from which he wrote on Friday 15 May:

> Came on here yesterday. But such roads – truly like the Transvaal! This morning, on awakening, I for the first time felt tired. But it is all right now. What a sad sight, the home here! The father [has been] left with ten children, ten motherless children, the youngest only three. The eldest daughter is now better, but still weak in health. The second daughter is the only mother, caring for all. Miss Piton, our graduate, is in the home, and acts as auntie – a great comfort to them.
>
> Services began this afternoon in pouring rain. I am humbly asking the Father to command it to cease. ... I am trusting for the full revelation of Christ in the heart, in a peace and rest never for a moment disturbed. The high-priesthood of Hebrews and the power of an endless life are very precious. I have begun writing a Dutch book on Hebrews, which I look to God to bless very much.[6]

---

4. ibid., p. 438. 'P.D.R.' was Rev. P.D. Rossouw, a fellow worker of Murray.

5. ibid., p. 439.

6. ibid.

Lessons on the Epistle of Hebrews had been the subject of study at the ministerial conference at Somerset East the previous month. Murray was so taken with the profound and illuminating truths in that book of Scripture that, even as he carried out his subsequent evangelistic tour, he penned the opening chapters of a devotional exposition of the epistle which two years later was published as *Ziende op Jezus* (Looking unto Jesus).[7]

From Lady Grey, Murray turned back and made his way nearly ninety miles south and west to Molteno. Meetings were held there and at Sterkstroom (seventeen miles southeast of Molteno) in the latter part of May. After ministering at Molteno on Sunday 24 May, Murray reported of the days immediately following:

> Our Monday morning meeting was something very beautiful. Testimonies in abundance, and very clear, of blessing received by people who had long feared the Lord, but had not known what salvation by faith was. And some twenty confessions of conversion.
>
> Monday afternoon to Sterkstroom, for that evening and Tuesday. Had some clear cases of entrance into light and joy. Returned to Molteno yesterday [Wednesday]; a number of people came up again. … Along the road, much proof of God's blessing on the services, and so many testimonies to the effect: 'I thought I must be, or get, or do something, and now I see it was all wrong. I now trust the living Jesus.' The joy is great in many hearts.[8]

When Spencer Walton had returned to South Africa two years earlier as Director of the Cape General Mission he brought with him his young wife, Kathleen. Both their hearts had been strongly drawn to Swaziland as the location where the CGM should establish its first foreign work among black Africans. (Swaziland bordered on the eastern side of Zululand which was located northeast of Natal.) In fervent, faith-filled prayer, the Waltons claimed 'Swaziland for Christ'.

---

7. *Ziende op Jezus* was a large volume, 130 chapters and 542 pages in length. One year after its publication in Dutch the work was issued in English under the title *The Holiest of All*.

8. Du Plessis, *The Life of Andrew Murray*, p. 439.

But in March of 1890, just six months after arriving in South Africa, Kathleen died. When sympathetic friends collected a modest fund to commemorate her brief career, Murray suggested no more fitting memorial could be devised than the establishment of a mission in the country that had come to be so much on her heart and in her prayers. In 1891 Murray accompanied Spencer Walton in visiting Swaziland. That same year the Cape General Mission sent its first foreign missionary to found Bethany, a mission station among the Swazis. In the years to follow, additional CGM stations were established throughout Swaziland.[9]

In 1892 Rev. J.R. Albertyn was called to serve as Murray's associate pastor at Wellington. With understandable reserve at the prospect of becoming the assistant to such a prominent minister, Albertyn candidly wrote Murray, 'What would happen if I cannot agree with you?' Murray responded good-naturedly, 'Come along, my brother. I will agree with you, only be sure you are always in the right.' A lasting and 'very tender affection' developed between the two ministers. Albertyn was ardent, spiritually minded and a gifted preacher. He accepted the call to Wellington's DRC with the understanding that Murray would be free to travel and have evangelistic services when he wished. Albertyn exercised his own gifts in that direction as well, and in his later years of ministry traveled a good deal also, building up and strengthening the Church in various locations.

The Murrays vacated the parsonage in which they had lived for twenty-one years, making it available as the Albertyns' residence. Murray and his family relocated to Clairvaux, a house that Murray had built on part of the Training Institute property. This would be their home till Murray's death twenty-five years later. Clairvaux did not offer the spacious grounds of the parsonage, being flanked as it was by the Training Institute buildings not far away on one side

9. ibid., p. 387. In 1894 the Cape General Mission absorbed the South-East Africa Evangelistic Mission and became the South Africa General Mission. The SAGM quickly expanded the scope of its foreign missionary enterprise by establishing new works in Zululand, Tembuland, Pondoland, Bomvanaland, Natal, Gazaland, Nyasaland and northern Rhodesia.

and by Sunnyside, a modest dormitory for institute students, nearby on the other. However, the expansive view that spread out before Clairvaux was far superior to that afforded by the parsonage. Du Plessis provides an appealing description of Clairvaux's scenic setting:

> Situated on a ridge above a little valley, it overlooks smiling gardens and broad green vineyards, with a background of low hills bedecked with waving cornfields and dotted with old oak-embowered Dutch homesteads. The house is girt about on the sunny north with a broad stoep, and on this stoep, when the weather was kind, Mr Murray used to receive his visitors, transact his business, and write his books. He never wearied of the outlook – to the right, the lofty Drakenstein Mountains, snow-capped in winter, on which the westering sun would cast the most marvelous colors, from pale blue to rich purple and flaming red; before, the view which has just been described; to the left, the long hill-slopes reaching down to the Berg River. It is a quiet pastoral scene, remote from the dusty highways of life. ... The whistle of a distant train or the rattle of a passing vehicle may occasionally break the silence but cannot disturb the settled quiet of this home among the vineyards.[10]

Throughout 1893 and 1894 Murray's writing output in both Dutch and English continued to be considerable, with his publication of eleven volumes of various lengths.[11] One of those works, *Be Perfect*, was begun by Murray on the last day of the family's annual vacation at their favorite seaside retreat on Kalk Bay. As other members of the family were busily engaged with preparations for departure, Murray, 'undisturbed by the bustle and confusion', sat contentedly at the window overlooking the sea. There he was composing the opening chapter of a fresh message from the Lord which he believed he had been divinely commissioned to deliver in printed form.

Another work produced around that time was *Wholly for God*, the first of six volumes of selections from the writings of William

---

10.   ibid., pp. 484-5.

11.   Among those eleven were *Ziende op Jezus* (Looking unto Jesus) and *The Holiest of All* mentioned earlier in the present chapter.

Law that Murray eventually had published.[12] Law (1686-1761) was an English clergyman and Christian mystic whose numerous books on practical divinity Murray greatly appreciated. While Murray read with interest and appreciation the works of a number of Christian mystics, he was most attracted to Law's writings. Murray possessed the nine-volume 1762 edition of Law's *Works* and especially appreciated his treatises on *An Affectionate Address to the Clergy, The Spirit of Christ, The Spirit of Love, Christian Perfection* and *A Serious Call to a Devout and Holy Life*.[13]

Murray, however, did not embrace all of Law's teachings, as the latter's mysticism had led him to depreciate the value of Scripture, minimize the worth of the Church as a visible divine institution, deny the imputation theory of the atonement, reject the doctrine of divine sovereignty in election and predestination, and manifest a definite pantheistic tendency. In Murray's prefaces to his first two collections of Law's writings, he dissociated himself from the mystic's unorthodoxy. In introducing the 1895 collection, *The Power of the Spirit*, for instance, Murray states:

> In publishing a new volume of Law's works I owe a word of explanation to the Christian public, and all the more because some with whom I feel closely united have expressed their doubt of the wisdom of giving greater currency to the writings of an author who differs markedly in some points from what we hold to be fundamental doctrines of the evangelical faith. ... It is because I believe his teaching to supply what many are looking for that I venture to recommend it. I do so in the confidence that no one will think that I have done so because I consider the truths he denies matters of minor importance, or have any sympathy with his views.[14]

---

12. The subsequent collections from Law's writings published by Murray included: *The Power of the Spirit* (1895); *The Divine Indwelling* (1896); *Dying to Self* (1898); *The Secret of Inspiration* (1916); *God in Ons* (God in Us, 1916).

13. *A Serious Call to a Devout and Holy Life*, Law's most popular work, was initially published in 1728 and had a marked influence on John and Charles Wesley, George Whitefield and other leaders of Britain's eighteenth-century evangelical revival.

14. Du Plessis, *The Life of Andrew Murray*, pp. 455-6.

When the Colony's DRC Synod convened in 1894 Murray, then sixty-six years of age, was selected as its Moderator for the sixth and final time. The Synod debated and ultimately adopted with 'remarkable unanimity' the recommendations of the committee that had been appointed four years earlier to research the issue of promoting increased study and use of the Dutch language in Cape Colony's schools. Among the committee's recommendations were the following: beginning students should be instructed in their mother tongue, as was the case in other bilingual countries; in all schools certain key subjects, especially history (sacred and secular) and descriptive geography, should be taught in Dutch; inspectors of schools where instruction was given in English and Dutch should be able to examine students in both languages.

In time these and similar efforts by other organizations and individuals were successful. The Dutch language came to be used in public schools, university examinations, the civil service and courts of law. The crowning success of these efforts came in 1910 when the various states of South Africa were united, at which time the 137th article of the Act of Union stated that 'both the English and Dutch languages shall be official languages of the Union'.[15]

Another significant concern addressed at the 1894 Synod was the problem of the 'poor whites'. In recent years, in mining centers like Johannesburg and Kimberley, as well as in other metropolitan areas, there had been an 'ominous increase of a class of indigent white people who had been trained to no trade, appeared to possess no regular means of subsistence and threatened to become a burden and a danger to the community'.[16] The DRC Synod discussed 'with great earnestness' how to improve their condition and provide them with suitable employment.

In the decades that followed the Church and Government in South Africa worked cooperatively in attempting much in behalf of the indigent white element. Industrial schools were established at various centers throughout the country, labor colonies were set up in

---

15.   ibid., p. 409.

16.   ibid., p. 405.

different provinces and a system of education was provided for even the poorest children in special institutions. Despite those diligent efforts the 'poor white' issue continued to be a marked problem.

23

NOTABLE OVERSEAS MINISTRIES
1895

Due to Murray's growing reputation in other parts of the world through the broad distribution of his books he was invited to speak at a number of Christian conferences in Europe and America in 1895. Murray was introduced to the Christian public of Great Britain in a flattering, colorful article about him that was printed, along with his picture, in the 6 December, 1894 issue of the *British Weekly*. The article, written by Rev. Henry Vicars Taylor (then the minister of Wellington's Presbyterian Church), stated in part:

> Andrew Murray, if any man, may justly claim the title of catholic, for his sympathies are unfailingly given to each one who loves the Lord Jesus in sincerity and truth.'We are Christians first and Dutch Reformed afterwards,' he said with vehemence when addressing the delegates from other Churches who came to the opening of the recent Synod. And this saying gives the note of his life. He desires to be known as a Christian, as a follower of Jesus simply, and he seems to examine every one he meets for the Christian element in him. That is the impression left on the mind when one is in conversation with him. ... You cannot help saying to yourself, 'This man wants me to belong to Jesus Christ.'
>
> He is, I suppose, well known to most readers of religious literature by his devotional books, notably *Abide in Christ*. His nature is profoundly devotional; he carries with him the atmosphere of prayer. He seems always wrapped about with a mantle of adoration.
>
> When preaching or conducting a service his whole being is thrown into the task, and he glows with a fervency of spirit which it seems impossible for human flesh to sustain. At times

he startles and overwhelms the listeners. Earnestness and power of the electric sort stream from him, and affect alike the large audience or the quiet circle gathered round him. In his slight, spent frame, of middle height, he carries in repose a volcanic energy which, when he is roused, bursts its barriers and sweeps all before it. Then his form quivers and dilates, the lips tremble, the features work, the eyes spasmodically open and close, as from the white-hot furnace of his spirit he pours the molten torrent of his unstudied eloquence. The thin face and almost emaciated body are transfigured and illumined. The staid, venerable minister of the nineteenth century, with the sober, clerical garb and stiff white tie, which is *de rigueur* [proper] among the Dutch clergy, disappears, and an old Hebrew prophet stands before us – another Isaiah with his glowing imagery, a second Hosea with his plaintive, yearning appeals. Audiences bend before the sweeping rain of his words like willows before a gale. The heart within the hearer is bowed, and the intellect awed. Andrew Murray's oratory is of that kind for which men willingly go into captivity.[1]

Murray and Emma embarked from Cape Town for Britain aboard the steamship *Norman* on 8 May, 1895. While in England they stayed in the home of a Mr and Mrs Head of Wimbledon. A Reception Breakfast was held for the Murrays at London's Exeter Hall. It was attended by about 120 leading Christians of all denominations, including representatives from England, Scotland and Ireland. At the China Inland Mission's annual Mildmay Conference held around that time Murray delivered three messages and administered the Lord's Supper to a large gathering of 1,400 communicants. After one of those messages Mrs Head reported:

In the evening Mr Murray gave a wonderful address so full of power and fire! We were quite amazed at the dear old man. He is so thin and worn-looking, and certainly such addresses must use up his bodily as well as spiritual strength. We feel indeed that he has come to this land as God's messenger, and he is so

---

1. Du Plessis, *The Life of Andrew Murray*, pp. 442-3.

simple, depending utterly on the Lord to use him as His channel of blessing to His people.[2]

Shortly thereafter Murray ministered at a convention in Guildford, thirty-two miles southwest of London, delivering four addresses during the week and preaching twice on Sunday.

While appreciated by most, Murray did have some critics. Mrs Head related:

> The following incident made a deep impression. One evening when the whole party returned together from a great meeting where a rapt and crowded audience had been addressed by Mr Murray, he found awaiting him a letter from a well-known man, filled with severe censures upon him for teaching error. The way the criticism was expressed stirred indignation in all, *except for Mr Murray*. He only said in his gentle way that if he had been teaching anything wrong, all that he asked was that the Lord would show this to him, that he might make it right. Quite simply they knelt down, and put up that petition; then rising they went in peace to rest. Next day being Sunday, Mr Murray stayed in bed to rest. For his own guidance he wrote these lines:
>
> In Time of Trouble Say:
>
> *First*, He brought me here; it is by His will I am in this strait place: in that fact I will rest.
>
> *Next*, He will keep me here in His love, and give me grace to behave as His child.
>
> *Then*, He will make the trial a blessing, teaching me the lessons He intends me to learn, and working in me the grace He means to bestow.
>
> *Last*, In His good time He can bring me out again – how and when He knows.
>
> Let me say I am here,
>
> (1) By God's appointment.   (2) In His keeping.
> (3) Under His training.   (4) For His time.

Of that incident, Mrs Head concluded, 'Next day Mr Murray went straight to the writer of the letter and by his loving intercourse made

---

2.   Douglas, *Andrew Murray and His Message*, p. 161.

him his faithful friend.'[3] Du Plessis reveals further circumstances which attended that same occasion:

> When Mr Murray visited England in 1895 ... he was suffering from a weak back, the result of an accident in Natal some years previously, when he was thrown violently out of a capsizing cart. He was due to speak one evening at Exeter Hall, and it seemed as though he would be unable to fulfill his engagement. Some expressions he had employed [while preaching], too, had given offence and provoked hostile criticism, so that mental suffering was superinduced on physical. When his sympathetic hostess, Mrs Head, brought him his breakfast, she informed him that a lady had called in sore trouble, and anxious for a word of advice. 'Well, just give her this, that I have been writing down for myself,' said Mr Murray. 'It may be that she will find it helpful.'[4]

He handed her a sheet of paper bearing the heading 'In Time of Trouble Say' which contained the reflections already stated. Andrew Murray's name appeared at the bottom of the page along with a Scripture reference, Psalm 50:15, which declares the Lord's promise, 'And call upon me in the day of trouble: I will deliver thee, and thou shalt glorify me'. Murray's friends were so taken with the valuable perspectives he had encapsulated for times of adversity that they had them printed on colored card stock and distributed in large numbers.

During July Murray was the principal speaker at the yearly Keswick Convention. Rev. Evan Hopkins, editor of the *Life of Faith*, reported:

> The main feature of this [twenty-first] Convention has been the presence of our beloved brother, the Rev. Andrew Murray of South Africa, whose addresses have come home to so many with peculiar power. ... As message after message was enforced by one who has evidently been the marked minister of God this time, it seemed as if none could escape, as if none could choose but let Christ Himself, in the power of His living Spirit, be the One to live, although the

---

3.   ibid., pp. 162-3.

4.   Du Plessis, *The Life of Andrew Murray*, p. 477.

cost was our taking the place of death. ... As this was dwelt on more and more deeply as the days went on, especially at the solemn evening meetings, there came over some of us a memory of Keswick in 1879, when an awe of God fell upon the whole assembly in a way the writer has never seen equaled.[5]

Murray was pressed at the Keswick Convention to share his personal testimony of how he had come to live by Higher Life principles. At first he demurred. As Douglas explains: 'It is the only record of the kind Mr Murray has left behind him. He was ever fearing to draw the attention of his hearers from Christ to any experience.'[6] But in the end Murray acquiesced to the request. He introduced his personal experience by stating:

> When I was asked to give my testimony I doubted whether it would be desirable, and for this reason: We all know what helpfulness there is in a clear cut testimony of a man who can say: 'There I was, I knelt down, and God helped me, and I entered into the better life.' I cannot give such a testimony, but I know what blessing it has often brought to me to read of such testimonies for the strengthening of my own faith. And yet I got this answer from those who wished me to speak: 'Perhaps there are many at Keswick to whom a testimony concerning a life of more struggle and difficulty will be helpful.' 'If it must be so,' I replied, 'let me tell for the glory of God how He has led me.'[7]

Murray went on to share about his initial decade of ministry when he unsuccessfully sought to live for and serve the Lord consistently because he tried to do so in his own strength. He next related how God had gradually led him, over the course of several more years, into a greater dependence upon the Holy Spirit in living the Christian life.[8] Murray then concluded:

---

5. ibid., p. 444.

6. Douglas, *Andrew Murray and His Message*, p. 165.

7. ibid.

8. That portion of Murray's personal testimony was recorded on pp. 200-1 of the current volume.

I can help you more, perhaps, by speaking, not of any marked experience, but by telling very simply what I think God has given me now, in contrast to the first ten years of my Christian life. In the first place, I have learnt to place myself before God every day, as a vessel to be filled with His Holy Spirit. He has filled me with the blessed assurance that He, as the everlasting God, has guaranteed His own work in me. If there is one lesson that I am learning day by day, it is this: that it is God who worketh all in all. Oh, that I could help any brother or sister to realize this!

I was once preaching, and a lady came to talk with me. She was a very pious woman, and I asked her, 'How are you going on?' Her answer was, 'Oh, just the way it always is, sometimes light and sometimes dark.' 'My dear sister, where is that in the Bible?' She said, 'We have day and night in nature, and just so it is in our souls.' 'No, no; in the Bible we read, "Your sun shall no more go down" [Isa. 60:20].' Let me believe that I am God's child, and that the Father in Christ, through the Holy Ghost, has set His love upon me, and that I may abide in His presence, not frequently, but unceasingly.

You will ask me, Are you satisfied? Have you got all you want? God forbid. With the deepest feeling of my soul I can say that I am satisfied with Jesus now; but there is also the consciousness of how much fuller the revelation can be of the exceeding abundance of His grace. Let us never hesitate to say, This is only the beginning. When we are brought into the holiest of all, we are only beginning to take our right position in the Father.[9]

From England the Murrays sailed to the United States. Dwight Moody had invited Murray to be one of the chief speakers at the Northfield Bible Conference that summer. For two weeks Murray spoke each morning on the themes then absorbing his thinking – the feeble religious life of the churches and the need for believers to live the Christian life based on faith in God and His Word. In addition to the general public more than 400 ministers attended the conference. From Northfield Murray traveled to Chicago where he spoke twice daily at a five-day convention. There, and afterward in New York, Boston, Toronto and other places, the meetings were

---

9.   Du Plessis, *The Life of Andrew Murray*, pp. 448-9.

crowded despite the hot summer weather. Another prominent preacher-writer, A.T. Pierson, joined Murray in ministering at those conventions.

After recrossing the Atlantic Murray was the featured speaker at a 'remarkable succession' of meetings in Holland during the month of October. In the Cathedral at Utrecht a throng of two thousand people eagerly listened as he preached from the very pulpit before which he had made public profession of his faith in Christ fifty years earlier. In Amsterdam, Rotterdam, Haarlem, The Hague, Groningen and other cities large crowds flocked to hear him speak, and the services were characterized by 'deep earnestness and real spiritual awakening'.

Following brief visits to Scotland and Ireland Murray returned to London for a final convention, 20-22 November, at Regent Square Church and Exeter Hall. Without using preaching manuscripts or notes Murray delivered seven sermons, each about an hour in length, during the three-day conference. Newman Hall, F.B. Meyer and Charles Spurgeon's son, Thomas, were among the other well-known ministers who 'took some part' in the meetings, though they did not preach. More than 2,000 people attended the Thursday and Friday evening services at Exeter Hall. Half an hour before those meetings were to begin it was difficult to find an available seat, and that pre-service interval was filled with the singing of hymns.

As a result of Murray's 1895 preaching tour to Europe and America, his writing ministry flourished to remarkable proportions that year and the next. In addition to seven of his addresses being printed as pamphlets, an astounding fifteen Murray books or booklets were published in six different countries during those two years alone!

24

STUDENT MINISTRIES AND
MINISTRY MILESTONES
1896–1899

Having returned to South Africa, Andrew Murray continued to actively promote foreign missionary developments there during 1896. That year Luther R. Wishard, a key player in the earlier development of the international Student Volunteer Movement for Foreign Missions, visited South Africa from the United States. Aided by Rev. Donald Fraser, who was en route to Nyasaland as a missionary, Wishard organized the Student Christian Association of South Africa (SCA). Two small bands of Missionary Volunteer Students that had previously formed at Stellenbosch's Theological Seminary and Wellington's Training Institute were now incorporated into the SCA. Murray warmly welcomed Wishard and Fraser and 'threw all his influence' into promoting their movement. Throughout the remainder of his life Murray nearly always attended the SCA's annual conferences and usually presented several addresses.

In 1897 Murray undertook his eighth evangelistic tour, this one to the Orange Free State and Transvaal. His youngest daughter, Annie, later related:

> Soon after his return from England ... he undertook a tour into Northern Transvaal where his testimony was mightily owned by God. It was an evangelistic tour and he preached almost every night, even if it were only a farmhouse congregation. In the Standerton District he was thrown out of the cart which was conveying him to his next appointment, and by the fall his arm

was broken. He bandaged it as well as he could, applying cold water compresses, and he preached that evening as usual. The broken arm was made a matter of prayer, and so complete was the healing that some months later he showed it to a friend of his, who was a doctor, and asked him if it had ever been broken. He assured him that it had been broken but had been most remarkably and perfectly set.[1]

That same year, 1897, Murray held Higher Life conferences at Durban and Pietermaritzburg in Natal and at Port Elizabeth on the Colony's southern coast. Travel distances and costs made it impossible for many who desired to attend Wellington's annual Keswick Convention to do so. Instead arrangements were made for similar conferences to be held in various towns throughout the country, including Cape Town, Johannesburg, Kroonstad, Port Elizabeth, Pietermaritzburg and Durban. Some of those conferences convened annually while others were held less frequently.

Large numbers of both Dutch and English residents of Natal made their way to the 1897 Durban conference. The Dutch attendees came in their ox wagons and camped in Victoria Park. Murray spoke on the theme of 'Absolute Surrender'. One conference attendee reported: 'The effect of the convention on the lives of many a Christian was permanent. But perhaps the outstanding feature of this convention was the number of ministers and missionaries who attended, and who from that time became themselves flames of fire.'[2]

At one of the Natal conferences a speaker protested against the extravagant language employed by some people who attended 'holiness conventions'. To the speaker's strictures Murray responded sagely: 'Yes, some sincere and godly people, in the overflowing fullness of their experience of a new truth, may not always express themselves wisely. But we must not reject the experience because of the vagaries which may accompany it. It reminds me of the olden days when we used to travel by ox wagon. At the end of the day's

1. Douglas, *Andrew Murray and His Message*, p. 200.
2. ibid., p. 172.

journey the first thing to be done was to light the fire, boil the water and put in the meat. While we watched the cooking process we saw the scum rise to the surface. That we skimmed off and threw away, but the meat we did not throw away.'[3]

When criticized himself, Murray characteristically responded non-defensively. An acquaintance once came to him 'in great distress over false reports'. In response Murray quoted the latter half of Psalm 31:20: 'Thou shalt keep them secretly in a pavilion from the strife of tongues.' On another occasion a loyal friend strongly resented some 'damaging criticisms' that had been leveled against one of Murray's published addresses. The supporter prepared a written vindication, which he read to Murray and asked his advice about publishing it. 'Do you think this reply will convince our critic?' Murray asked.

'No, I don't suppose it will,' came the reply.

'Then what will be the use of publishing it?' Murray concluded. 'It will only lead to further controversy, from which nothing will be gained.'[4]

Not long after the inauguration of Wellington's Keswick Convention several years earlier Murray was conversing with members of the Cape General Mission (afterward the South Africa General Mission) about the spiritual needs of the country's innumerable rural districts. 'How I wish the teaching we have here could be given in the small towns and villages throughout the land,' Murray stated. He then asked, 'Could not the Mission arrange for the villages to be visited?' Answering his own suggestion, he then encouraged, 'You will not find it easy work, but the need is very great. Go ahead with it, and I will pray to God to bless your efforts.' Douglas adds:

> This led to the starting of 'Village Work' in connection with the S.A. General Mission. No branch of the Mission's activities has been more wonderfully owned and used by God than this; thousands

---

3.   Du Plessis, *The Life of Andrew Murray*, p. 505.

4.   ibid., p. 506.

have been reached by the Gospel in this way, and numbers led into a life of full deliverance and victory.[5]

It was also at Murray's instigation that the hymnbook *Hymns for Life and Service* was compiled and produced for use at Higher Life conferences throughout South Africa. At one of the convention council meetings he mentioned the need for such a special hymnbook. Turning quickly to the convention song-leader, Murray stated, 'I think we must ask you to undertake the work for us.' When the new recruit mentioned the considerable labor and difficulty that would be involved in such an undertaking, Murray placed his hand on the man's shoulder and, with a twinkle in his eye, said simply, 'Never mind, my dear brother. You do the work and we will promise to pray for you.' Although the sale of the publication had to be limited to South Africa due to copyright restrictions on many of the songs, more than 50,000 copies of the lyrics-only edition were sold.

Another ministry Murray helped promote in 1897 was the Christian Endeavor Movement (CEM). The Young People's Society of Christian Endeavor had been founded sixteen years earlier by Rev. Francis Edward Clark in Portland, Maine. The society sought to lead youth to faith in Christ then train them to serve Him. The interdenominational youth ministry grew rapidly and soon became an international movement with thousands of affiliate Christian Endeavor societies. Miss Bliss of the Huguenot Seminary established a Christian Endeavor society in Wellington, and not long thereafter seven societies joined together to hold Cape Colony's first CEM convention.

The Colony's growing youth ministry received a boost in 1897 when Francis Clark visited South Africa. Murray greatly enjoyed interacting with this individual who shared his concern for ministering to the spiritual needs of young people, and he did all he could to make Clark's visit a success. Ever after that Murray remained an active supporter of the CEM.

---

5. Douglas, *Andrew Murray and His Message*, pp. 174-5.

When the DRC Synod met later that same year, the sixty-nine-year-old Murray let it be known that if nominated for another term as Moderator he would definitely decline the nomination. As a result his brother-in-law J.H. Hofmeyr was selected as his successor. Murray had served six terms as Moderator, including the past four terms (comprising fourteen years) consecutively. So great was the Synod's esteem of Murray and its appreciation for his many years of capable service that it presented him with a golden watch and chain, an honor that no other Moderator had received.

The following year, 1898, Murray's alma mater, the University of Aberdeen, conferred on him the honorary Doctor of Divinity degree. That honor was given him in acknowledgement of the widespread positive influence of his many books with their various theological and devotional themes.

Murray's seventieth birthday and the fiftieth anniversary of his ordination to Christian ministry fell on Sunday 9 May, 1898. Unfortunately, the weather was uncooperative that day, with rain falling in torrents. As a result the worship services were poorly attended because many congregants who lived in the country were unable to make it to town. Professor N.J. Hofmeyr was the guest speaker that morning. The following day, though inclement weather continued, a large number of ministers gathered to honor Murray and Emma. After a public address rehearsed the highlights of Murray's half century of ministerial service, his colleagues presented him with a gift of furniture for his study.

On Tuesday the celebration continued, this time involving teachers and students from Wellington and the surrounding area. The *Huguenot Seminary Annual* reported:

> All the teachers of the district were invited to meet Mr and Mrs Murray at tea on Tuesday, and they with a few friends sat down to the number of one hundred. There was a wonderful charm in the spontaneity of the tribute laid at Mr Murray's feet. More than one said, 'I am what I am because of Mr Murray's interest in me.' The gathering of the scholars, over a thousand strong, marked a gala day. They marched in procession, with banners flying, to

the Dutch Church. The young people had embowered an open carriage with flowers, and in this Mr and Mrs Murray sat at the Parsonage gate, watching the procession, each section giving them the Chatauqua salute [by waving a white handkerchief] as they passed. When he entered the church, all stood, and there was a wonderful fluttering of handkerchiefs in greeting from the different schools. It was a beautiful gathering up of Mr Murray's loving interest in the young people.[6]

That week more than 200 congratulatory telegrams were received by Murray from all parts of the country. Those came from Cape Colony's Governor, the Prime Minister, the Colonial Secretary, other prominent public officials, pastors and missionaries, teachers and farmers, old and young, all expressing their appreciation for Murray's broad and beneficial influence. The telegram from the Cape Town Ministers' Association stated: 'The Ministers' Association send hearty greetings. We thank God for your work, friendship and help, and pray you may long be spared. Heb. 6:10.' Douglas comments:

> Well might they mention his friendship, for his love to all ministers of all denominations was very tender. When well over seventy he used to catch the 6:15 morning train to Cape Town, reaching there at nine so as to be able to attend the monthly breakfast conference of the Ministers' Association, and he much enjoyed the fraternal intercourse.[7]

Later in 1898 Murray visited the Orange Free State to take part in the jubilee celebrations of the four congregations – Bloemfontein, Winburg, Smithfield and Fauresmith – that had formed when he first came as their minister half a century earlier. He carried out his ministry opportunities so energetically on that tour that Emma, who was traveling with him, reported, 'I fear sometimes he will be laid to rest in this country of his first love.' But she also divulged,

---

6.   Du Plessis, *The Life of Andrew Murray*, p. 371.

7.   Douglas, *Andrew Murray and His Message*, p. 148.

'I have ceased to be anxious about him but just trust. It is God who gives him strength and will give it as long as He sees best. But someone remarked that when he is gone, six ministers will not do his work.'[8]

Another special gathering took place in Wellington on Saturday 17 December of that same year, when the twenty-fifth anniversary of the establishment of the Huguenot Seminary was celebrated. That morning a procession of some 600 current and former students made its way to the Dutch Reformed Church. There they joined 'a large assemblage of guests and friends' who had gathered to mark the significant occasion. Murray expressed deep gratitude over the fact that nearly 1,000 teachers had gone out from the seminary during its quarter-century of operation.

A further highlight of the day was the opening of Cummings Hall, the first building of the new Huguenot College for women that had been established that same year. When asked by his associate pastor, J.R. Albertyn, what he would wish to receive as a jubilee gift, Murray replied 1,000 pounds to pay off the debt of the newly-opened women's college. That desire was made known and donations totaling that amount were readily contributed.

In addition, a girls' industrial school had been founded in Wellington earlier in the year. Started largely on Emma Murray's initiative, the industrial school enabled poor white girls to receive an education and training in various practical skills.

Andrew Murray's writing ministry had continued to thrive. In the three years from 1897 to 1899 he published another remarkable total of seventeen books or booklets on a variety of subjects. In addition to Scripture, which was always the primary source of his devotional reflections, Murray likely received additional food for thought for two of those volumes, *The Mystery of the True Vine* and *The Fruit of the Vine*, by observing and contemplating the vineyards that flourished all around Wellington.

In the first decade of its existence, 1889-1899, the missionary staff of the DRC's Nyasa Mission had increased from two

---

8.   ibid., pp. 150-1.

missionaries to fourteen. Wherever the missionaries traveled they found indigenous people eager to hear God's Word. Even at remote villages it was not uncommon for attentive audiences of 500 or more individuals to gather for that purpose. Schools were crowded with children desiring to be instructed. The demands were so great that the missionaries were in danger of overtaxing their strength. Likely in March or April of 1899 A.C. Murray wrote to his sending agency, the Ministers' Mission Union (MMU): 'You have been praying that God would open the door to the Word. That is no longer necessary. There are so many open doors that we are thrown into a condition of great perplexity.'

Murray immediately held a meeting of the MMU Committee in the study of his home at Wellington. The Committee drafted a letter that was sent to all supporters of the Nyasa Mission. The correspondence encouraged all its readers to devote at least half an hour to prayer on Ascension Day, 11 May, seeking the Lord's ongoing blessing on the mission's ministry. People were asked to pray especially that: more individuals would offer themselves for foreign service and that God's people would willingly support them with their sacrificial financial giving; all Christian workers and converts in Nyasaland would be filled with the Holy Spirit; over the course of the next five years the Nyasaland missionary force would 'be at least doubled'.

For several years, however, tensions and hostility had been mounting between South Africa's Dutch and British factions, leading the country to the brink of civil war. In fact, within six months of the MMU's letter having been sent, the Boer War erupted and became the all-engrossing focus of public attention. Under such absorbing circumstances it seemed unlikely that sufficient interest and support would be available to send additional missionaries to Nyasaland. The outcome of the MMU's appeal would not become clear for years.

In July, 1899 Murray went to visit his dying brother William who had succeeded him as the minister at Worcester some thirty-five years earlier. Upon his arrival, Murray greeted William by saying, 'I have come to preach for you, as you are ill. What shall I say?'

'Give a powerful testimony,' sixty-nine-year-old William responded.

Sunday morning, 16 July, Murray employed as his sermon text the words of Joseph the patriarch as he neared death, 'I die, but God will surely visit you, and bring you up out of this land unto the land which He sware to Abraham and Isaac and Jacob' (Gen. 50:24). As the final hymn of that solemn and touching service was being sung a message was conveyed to the pulpit that William had passed away. The following Wednesday Murray preached his brother's funeral sermon, expounding on Joshua 1:2, 'Moses My servant is dead; now therefore arise, go over this Jordan unto the land which I do give unto the children of Israel.'

25

PRELUDE TO WAR
1895–1899

In 1886 the world's largest gold field was discovered at a watershed known as Witwatersrand (white water ridge), about thirty-five miles south of Pretoria, the capital city of Transvaal. Thousands of prospectors, mainly from Britain but also from many other countries, immediately flooded into the region. Seemingly overnight Johannesburg sprang up as a shanty town, with 'uitlanders' (foreigners) soon outnumbering Dutch residents there and along Witwatersrand. The Dutch remained the majority population in the Transvaal and sought to maintain control over their province and its lucrative new resource. Dutch officials imposed taxes and tariffs on the gold industry, granted unpopular monopolies,[1] and required an unreasonable fourteen-year residential period before uitlanders could qualify for 'the franchise' (the right to vote).

By 1895 a 'Reform Committee', composed of sixty aggrieved uitlanders in Johannesburg, began contemplating an armed revolt. They were quietly encouraged by Cecil Rhodes, Cape Colony's Prime Minister who desired to promote British expansionism throughout the entire continent of Africa, 'from the Cape to Cairo'. Rhodes, acting largely independently insofar as other British officials were concerned, supplied rifles and ammunition with which the Reform Committee and its supporters could carry out an uprising. He also provided a troop of around 500 well-armed men

---

1. The most irksome was the so-called 'dynamite monopoly' which forced mining companies to purchase that much-needed commodity at steeply-inflated prices from a non-British supplier.

from Rhodesia and Bechuanaland, north of Transvaal, to support and help assure the uprising's success. Most of those men served as part of the police force that protected the interests of the British South Africa Company (BSAC). Founded and chaired by Rhodes, the BSAC carried out mining enterprises in various countries in southern Africa.

The troop was under the command of Dr Leander Starr Jameson, Rhodes' loyal Administrator of the BSAC. When the uitlanders failed to take up arms the impatient Jameson, without Rhodes' permission, led his men across the northern border of Transvaal on 29 December. He intended to hustle to Johannesburg before the Boers could mobilize their forces, and there he would help initiate the uprising. But what became known as the Jameson Raid met with disastrous and humiliating results. A Boer commando surrounded the invading column about ten miles outside of Johannesburg on 2 January, 1896, killing or wounding sixty-five of Jameson's men.

Jameson and his surviving men were captured and the members of Johannesburg's Reform Committee were arrested. Rhodes was forced to resign his positions as the Colony's Prime Minister and as BSAC's Chairman. Jameson was turned over to the British Government for prosecution and served a fifteen-month sentence in London's Holloway Prison. But he was hailed as a hero by the British press both in England and at the Cape.[2] Members of Johannesburg's Reform Committee were tried in Transvaal court and convicted of high treason. The committee's four leaders were initially sentenced to death by hanging, but their sentence was quickly commuted to fifteen years' imprisonment. The other committee members were fined 2,000 pounds each, but Rhodes paid the fines for all of them.

In the three and a half years that followed the Jameson Raid, relations between the Dutch and British in South Africa continued to deteriorate. British subjects living in the Transvaal appealed to Cape Colony's British Government for assistance in redressing

---

2.   Several years later Jameson was appointed as Cape Colony's Prime Minister, a position he filled from 1904 to 1908.

the perceived injustices they continued to experience under that republic's Dutch officials. Transvaal's leaders were unwilling to give in to the demands of either the uitlanders or the Colony's British officials for fear of losing the right to govern their own republic. Unhealthy degrees of pride and stubbornness, 'inveterate suspicion' and 'imperious diplomacy' on both sides made matters more difficult and hampered efforts at reconciliation.

Gradually most (though not all) British leaders both in South Africa and Britain came to believe that going to war against the Transvaal was justified for two primary reasons: to protect its subjects in the Transvaal from suffering 'oppression and injustice'; to assure that Great Britain would remain the paramount power in South Africa. In the middle of 1899 Britain began sending increased levels of troops, weapons and other supplies to South Africa, stockpiling those along the Transvaal's border. When Transvaal officials asked the reason for this build-up they were told, with unsatisfactory vagueness, that it was 'for all eventualities'.

Meanwhile, in recent years the Transvaal Government had been increasing its own supplies of modernized weapons and ammunition for just such an eventuality. The Boers did not intend to seek to establish a Dutch-governed South Africa, but Boers in both Transvaal and Orange Free State were fiercely determined to maintain their independence and the right to govern their own republics.

Not a few officials on all sides of the impending conflict made repeated and diligent efforts to avert it. Marthinus Theunis Steyn, President of Orange Free State, knew that if Britain and Transvaal went to war his own republic would be dragged into the conflict. So he urged the primary governmental leaders of Cape Colony and Transvaal to meet face to face at Bloemfontein, the OFS capital, to work out their differences.

Sir Alfred Milner, Governor of Cape Colony and High Commissioner for South Africa, and Paul Kruger, four-term President of Transvaal, accordingly met at Bloemfontein from 31 May till 5 June, 1899. Negotiations broke down when the two men could not agree upon whether the residency requirement for Transvaal uitlanders to gain voting privileges should be reduced to five or seven years. In August the Transvaal offered to lower the requirement to five years if the British agreed not to interfere with the republic's domestic problems in the future. The British Cabinet in London responded on 8 September by voting unanimously to repudiate the claims of the Transvaal to be a sovereign international state and by ordering an increase in the number of British troops in South Africa to 22,000.

Throughout his ministerial career Andrew Murray had normally maintained silence with regard to political issues. At the prospect of imminent war, however, he wrote a short series of articles that were published in the *South African News*. The purpose of the articles was to affirm the rights of the Dutch to govern their own republics without the British interfering in those affairs. Originally Murray intended to write six articles but only three had been published before war was declared. After that Murray considered it 'inadvisable and useless' to continue publishing perspectives that were diametrically opposed to the policy of the British Government for South Africa.

Just days before war was declared, Murray wrote an impassioned 'Appeal to the British People' for peace. He began:

> As the oldest minister in the Dutch Reformed Church, as one known, and sometimes even misjudged by my own people, for my loyalty to British interests, as one not unknown in England as a teacher and a worker in the service of God and humanity, I venture, at the urgent request of many in this country, to make this appeal for peace.
>
> I implore the rulers and people of the greatest Christian nation in the world not to make war on the youngest and smallest of its free States.[3]

After posing the question 'What is it that makes war necessary?', Murray briefly demonstrated that it was not the suzerainty of the Queen, British supremacy in South Africa or the voting-rights

---

3.   Du Plessis, *The Life of Andrew Murray*, p. 424.

issue. Those matters were already being addressed or, in some cases, were actually non-issues. Murray then asserted:

> The one cause of the war is the independence of the [Transvaal] Republic. It refuses to be dictated to in internal affairs. It is willing to allow discussion and friendly counsel, has proved itself ready to act on it, and consented to a joint commission of inquiry. The one object of the originators of the agitation which has led to the war is to destroy the independence of the Republic, either by gradually giving uitlanders a preponderating influence, or making it a British Colony.[4]

Murray next pointed out some of the 'serious mistakes' British officials had made in assessing the situation with the Boers, misjudgments that underscored the inadvisability of going to war:

> We have reason to know that the English Government was led to believe that President Kruger would yield, and that there would be no war; that the Orange Free State would keep out of the war; and that it would be possible to secure the cooperation of the Dutch inhabitants of [Cape] Colony. And so the Government adopted a threatening tone, and spoke of an ultimatum before it was ready, and so gave the Republic cause and opportunity to begin the war, while Natal, Mafeking and Kimberly [all under British control] are insufficiently defended. Any day may bring the tidings that war has broken out. If disaster comes at the opening of the campaign, there is no reason to think that such disaster will be the last or the worst.[5]

Murray then set forth his appeal and recommendations for pursuing peace rather than war, in terms that were both earnest and eloquent:

> On behalf of a hundred thousand of the Dutch-speaking people of our Church in this Colony, I implore the British people to pause and adopt a different policy. I ask whether the nation which in the whole world makes the loudest boast of its liberty, and what it has done for liberty, ought not to consider the

---

4. ibid., p. 425.

5. ibid.

liberty of the Republic as sacred and inviolable as its own, and to make this the basis of all its negotiations. Give the Republic the generous assurance of this. Do not meet it with dictation or threats, which have so signally failed. The Boer mind, which resists intimidation, can be reached by reason and conciliation. (1) Let the threatening of war be withdrawn, and proposals be made to return to a peace footing. (2) Let the suzerainty of the Queen and the independence of the Republic be left as settled by the Conventions. (3) Let a Joint Commission inquire into the uitlander grievances, and take time – months, if need be – to find a way out of the difficulties with which the whole relationship of the two races is beset. (4) Let England and the Republic offer each other the hand of friendship, and the assurance that they desire to meet and act in the spirit of conciliation and mutual confidence.

I make bold to undertake that the decision of such a Joint Commission would receive the support of every South African who now condemns the war as needless and unrighteous.

The horrors of war are too terrible; the sin and shame of war are too great; the folly of war is too monstrous; the penalty of war is altogether too awful for England to inflict it on this country.

I believe with my whole heart that in many respects Britain is the noblest, the most Christian nation in the world, its greatest power for good or evil. I cannot believe that the English Cabinet, if it had not been misled by one-sided and false representations as to the necessity, the duration, the results of the war, would ever have threatened it. I cannot believe that the British people will give its sanction to a war that, even if England conquers, can end in nothing but the extinction of two free Republics, in the extermination of tens of thousands of men who are determined to die for their liberty, in the alienation of our whole people, and the perpetuation of race-hatred for generations to come.

Once again I beseech the Christian people of Great Britain to rouse themselves, and to say, 'This war shall not be.' Let every lover of peace make his voice heard. And let every one who knows how to make his voice heard in heaven above, join us in one unceasing supplication to God that peace may be restored. There are thousands of God-fearing people in this land praying without ceasing for peace. I call upon all God's children: Kneel down beside us, present yourselves as one with us, and see if our God may not even yet send deliverance. ...[6]

Murray's appeals met with a mixed reception in South Africa, Britain and the United States:

> Among the Chauvinists Mr Murray's attitude towards the war policy provoked the greatest resentment and anger. The more violent section of the English colonial Press heaped abuse upon his head, and flung at him many opprobrious [contemptuous, reproachful] epithets, of which 'Pecksniffian humbug' and 'lying priest' may be taken as extreme examples. In Great Britain, except among the staunch little circle of 'pro-Boers', his appeal fell upon deaf ears. But in America, where his three papers on the situation were issued in pamphlet form, his words won a large measure of sympathy for the Boer cause.[7]

On 29 September the British Cabinet issued an ultimatum in which it demanded: that the Transvaal repeal all legislation passed since 1881 which affected the rights of uitlanders; that it grant home rule (self-government) to the inhabitants of Witwatersrand; that the Transvaal 'surrender' its rights to import arms through Mozambique; that the Transvaalers disarm. The Cabinet had to know such an ultimatum would be rejected. Likely in hopes of buying more time to prepare before the commencement of hostilities, the Cabinet delivered its ultimatum to South Africa by mail steamer rather than by telegraph.

Even before Transvaal officials received that communication they had issued and delivered an ultimatum of their own. In it they demanded that the British must withdraw their troops from the Transvaal border, remove from South Africa all troops that had arrived since 1 June, and send back the troops currently bound for South Africa on the high seas. That ultimatum was delivered to London on 10 October with the stipulation that unless an

---

6. ibid., pp. 425-6.

7. ibid., pp. 426-7.

'immediate and affirmative answer' was received by five o'clock in the afternoon on the next day (Wednesday 11 October), the Transvaal would consider the British to have declared war. The ultimatum was received in London with outrage and derision.[8]

---

8. Details concerning the ultimatums are taken from: Byron Farwell, *The Great Anglo-Boer War* (New York, Hagerstown, San Francisco and London: Harper & Row, 1976), pp. 46-7.

26

'THE HORRORS OF WAR ARE TOO TERRIBLE'
1899–1902

The Boers, hoping to gain an advantage by launching the first offensive, lost no time in acting on their ultimatum. Some 38,000 citizen-soldiers (23,000 from Transvaal and 15,000 from Orange Free State) were assembled and ready to go to war on 12 October. The Boer army was made up of all able-bodied men who were able to respond to the summons to join the fight to preserve the freedom of their republics. These were not highly trained soldiers but ordinary 'burghers' (citizens); most of them were farmers. However, the vast majority of them were skilled on horseback and expert marksmen. Nearly every man came with his own horse and rifle, dressed in everyday work clothes.

Britain, by contrast, had 22,000 trained soldiers in South Africa at the outset of the conflict. Throughout the course of the war, however, more than 450,000 British and allied soldiers served compared to less than 90,000 Boers, including Cape Boers and a small number of foreign volunteers sympathetic to their cause.

The first battle took place on Friday 20 October, near Dundee, in Natal. Thus commenced the Second Boer War, also known as the Anglo-Boer War by most South Africans. Both sides wrongly expected the war to be of short duration, as had been the First Boer War in 1881. The Boers did not think the British would be willing to pay the necessary price in terms of lives and monetary expense in order to subdue them. The Boers also wrongly supposed the international community would intervene on their behalf if the conflict lasted more than a few months. The British, on the other hand, underestimated the Boers' military capabilities and the extent of their determination to maintain their independence.

The war unfolded in three phases. First, the Boers made pre-emptive strikes into British-held territory in Natal and Cape Colony by laying siege to British garrisons at Ladysmith, Mafeking and Kimberley. The Boers also prevailed in a series of smaller-scale engagements that took place during a failed British counter-offensive to relieve the sieges. In the second phase, from January to September 1900, after greatly increasing the number of its troops, the British army carried out another offensive and succeeded in bringing the sieges to an end. After securing Cape Colony and Natal the British invaded the Transvaal, capturing Pretoria, the republic's capital, that June.

In phase three, beginning in March of 1900 and continuing for more than two years, the Boers resorted to carrying out guerrilla warfare by attacking such targets as British troop columns, railway and storage depots as well as telegraph sites. The British army, in order to cut off supplies to the guerrilla fighters, adopted a scorched earth policy in which they destroyed Boer farms and moved civilians (mainly women and children) into concentration camps.

Even after the British army controlled all the railways and nearly all the towns, and the Boers were reduced to carrying out guerilla warfare, Murray still believed that the Dutch were justified in continuing to fight in order to preserve the independence of their republics. More than one delegation was sent to Boer leaders in hopes of persuading them to lay down their arms, but without success. In one such failed attempt, Murray and other DRC ministers declined to support a proposed surrender, as a journal of the day reported:

> The report of the Peace Envoys shows that the mission was an entire failure. The Rev. Dr Murray was immovable in declining to do anything unless the British Government acknowledged the independence of the Republics. The other Dutch ministers, the report says, simply piped after Dr Murray.[1]

---

1. Du Plessis, *The Life of Andrew Murray*, p. 427.

In 1900 Murray and fellow DRC pastors, in conjunction with ministers of the Anglican Church and other denominations in South Africa, issued a joint call to prayer in which all Christians were encouraged to unite in requesting:

(1) That under the guidance of the Holy Spirit the deepest desire and prayer in all our hearts – deeper than even personal or national feeling – may be that of the blessed Son of God, 'Father, glorify Thy name!' [John 12:28]

(2) That God in answer to prayer may make a speedy end to the war, and bring about a sure, righteous and abiding peace, which shall promote the glory of His name and harmony among men.

(3) That believers may be willing to learn the spiritual lessons of humiliation which God desires to teach us by His chastisements, so that each of us may personally receive the hidden blessing which God purposes to bestow.

(4) That God would discover [reveal] and judge all the causes which have led to this war, or can lead to any future wars.

(5) That the Holy Spirit may at this time glorify Christ, by granting to us that we may know Him in a wholly new sense as the Prince of Peace between man and man, people and people.

(6) That we ourselves, and all God's children on both sides, may be so kept by the power of God's almighty grace, that we may be true peacemakers, and that a spirit of gentleness, forbearance and brotherly love may be shed abroad in all hearts by the Holy Ghost.[2]

In addition to prayer, Murray and other pastors ministered to Boer prisoners as they began to be gathered into camps not long after the war commenced. At first these prisoners were detained in camps at the Cape. But eventually more than 90 percent of the 28,000 Boer soldiers taken as prisoners were sent overseas to Saint Helena, Ceylon, India and Bermuda. Douglas reveals of Murray's ministry to prisoners:

---

2. ibid., pp. 427-8.

With true spiritual statesmanship Mr Murray applied himself unwearingly to supply their souls' needs. It was no easy task to find deeply concentrated spiritually-minded men who would be acceptable to both Boer and Briton. When the right man was found it required endless correspondence to remove the many obstacles that beset his way to the camps. When no one could be found for Sea Point Camp [in northern Cape Town], Mr Murray twice took charge for some weeks, and held three services daily during the whole period.[3]

Murray was also able to minister to thousands of Boer POWs in the camp at Simon's Town, thirty miles south of Sea Point. There he preached from Psalm 142:7: 'Bring my soul out of prison, that I may praise Thy name.'

Twice Murray received urgent invitations (the second one came from Dwight Moody) to be one of the featured speakers at an Ecumenical Missionary Conference that was to be held in New York in 1900. Murray declined the invitations, believing it would not be appropriate for him to leave South Africa in its time of crisis. However, he started contemplating whether there was any special message he would have been compelled to deliver had he been able to attend the conference.

When the report of the conference reached him, he eagerly perused it to discover what solution the conference had proposed for a primary concern it had addressed – how the moral and spiritual energies of the Church could best be translated into a vigorous, effective missionary offensive. In his typical straightforward fashion, Murray afterward commented:

> I found many important suggestions as to how the interest in missions may be increased. But, if I may venture to say it, the root evil, the real cause of so much lack of interest, and the way in which that evil should be met, was hardly dealt with. While indirectly and implicitly it was admitted that there was something wrong with the greater part of professing Christians, the real seriousness and sinfulness of the neglect of our Lord's command,

---

3. Douglas, *Andrew Murray and His Message*, pp. 151-2.

and the problem as to what the missionary societies could do to effect a change, certainly did not take that prominent place which I thought they deserved.[4]

As a result Murray wrote the book *The Key to the Missionary Problem*, which addressed those issues head-on. He asserted that 'missions are the chief end of the Church' and 'the chief end of the [pastoral] ministry is to guide the Church in this work and fit her for it'. Repeatedly in the volume he emphasized these related premises: 'the missionary problem is a personal one; every believer is a soul-winner; every minister holds office under the Great Commission; the missionary enterprise is the work not merely of all but of each.'[5] He heavily emphasized that if the Church was to fulfill its missionary responsibility it needed to be revived and empowered by the Holy Spirit: 'The Pentecostal commission can only be carried out by a Pentecostal Church in Pentecostal Power. ... We have given too much attention to methods and to machinery and to resources and too little to the Source of Power – the filling with the Holy Ghost.'[6]

When the book was published in 1901 it received extraordinary reviews. Dr Alexander Maclaren, a prominent British minister, stated, 'It is the *Key to the Missionary Problem* indeed, but it is also the key to most of our problems, and points to the only cure for all our weaknesses.' Dr F.B. Meyer, another popular British pastor, declared, 'If it were only read universally throughout our churches, by ministers and [lay] people alike, I believe it would lead to one of the greatest revivals of missionary enthusiasm that the world has ever known.'[7] On a far less formal basis, one enthusiastic and visionary reader of the volume wrote Murray from England:

I have been greatly profited by reading your book on Missions, and I cannot help thinking that some effort should be made to

---

4. Du Plessis, *The Life of Andrew Murray*, p. 389.

5. ibid.

6. Douglas, *Andrew Murray and His Message*, pp. 328-9.

7. Du Plessis, *The Life of Andrew Murray*, p. 391.

bring it to the notice of every member of the various Churches. I respectfully suggest the issue of a million copies (to start with) at one penny each![8]

Murray's writing ministry hardly slackened through the war years. From 1900 to 1902, besides *The Key to the Missionary Problem*, he published six other books (two of which were released in both English and Dutch) as well as two booklets.

As the war dragged on and as more and more Dutch women and children were confined in the concentration camps, conditions soon became deplorable, then fatal. More than 100,000 Dutch women and children were detained in a total of forty-five tented camps. The intention was to adequately care for them there while preventing them from communicating with Boer soldiers still in the field. In addition, sixty-four other internment camps were thrown up for some 107,000 black Africans who were displaced by the war. Inadequate shelter from severe weather conditions, overcrowding, poor hygiene and sanitation, meager food supplies and lack of proper medicine and medical treatment led to malnutrition and endemic diseases such as dysentery, typhoid and measles. Tragically, as a result, over 26,000 white women and children and more than 14,000 blacks perished in the concentration camps. Eighty-five percent of the whites who died in the camps were children under sixteen years of age; they comprised fully half the Boer child population![9]

Eventually the strain of the war 'told terribly' on Murray, who turned seventy-four years old in May, 1902, the same month the war finally drew to a close. Douglas relates:

---

8. ibid., p. 476.

9. It does not appear that Andrew Murray ministered in any of the concentration camps for women and children or for blacks. Murray biographer J. du Plessis served for six months as chaplain in the Women's Camp at Aliwal North (on the Orange River, thirty-seven miles west of Lady Grey), where 5,000 individuals were detained. At one time, during October 1901, an average of thirteen people per day were buried there (Du Plessis, *The Life of Andrew Murray*, p. 430).

He felt for both sides, his own children and relatives suffered by it, and finally his health gave way. Then the Lord in mercy made it possible for him to go with his wife and two daughters to Switzerland, through the kindness of two Christian ladies in Cape Town. Here he could give himself to prayer but his tender heart was spared the harrowing tales of suffering which he could not relieve.[10]

The Murrays left for Europe some time early in 1902 and returned to South Africa in July, 1903. Little else is known of Murray's recuperation in Switzerland. It is not clear if he did any public speaking during that visit to Europe.

By the time the war ended a staggering 75,000 lives had been lost in the conflict. 22,000 British and allied soldiers had died (7,800 were killed in battle while the rest perished from disease). Between 6,000 and 7,000 Boer soldiers died in battle. Around 6,000 blacks perished on battlefields. For Britain the Second Boer War was the longest and costliest conflict it waged in the century between 1815 and 1914. It cost Britain 20,000,000 pounds to prosecute this war, which lasted three months longer than the Crimean War (1853-1856). The Anglo-Boer War claimed the lives of more British soldiers than did the Crimean conflict, though more died of disease in the Crimea.

The Treaty of Vereeniging, signed on 31 May, 1902, officially ended the war. The treaty also brought to an end the Transvaal Republic and Orange Free State as independent Boer republics and made them part of the British Empire. However, the Boers were given 3,000,000 pounds for reconstruction and were promised eventual limited self-government, which was granted in 1906 and 1907. In 1910 Transvaal Colony and Orange Colony were joined with Cape Colony and Natal Colony, collectively forming the Union of South Africa, which was established as a self-governing Dominion of the British Empire.

---

10.   Douglas, *Andrew Murray and His Message*, p. 152.

27

SHOWING FORTH GOD'S POWER
1903–1908

With the commencement of the Boer War came the very real and reasonable concern that the cause of foreign missions might be neglected due to the absorbing nature of the crisis. In the all-wise workings of Providence, however, interest in and support for missions were actually promoted and strengthened as a result of the war. With regard to the 1899 appeal of the Ministers' Mission Union for additional workers and financial support so its Nyasaland missionary staff could be doubled in five years:

> Gifts of money, frequently from unsuspected sources and some-times in comparatively large amounts, streamed into the [MMU] treasury. The sympathy which had been awakened in the hearts of the Dutch-speaking public for those who were sufferers through the war was extended to every form of philanthropic activity, and not the least to the missionary cause.[1]

In addition, an increased number of capable young men offered themselves for foreign missionary service. As a result, in 1903, one year after the end of the war and within only four years of having sent out its 1899 prayer appeal letter, the MMU Committee was delighted to report that the number of workers had already doubled, with twenty-eight missionaries now serving in Nyasaland.

Still further, through the faithful ministries of chaplains, hundreds if not thousands of Boers had been led to saving faith in

---

1. Du Plessis, *The Life of Andrew Murray*, p. 379.

Christ in the prisoner of war camps at the Cape and at St Helena, Ceylon, India and Bermuda. As they returned to South Africa after the war, more than 150 of those new converts committed themselves to receiving the necessary training, then devoting their lives to foreign service. The Boer Missionary Institute at Worcester was founded early in 1903 for their reception and training.

While passing through London en route to returning home to South Africa in July, 1903, Murray visited Mr and Mrs Head, who had been his hosts during his ministry in England seven years earlier. One morning F.B. Meyer joined the Heads and the Murrays for breakfast. The others listened with interest as the two pastor-authors questioned each other about what they intended to write next. Presently Murray's daughter, Annie, raised a laugh from the group by exclaiming, 'Oh, Father has eight books on his brain!'

Though details are no longer known, Murray experienced 'a serious accident' in a London street around that same time and needed to be taken to a hospital. News of his injury traveled back to a lady and her young son, Alec, whom the Murrays had recently befriended while staying at the same motel in Switzerland. Murray had shown interest in Alec, age five, and the youngster quickly became fond of the aging gentleman. When Alec's mother wrote back to the Murrays, the boy asked her to enclose a pressed pink for Mr Murray 'because flowers are so comforting'.

Later that year Murray attended his final Cape Colony DRC Synod. (By the time the next Synod was held in 1906, Murray had retired so no longer qualified to participate in the proceedings.) Though seventy-five years old and beginning to battle deafness, Murray was still held in highest esteem by his contemporaries and exercised considerable sway in the 1903 Synod deliberations. His wife, Emma, reported:

> He is interested in what is going on but too deaf to always listen quietly, while he is invaluable in giving advice. He attends committee meetings for schools and missions and often makes his influence felt. When he does speak in Synod his words carry weight and he

feels that being here he can often overrule things for good, as he generally has his way.[2]

The Nyasa Mission had become large enough that it was thought advisable to turn over its supervision to the DRC Synod. The 1903 Synod established the General Missions Committee to oversee various missionary enterprises. Murray was appointed as the GMC's Chairman, a responsibility he fulfilled until his retirement from active pastoral ministry three years later. By that time Murray had helped guide the mission policy of the Colony's DRC for half a century, ever since he, N.J. Hofmeyr and J.H. Neethling were elected to form a new Missions Committee at the 1857 Synod.

Supervision of Wellington's missionary Training Institute was also entrusted to the Synod at its 1903 meeting. Ongoing growth at the school soon made additional accommodations necessary. As a result, Murray Jubilee Hall was erected then publicly dedicated on Murray's seventy-seventh birthday in May, 1905. In Murray's lifetime more than 200 students graduated from the institute, with the 'vast majority' of those going on to serve as missionaries or teachers in the DRC's foreign and home mission fields.

Murray undertook his ninth evangelistic tour in 1904, again returning to Transvaal and Natal. A witness of Murray's ministry exertions in the Transvaal at that time would later recall to his daughter Mary:

> His power for work was something unusual. One day your mother said to him, 'I think we ought to go home now, we are getting old.' He said, 'Speak for yourself only, Mother. I don't want to die, there is much to be done still.' I was often astonished at the amount of work he got through, even when traveling or having special services.
>
> ... I often look back to the days he spent with us. It was a benediction to have him in the house. What made a great impression upon me at such times was the perfectly natural way in which he would take everything to the Lord in prayer. One day there was an argument with another man who was helping with

2. Douglas, *Andrew Murray and His Message*, pp. 152-3.

special services here; this man was rather bent on having his own way. We were at dinner, and all at once Mr Murray said, 'Let us ask God!', and we all knelt down at table while he prayed. It seemed to me that the man looked rather ashamed of himself when we got up; at least he did not continue the argument.

This was surely an unusual and evidently very effective way of dealing with an overbearing brother. Dr Murray had wonderful tenderness and skill in dealing with such persons, and his patience seemed never to fail.[3]

As it turned out, due to a further injury sustained in yet another cart accident, this would prove to be Murray's final such evangelistic tour.[4] His daughter, Annie, would eventually relate:

Some years later[5] he was thrown, along with Mrs Murray, from a cart again, when he was on a similar tour in Natal. He was seriously hurt in the leg and back. This time the relatives insisted on calling in a doctor, and though he did not give up his tour, he was never perfectly restored and had to give up traveling by cart again.

Some time afterwards, one cool evening at Clairvaux, I was sitting on the stoep with him, and he said to me in his humble way: 'My child, I would so much like to hold evangelistic meetings but God does not see fit to heal me.' He sighed as he said this and I felt it was a mystery that when God was using him so mightily as a soul winner that this accident should have happened. But it was his Peniel [Gen. 32:30]. He became through this experience a prince who prevailed with God in prayer. He was led through this seemingly strange providence into a deeper prayer life, and was taught what the power of intercession really was. The Church of God at large

---

3. ibid., pp. 256-7.

4. Du Plessis, *The Life of Andrew Murray*, p. 524 states this tour was to Transvaal while Annie Murray (as cited in Douglas, *Andrew Murray and His Message*, p. 200) indicates it was in Natal. Presuming the various accounts of both du Plessis (p. 477) and Annie Murray (in Douglas, p. 200) are accurate, 1904 was the third time Andrew Murray was injured in a cart accident while on an evangelistic tour.

5. After the 1897 cart accident in Transvaal as recorded on pp. 263-4 of the present volume.

little knows what it owes to those prayers. His remarkable books on prayer were written after that accident, and the influence they have exercised cannot be measured nor told by man.[6]

Murray's brother Charles died of an 'internal tumor' on 23 September, 1904. He was seventy-one years old. His thirty-eight years of pastoral ministry at Graaff-Reinet had been 'much blest'. Little more than three months later a much more grievous bereavement befell Andrew Murray when his wife's life suddenly and quite unexpectedly came to an end. Emma had been her husband's affectionate, supportive partner in life and ministry for forty-eight and a half years. Du Plessis summarizes some of the highlights of her decades of devoted service:

> Owing to the father's prolonged absences from home on evangelistic errands, the training of [their] children devolved to a large extent upon Mrs Murray. And she acquitted herself of her task with exemplary devotion, earning the lasting gratitude and deep affection of all her sons and daughters. So long as life endured her zeal in service of the Master never slackened. To her work in Bloemfontein, especially in connection with Mr Murray's rectorship of the Grey College, we have already referred. During the revival of 1860 she instituted a ladies' prayer meeting at Worcester which has been continued down to the present day [1919]. She was the first to introduce children's work circles for the missionary cause, both at Worcester and in Cape Town. On behalf of Sunday School work her efforts were untiring. As her children grew up and set her free from domestic duties, the sphere of her activities was enlarged. At Wellington the Huguenot Seminary, the Mission Training Institute, and Friedenheim – a training school for women workers – owe much to her fostering care. In 1898, chiefly on her initiative, an industrial school for poor white girls was opened, which supplied a felt need and achieved a large measure of success. Mrs Murray was also president, from its inception, of the *Vrouwen Zending Bond* (Women's Missionary Union), and much of the marvelous growth and wide influence

---

6. Douglas, *Andrew Murray and His Message*, pp. 200-1.

of this society may be traced to her unceasing interest and wise counsels.[7]

Emma suffered greatly from rheumatism in her later years. Toward the end of 1904 an 'unusually severe' attack of rheumatism compelled her to keep to her bed but no serious consequences were foreseen. Suddenly, however, she lapsed into unconsciousness due to a blood clot to the brain and died on 2 January, 1905, at sixty-nine years of age. Her husband and four daughters were gathered around her bed at her passing. 'It was wonderful to hear his prayer of thanksgiving, immediately after her passing away,' Annie later revealed, 'because of what she had been to him and her children. It took us into the very vestibule of heaven.'[8] Murray preached the following Sunday, employing Philippians 1:23 as his sermon text, 'with Christ, which is far better'.

For a time Murray's sorrow at the loss of his life partner seemed nearly unbearable. As a diversion from his grief, he threw himself into his work. But the overall strain proved too much, and he suffered a slight stroke that confined him to his bed for a few weeks. After he recovered he divulged to Annie, 'I now begin to see the glory of God's will.'

The following year, 1906, Murray retired from pastoral ministry. He turned seventy-eight that year and had served as a DRC minister for fifty-seven years, thirty-five of those at Wellington. However, he had no intention of retiring from active Christian service. Rather, he planned to continue serving Christ and His Kingdom through his speaking and writing ministries as well as by his ongoing promotion of various Christian causes.

A writing project that engrossed a considerable amount of Murray's time and attention that year was the compilation and publication of a forty-two page quarto booklet entitled *The Kingdom of God in South Africa: A Brief Survey of Missions South of the Zambesi*. The booklet provided a description of the ministry

---

7. Du Plessis, *The Life of Andrew Murray*, pp. 485-6.

8. Douglas, *Andrew Murray and His Message*, p. 153.

as well as statistical information about each of the thirty-one missionary societies laboring in the sub-continent. In introducing the brief work, Murray stated:

> The need has long been felt of a little book in which the work of the different Societies laboring for the extension of Christ's kingdom could be set forth in such a way as to make every worker acquainted with his fellow-laborers in the Lord's harvest field. ... As we all meet within the pages of this little book, we shall know each other better ... And where we thought that we had reason to criticize or disapprove of the spirit or the method of our brother, closer knowledge of his work and the remembrance that our Lord is with him will stir our hearts to that forbearance and love which will make our prayer fervent and effectual.[9]

John R. Mott, Chairman of the Student Volunteer Movement for Foreign Missions, came to minister for two months in South Africa, beginning in mid-April, 1906.[10] Mott and his wife Leila visited Murray at Wellington:

> At Wellington both Motts satisfied a longing of years in meeting in his home 'Clairvaux' the aging Andrew Murray, who could rightly have been called the patron saint of the South African student movement because of the aid he had given Wishard in 1896. John had discovered Murray's devotional tract *With Christ in the School of Prayer* while an undergraduate at Cornell, and his *Key to the Missionary Problem*, which laid the burden of responsibility for missions on the local pastor, was a stimulus to Mott as he planned *The Pastor and Modern Missions* and now discussed the issue with Murray. ... Mott now sought his advice on the strategy of his [present] tour. Murray called on Leila briefly one evening, affording her the opportunity to tell him 'how much he was loved in America'. He in turn spoke of the 'precious fellowship in Christ'.

---

9.   Du Plessis, *The Life of Andrew Murray*, p. 393.

10. C. Howard Hopkins, *John R. Mott, 1865-1955, A Biography* (Grand Rapids: Eerdmans, 1979), pp. 294-300 summarizes Mott's South Africa ministry tour.

She recorded in her diary that he made 'an impression of saintliness such as few if any men ever have upon me'.[11]

Mott ministered in churches and schools of various denominations in all four of South Africa's colonies. He was the featured speaker at student missions meetings as well as mass evangelistic rallies that drew up to 3,500 people. Mott's larger campaigns were held at Capetown, Stellenbosch, Paarl, Wellington, Grahamstown, King Williamstown, Lovedale, Bloemfontein, Johannesburg, Pretoria, Pietermaritzburg and Durban. The 'principal event' of Mott's ministry tour was the Student Missionary Conference at Capetown, 17-20 May, which was said to be the largest student gathering ever held in South Africa. Mott spoke five times at the conference while Andrew Murray delivered a 'burning and prophetic message' entitled 'He Must Reign'.

The following year, 1907, the University of the Cape of Good Hope conferred on Murray the honorary Doctor of Literature degree. The official citation that was read when the honor was bestowed stated in part:

> Dr Murray is known throughout South Africa as a preacher of great intellectual power and spiritual insight; and his works, translated into many foreign languages, have received a wide recognition in Europe and America. Through a ministry extending over nearly sixty years Dr Murray has been an earnest advocate of that system of national education in which the work of the public school is strengthened by the influence of the well-regulated school-home.[12]

After rehearsing Murray's part in founding Grey College in Bloemfontein, the YMCA in Cape Town and a number of educational institutions in Wellington, the citation concluded:

> Through his counsel and example in the work of national education in South Africa Dr Murray has contributed in no ordinary measure

11. ibid., p. 296.

12. Du Plessis, *The Life of Andrew Murray*, p. 411.

to prepare the foundations on which the work of this University must rest. The University desires that the name of so distinguished a South African as Dr Murray may be connected permanently with its history ...[13]

Murray's eightieth birthday took place on 9 May, 1908. The next day, Sunday, he preached in Wellington from 1 Thessalonians 1:5: 'Our Gospel came unto you ... in power'. He began the message with the sentiment of Psalm 71:18 by stating, 'I am an old man. As I have grown old I have prayed that God would let me show forth His *power* to the generation to come.'[14]

For over two decades Murray had used his enormous influence to help gain a welcome for a number of evangelists from Britain and America who came to carry out ministries in South Africa. One of the earliest of those had been Henry Varley, a British associate of Dwight Moody who had deeply challenged the American evangelist with the immortal words, 'The world has yet to see what God will do with a man fully consecrated to Him.' In 1886, Varley conducted a series of 'remarkable' meetings in a number of South Africa's primary towns. Other foreign evangelists whose fruitful ministries to South Africa Murray helped to promote through the years included Spencer Walton, George C. Grubb, John McNeill, Mark Guy Pearse, Gelson Gregson, Charles Inwood, Rodney 'Gipsy' Smith, Donald Fraser, Luther Wishard, John R. Mott and F.B. Meyer. Du Plessis observes, 'Many of them might have found the doors of the Dutch Reformed Churches closed against them – for the South African Dutch as a people and as a Church are averse from *nieuwigheden* (novelties) – were it not that the Moderator [Murray] had given them his countenance and benediction.'[15]

F.B. Meyer's visit to South Africa came in 1908. He testified:

From the first the ministers of the Dutch Reformed Church showed me much Christian courtesy. ... All were prepared to

13. ibid., p. 412.

14. Douglas, *Andrew Murray and His Message*, p. 226.

15. Du Plessis, *The Life of Andrew Murray*, p. 440.

accept the lead given by the venerable Dr Andrew Murray, who came from Wellington on purpose to attend the meetings [in Cape Town], and took part in prayer and benediction. I can never forget or repay his kindness.... [N]otwithstanding his eighty years, his intellect is as bright and his natural force almost as vigorous as when he visited England fifteen years ago. He is honored and loved throughout the [Cape Colony Dutch Reformed] Church of which he is the recognized father and leader, and beyond. It was of untold help, therefore, that my earliest meetings should receive his endorsement and his blessing.[16]

That same year the growing mission work of the Colony's DRC found itself faced with a serious deficit of some 2,500 pounds. The General Mission Committee issued a request for universal prayer about the concerning situation on Pentecost Sunday, 7 June, and nearly every congregation in the denomination heartily complied. Murray preached at Wellington that day, taking Exodus 14:15 as his text: 'And the Lord said unto Moses, "Wherefore criest thou unto me? Speak unto the children of Israel, that they go forward".' As a result of Murray's stirring appeal that day to boldly advance the missionary cause, the Wellington Consistory decided to host a 'Missionary Congress' in order to consider the crucial issues that lay before them. The date for the congress was set for August and delegates were invited from near and far.

Annie Murray's diary entry on 8 July, 1908, describes a 'typical' day in her father's life at that time when he was at home:

Before breakfast, where he usually made his appearance before the sun was visible over the mountaintops, he stood gazing fixedly out the window to see the sun rise over Groenberg. ... At family prayer he used these expressions: 'We have just seen the sun rise. It is the evidence of Thine almighty power. It is the work of Thine omnipotence. In all nature around us Thy power is working patiently and persistently. May it work with like power in our hearts, taking away all sin and self-sufficiency, all pride and self-exaltation.'

---

16.   ibid., pp. 440-1.

At half past nine we set to work on Ephesians, and he began to dictate the chapter 'In the Heavenly Places'. The day being calm and fine, father sat outside on the stoep with a rug over his knees, enjoying the bright sunshine. Presently he described our old colored gardener April, aged eighty, with a large bag of forage on his back. 'Dear old man,' was father's comment, 'he is faithfulness itself.' ...

A telegram was then delivered, informing us that Mrs Searle (a faithful worker in the South Africa General Mission) was lying seriously ill in Tembuland. 'Let us stop a few minutes,' said father, 'and pray for her'; and immediately commenced: 'O Lord, let Thy presence fill the sick-chamber with Thy comfort and peace. And if it be Thy will, grant speedy and complete restoration.' The dictation was resumed and a few more pages completed, when a note arrived from Rev. Albertyn [Wellington's pastor], saying that Amy Luckhoff (the daughter of a beloved ministerial colleague) had died suddenly, and that he purposed going to the funeral. So a message of love and sympathy was quickly written down and dispatched with Mr Albertyn.

At half past ten a prayer meeting of local ministers was held in the study, to intercede for the approaching Missionary Congress. When this was over, the English mail had arrived with letters, books and periodicals – among the latter the ever-welcome *British Weekly*. Father next had a few kind words with two young ladies who were having eleven o'clock tea with us. ... A letter was next dispatched to Haldane (at that time member of Parliament), to see if he could obtain concession fares for visitors to the annual 'Keswick' Convention; and another letter to Charlie, with advice as to accepting the call to Rossville.[17]

At one o'clock we adjourned for dinner, when the books which had just arrived were exhibited – always a keen pleasure to father. On this occasion it was Amy Carmichael's *Overweights of Joy*,

---

17. After several years of successful service as a teacher and school inspector Andrew Haldane became a farmer in the Graaff-Reinet area. There he became a highly-respected member of the community and representative of the district of Alice in the House of Assembly. Charles had served for a time as a missionary in Nyasaland. After his wife's failing health forced him to withdraw from that malarial climate, he became the minister at Rossville (present-day Rhodes) in Eastern Cape Province.

and a large volume on *Santa Teresa* by Mrs. Grahame. Father was much pleased with the latter, read out the dedication, and quoted the Teresian vow: 'I have made a vow never to offend God in the smallest matter.' ...

After a short nap, we continued writing on the sunny stoep for an hour. When the article of six foolscap pages was finished, father said, 'I am deeply grateful that we have been able to complete this work. But it will all have to be done over again [revised].' Somewhat later Mrs Albertyn came over for a talk and advice on matters in connection with the Women's Missionary Union. Father was always a ready and most sympathetic listener, while his suggestions were invaluable.[18]

That year over 1,000 people, primarily younger men and women, attended the South African Keswick meetings at Murray's church in Wellington. A Johannesburg minister described Murray and his role in the meetings:

In the evening, when the congregation was still larger, Andrew Murray was present himself. When the opening notes of the organ had died away, a third minister [Murray] stole feebly into the rostrum where the other two were seated, and commenced the service with prayer. We felt as though a benediction fell upon us as we listened to his prayer. But how frail he seemed! A thin, lined face, spare form, long gray hair, and attenuated hands grasping the red velvet cushion in front. It was a pathetic picture – the picture of a prophet of a past generation. During that evening, and at each service through the convention when Dr Murray took some part in the proceedings, he seemed to overcome his weakness, and he amazed us with his fire and energy.[19]

The Missionary Congress held in Wellington that August was also well attended and produced 'momentous' results. A Laymen's Missionary Union was established and the first 700 pounds was pledged toward wiping out the General Mission Committee's

---

18.   Du Plessis, *The Life of Andrew Murray*, pp. 493-4.

19.   ibid., p. 493.

2,500-pound deficit. In addition to eliminating the deficit, it was decided to raise an additional 2,500 pounds to extend the work in the foreign field. A 'Missionary Crusade' was also planned, in which representative ministers would visit populous centers throughout the country, conducting congresses similar to the one at Wellington in order to further promote missionary zeal.

The first series of congresses were held at six widely-scattered locations – Klerksdorp and Johannesburg in the Transvaal, Bloemfontein in the Free State and Cradock, Oudtshoorn and Beaufort West in Cape Colony. Murray was looked to for leadership in this Missionary Crusade and, despite his advancing age, he rose to the challenge. He was the only one of the ministerial deputies who participated in all six of the initial set of conferences. Annie reported about a portion of one of those early journeys:

> We arrived by train at Kroonstad at 2:30 a.m., where the carriage was disconnected from the train and stood in the station yard. At 6:30 the Dutch minister, Rev. Mr v[an] d[er] Lingen, met us and took us to his house where we rested till breakfast at 8:30. 10-11 a.m., ministers' meeting; 11:30-12 noon, he visited all the old members of his Wellington congregation resident at Kroonstad. After dinner rested till the convention meeting at 4 p.m., which lasted till 5:30, and Dr Murray gave the principal address. Evening meeting, 7:30 till 9:30, when he again gave the chief address. Retired at 10 p.m., rose at 1:30 a.m. to catch the 2:30 a.m. train to Bloemfontein, where we arrived about 11 a.m. And after resting Dr Murray attended all the sessions of the Congress for the next two days, and gave the chief addresses. It was wonderful how fresh all the addresses were. One of his brethren remarked, 'He never repeats himself.' One secret of his power was that every message was newly received for the occasion. He did not offer stale bread to hungry souls.[20]

'Father, you will die in the train,' Murray's daughter Mary fretted. 'No, my child,' he properly predicted, 'I shall not. I shall die in my bed.'

---

20. Douglas, *Andrew Murray and His Message*, p. 233.

One Murray admirer wrote of him: 'Our old father and leader, Mr Murray, fills us continually with new astonishment and admiration. He is sometimes weary but never discouraged. The lion's share of the work falls to him. And though his strength has somewhat decreased, the old fire burns with undiminished glow.'[21] Du Plessis relates:

> Nevertheless, he bore all the vicissitudes of travel and all the strain of six successive conferences not only without apparent fatigue but with positive zest. And when he alighted from the train at Wellington he was in better health than when he had set out, and was already evolving plans for a second series of conferences at centers as yet unvisited.[22]

The Missionary Crusade was a tremendous success. Widespread interest in missions was aroused. The debt was completely eliminated. A number of congregations that had been indifferent or even antagonistic towards mission work became zealous supporters of the cause. Many churches doubled, tripled or even quadrupled their missions-giving. Not a few congregations decided to underwrite the salary of their own representative in the foreign field. By early in the following year – 1909 – 4,000 of the 5,000 pounds originally aimed at had already been contributed. When the campaign drew to a close some time later, no less than 10,000 pounds had been raised for foreign missionary endeavor.

One aspect of Murray's ministry that had decreased noticeably since the end of the Boer War was the publication of his written works. In those six years, 1903-1908, he published thirteen pamphlets and booklets but only two new books. However, writing would continue to be a significant facet of his ministry to the end of his life.

---

21. Du Plessis, *The Life of Andrew Murray*, p. 381.
22. ibid.

28

FRUITFUL SUNSET YEARS
1909–1914

Throughout his more settled decades of ministry at Wellington and in semi-retirement Andrew Murray did a substantial amount of reading, especially in particular areas of study that interested and concerned him. 'Novels he could not and would not read, but biographies were his delight,' Murray's daughter Annie related. His bookshelves contained the biographies of such prominent Christians as George Fox, David Brainerd, John Wesley, William Burns, Andrew Bonar, George Muller, Dwight Moody, Hudson Taylor, John Williams, Robert Moffat and Count Zinzendorf. With his passion for promoting education, Murray read rather extensively in that field. In addition to the biographies of a number of educators, including Mary Lyon, Fidelia Fiske, Edward Thring, Almond of Loretto, Hannah Pipe and Dorothea Beale, he read the didactic works of several educationalists.

Murray's appreciation for Christian mysticism led him to value not only the works of William Law, Dora Greenwell and Frances Bevan, but also the biographies of Madame Guyon, Catherine of Siena and Saint Teresa of Avila. Other writers whose works Murray admired included Alexander Whyte, P.T. Forsyth, Bishop Handley Moule, John R. Mott, Charles Wagner, A.E. Garvie, W.M. Clow and the German professors Harnack and Eucken. During the latter years of his life Murray collected many works on prayer, being especially impressed with W. Arthur Cornaby's *Prayer and the Human Problem* and E.M. Bounds's classic *Power through Prayer*.

All through his mid-eighties Andrew Murray was able to continue his considerable traveling ministries. Annie summarizes:

> During the next six years [1909-1914] he traveled much up and down the country, usually taking one long tour each year, lasting from three to five weeks, and then shorter journeys as opportunity offered. The winter tour almost always included the annual conference of the Christian Students' Association where he usually gave several addresses. He generally attended other conferences also, such as the Laymen's Missionary Union. Often he was invited to take part in the services connected with the opening of new churches, and communion seasons often gave him the opportunity for preaching two or three sermons. [On one occasion,] going to Johannesburg for a 'Keswick' Convention and Missionary Congress, and the ten days of prayer at Pentecost, he preached twenty-eight times in twelve days, and it was *preaching*. From a full heart he would pour out praise and thanksgiving for traveling mercies, and intercessions on behalf of the work, and for the friends he had met as we drew near home after these tours.[1]

Douglas relates of Murray's preaching at a SCA conference around that time:

> Some of his hearers at a convention of the Students' Christian Association held in Cradock ... noticed with interest the clouds of dust which rose from the pulpit cushion when he began his sermon, but ere it was finished the dusting had been completed. Yet he was never violent or unrestrained, but just glowing with intensity.[2]

On another occasion during that general time period Murray preached at the Wesleyan Metropolitan Church in Cape Town in conjunction with a new missionary enterprise that was being launched in Sudan. A former student at Wellington's Huguenot Seminary and College, who was now a missionary candidate to Sudan, was at the meeting. She revealed:

1. Douglas, *Andrew Murray and His Message*, pp. 233-4.
2. ibid., p. 51.

A lady was sitting close to me, and as Dr Murray went up the pulpit steps, frail and gray and old, she asked: 'Who is that old man? What a shame to make him go up those steps to preach.' I smiled inwardly and thought, 'My dear lady, you will be surprised tonight.' Dr Murray got up, he seemed to grow tall and majestic. In regard to the new work in the Sudan he once more spoke according to the oracles of God. 'Forward' was his cry.[3] Well, my lady was surprised, and more than surprised, pity made way for reverence. 'What a voice for such a body!' she exclaimed. Clear as a bell, irresistible in its power and command, the all victorious *forward* rang forth in tones which knew no hesitation or defeat.[4]

For many years Murray had underscored the vital importance of prayer. During the closing years of his life, however, that emphasis became even more pronounced. One manifestation of that was his response to the World Missionary Conference (WMC) held in Edinburgh, Scotland, in June, 1910. Some 1,300 delegates, most of them representing major Protestant denominations and missionary societies from North America and Northern Europe, attended the gathering. Their unifying focus was how to fulfill what had become the watchword of the powerful Protestant missionary movement at that time, 'The Evangelization of the World in This Generation'. Nine volumes were published, containing major reports on various aspects of world missions considered at the WMC, as well as a description of the proceedings and major speeches delivered at the convention.

Murray scanned those works with eager interest. 'To which volume, do you think, did I turn first?' he asked J. du Plessis.

'To the volume on *Carrying the Gospel to All the Non-Christian World*, I suppose,' came the reply.

'Not at all,' revealed Murray. 'What interested me first and foremost was *The Home Base of Missions*.'

---

3. The young lady relating this incident, while still a student at Wellington, had heard Murray's stirring sermon there in June, 1908, when he employed Exodus 14:15 to urge the congregation to go forward in its advancing of the missionary cause.

4. Douglas, *Andrew Murray and His Message*, pp. 258-9.

Murray was, in fact, just at that time giving a great deal of thought to the condition of the Church (the home base), which he viewed as being in serious need of spiritual revitalization. Characteristically he put his thoughts to paper and the next year, 1911, published *The State of the Church – A Call to Prayer*. Murray's message in that volume resonated with a number of his ministerial brethren. P.J.G. de Vos, a professor at the Stellenbosch Theological Seminary,[5] addressed an open letter to his fellow ministers in which he deplored the Church's lack of spiritual power and suggested that they gather together and prayerfully seek to identify the source of that weakness. As a result, more than 200 ministers, missionaries and theological students attended a conference for that purpose at Stellenbosch in April, 1912. Murray participated in the conference and afterward reported:

> The Lord graciously so ordered it that we were gradually led to the sin of prayerlessness, as one of the deepest roots of the evil. No one could plead himself free from this. ... Such confessions gradually led to the great truth that the only power for a new prayer life is to be found in an entirely new relation to our blessed Savior. Before we parted many people were able to testify that they were returning [to their homes] with new light and new hope, to find in Jesus Christ strength for a new prayer life.[6]

Throughout the remaining five years of his life Murray continued to emphasize the crucial need for prayer. In that time he wrote several additional booklets comprised of short meditations on the subject. Once when a volume of sermons by a well-known preacher of the day was handed to Murray, he eagerly consulted the table of contents. 'There is not a single sermon on *prayer*,' he remarked with obvious disappointment, and laid aside the book as one which held no interest for him.

---

5. N.J. Hofmeyr, long-time professor at the Stellenbosch seminary, had died two years earlier, in 1909. Rev. J.H. Neethling, who along with Hofmeyr and John Murray had formed the Stellenbosch Triumvirate, had passed away in 1904.

6. Du Plessis, *The Life of Andrew Murray*, p. 472.

Another contributing factor to lower spiritual conditions in South Africa's DRC during 1911 and 1912 were political tensions that were running high and taking a toll within the Church. At the Colony's 1903 Synod, the first one after the conclusion of the Boer War and the last one where Murray served as Moderator, a committee was appointed to explore the possibility of the DRCs in Cape Colony, Orange River Colony, the Transvaal and Natal being united into a single Synod. The resulting Conference on Unity, in which Murray played an active role, was held at Colesberg in October, 1905. Eventually in 1909 a proposal was laid before each of the four existing Synods, recommending that all their congregations be joined into one denomination, to be called The Dutch Reformed Church of South Africa. The DRCSA would be governed by one unified Synod.[7] All four Synods approved the proposal.

In 1911 South Africa's Parliament passed an 'enabling bill' by which the four DRC Synods were empowered to unite into one, so long as a certain procedure was followed and specific conditions were observed. Namely, at least three-quarters of the 2,500 individuals who made up the consistories (church councils) of the 250 DRCs represented in all four of those provinces needed to vote in favor of the union in order for it to be approved. But when decided in 1912 by individual churchwardens rather than by more broadminded Synod representatives, the proposal failed miserably.

In September, 1912, Murray was visited by his nephew, Rev. A.A. Louw, who drew from his pocket a small, slender volume entitled *Uwe Zon* (Thy Sun). Louw remarked how handy it was to have such a portable book to carry around and read at odd moments, on a cart or train, at the railway station, just about anywhere and everywhere. The idea struck Murray as an excellent one, and he at once began to compose the first of an intended series of 'booklets

---

7. This recommendation was in keeping with political developments in South Africa at that time. As has already been noted, the next year (1910) Cape Colony, Orange Colony, Transvaal Colony and Natal Colony were all joined, collectively forming the Union of South Africa.

for the vest pocket'. The initial work in the series was entitled *Heere, leer ons bidden!* (Lord, teach us to pray). During the four years to follow Murray produced twelve *zakboekjes* (pocket manuals), each consisting of thirty-one brief meditations. Before Murray's death five of the booklets were translated into English, forming the 'Pocket Companion' series.[8]

Annie provides an enlightening description of Murray's rather exacting writing habits at that time:

> He sits up very straight in his study chair, and dictates in a loud, clear voice, as though he were actually addressing his audience. His hours of work are usually from 9 or 10 till 11 in the forenoon, during which time two or three chapters of a book are completed. He is very particular about punctuation, and always says: 'New paragraph' (pointing with long, slender finger to the exact spot on the paper where the new line must commence), 'full stop', 'comma', 'colon', 'semicolon', as the sense may require.[9]

Du Plessis continues the depiction:

> Should his secretary perpetrate some mistake or other in spelling, he would make some playful remark like, 'You will have to go back to the kindergarten, you know.' At 11 o'clock he would say, 'Now give me ten minutes rest'; or 'no, let us write some letters for a change.' Then half a dozen letters would be quickly dictated, in reply to requests for prayer for healing, for the conversion of unconverted relations, for the deliverance of friends addicted to drink, or, it might be, business letters. Occasionally a letter would be dictated for *De Kerkbode* on the state of the Church, or for the public press on some matter affecting the country.
>
> The manuscript of a new book was often kept inside the pages of an illustrated annual. 'Now bring me Father Christmas,'

---

8. Eventually all twelve of these booklets were published in English in the Pocket Companion series. Because each English title began with the words *The Secret of ...*, this was popularly called the 'Secret Series'. *Heere, leer ons bidden!* (Lord, teach us to pray) was entitled *The Secret of Intercession*.

9. Du Plessis, *The Life of Andrew Murray*, pp. 468-9.

he would say, and the manuscript pages of one of the *Pocket Companion* series would be produced from the covers of the journal which had shielded them from harm. When recovering from an illness, he often wrote in bed. He always dictated in a tone of great earnestness, and was specially anxious to get a great deal into a page. ... When near the end of the foolscap page, he said, 'Now the last four lines for a prayer.' And then he would fold his hands, close his eyes, and actually pray the prayer which ended the written meditation.[10]

Murray used to say that with his writing ideas he was like a hen about to lay an egg; he felt 'restless and unhappy' until he was able to get the burden of his message off his mind. As soon as a book was completed Murray liked to have it forwarded to the printer. But before a copy of the new manuscript was dispatched he often said to Annie, 'Now just a word of humble thanksgiving first.' Then, bowing his head over his study table, he prayed: 'Lord, we have been endeavoring to instruct others; may we ourselves learn the truths Thou seekest to impart. And do Thou richly bless this book to all its readers. Amen.'[11] With Annie's continued capable assistance, Murray published five books and sixteen shorter works from 1909 to 1913.

On Monday, 3 November, 1913, eighty-five-year-old Andrew Murray set out on an eleven-week ministry tour. Accompanied by Annie, he first traveled by train 235 miles east to Oudtshoorn. There he preached and chaired the three-day conference of the Laymen's Missionary Union. Murray then spent several days and preached at least once in his brother George's parish at nearby De Hoop. From there he continued on by rail some 200 miles north and east, to a conference at Graaff-Reinet. Murray preached twice on Sunday 23 November. That evening he spoke from 2 Chronicles 15:12 and reminded his audience that he had preached on that very Scripture text at a similar conference in the same location fifty-two years earlier![12]

---

10. ibid., p. 469.

11. ibid., p. 465.

12. See p. 144 [ch 12 p. 9] in the current volume.

After spending a few days at Broederstroom, the nearby farm of his son Andrew Haldane, Murray traveled by 'motor-car', sixty-one miles north and west to Murraysburg. That week and the next he ministered there, then at Middelburg and Burgersdorp. Murray led the dedication ceremony for the new DRC building at the latter location.

At midnight on Sunday 14 December, Murray and Annie set out by train for Bloemfontein and arrived there at ten o'clock the following morning. Murray preached that same evening and the next morning delivered a special address at the DRC on the theme of love. That brief address was presented in conjunction with the dedication of a war memorial that took place in Bloemfontein that same day. 'The Women's Monument' commemorated the tens of thousands of women and children who were the victims of the Boer War. A member of the Bloemfontein DRC who had sat under Murray's ministry there more than sixty years earlier, related of the old minister's love-discourse on this occasion:

> His voice, stronger even in the speaker's old age than that of most preachers (how it reminds us of the days when it made us tremble as he spoke of death and eternity!) still possesses the power of penetrating to the very depths of the soul. But the power it now wields is of a different nature, as anyone will understand when he set down the opening words of his address: 'We are assembled here to celebrate the festival of love – suffering, intercessory, benedictory, all-conquering love. The monument which is to be unveiled today is the monument of love.'
>
> He then spoke of the sufferings endured in the camps, and asked what could have been the divine purpose of it all. God's object was to lead souls through suffering to love. And that suffering brought them also to their knees. Many persons entered those camps not knowing what prayer was, and there learnt the secret. … The speaker also pointed to the danger which at present existed of dissension and schism among our people. What could prevent this? Only love. 'Let us go to the monument,' he said, 'with the words, "I yield myself to God, in the desire to seek not mine own." Let us go under the banner of God's love – suffering, praying, blessing, overcoming.'[13]

---

13. Du Plessis, *The Life of Andrew Murray*, p. 431.

The Women's Monument was a 120-foot-high obelisk, with bronze reliefs at its base that depicted the sufferings endured by the women of the two Boer Republics during the war. The monument had been erected primarily due to the tireless efforts of M.T. Steyn, President of the Orange Free State at the commencement of the war. Some 20,000 people attended the dedication ceremony, including military officers, politicians, ministers and other prominent individuals from all parts of the Union. Murray followed immediately after President Steyn in the ceremony's official procession. Both men, elderly and somewhat feeble, were assisted by escorts. One eye-witness of the procession testified of them: 'Shall we say what feelings stirred within us as we looked upon these two figures? We cannot. This only let us set down – *our two great men, each the first in his own sphere!*'[14]

Periodically throughout the ceremony Rev. J.M. Louw handed Murray, who by then was almost completely deaf, a scrap of paper, summarizing for him what was being said by various speakers. As the sun's intense rays bore down on the gathering, Christiaan de Wet, the most formidable Boer general during the war, extended an umbrella over Murray's head. 'Who is the good friend who is so kindly holding the umbrella above me?' the esteemed old minister asked. 'General de Wet,' he was informed. When Murray expressed his hearty thanks for the thoughtful service, de Wet himself responded, 'It is an honor worth paying for.'

At five o'clock that same afternoon Murray, Annie and Murray's sister Isabella were taken for a tour of various sites in Bloemfontein. Annie reported:

> In visiting the pile [large group] of buildings which mark the site of the present day Grey College, we touched at Andrew Murray House and saw in the hall an enlarged daguerreotype of father, which seemed to us a very good likeness. We then drove to the National Museum, father's old church – a long building with four small windows, the pulpit having been at the one end. Father himself was unable to get out of the motor [car], but was

---

14.   ibid., p. 430.

keenly interested, and insisted that we should see everything. 'Bloemfontein,' he reminded us, 'was my first love.'[15]

Leaving Bloemfontein Wednesday night, the Murrays traveled nearly 130 miles south by rail to Aliwal North, arriving there the next evening. Two days later, after journeying some 115 miles east and a little south, they came to Rossville (modern Rhodes), the parish of Murray's son, Charles. There the senior Murray preached twice on Sunday 21 December, as well as once on both Christmas Day and 'Old Year's Day'.

Murray and Annie began their homeward journey on Tuesday 6 January, 1914. Along the way Murray preached and addressed missionary union meetings at Barkly East, Lady Grey and George. He and Annie arrived home in Wellington on Tuesday, 20 January. Throughout the course of the eleven-week ministry tour they had traveled more than 1,900 miles.

---

15.   ibid., p. 496.

29

'A Voice on the Verge of Eternity'
1914–1916

High political tensions in the opening months of 1914 divided Dutch South Africa into two antagonistic groups and seriously threatened the unity of the DRC. The crux of the tensions had to do with differing perspectives over the ongoing promotion of Dutch nationalism. As had been the case throughout his ministerial career, so now in the closing years of his life Andrew Murray consistently sought to use his influence to promote a spirit of love, peace and unity, especially among fellow Christians, regardless of their nationality or political persuasion.

A former DRC minister, Daniel F. Malan, who had resigned his pastorate to devote himself to politics, stated in one of his speeches at that time: 'If the dissensions which divide our people are not healed, I cannot see how our Church can in the long run remain united. There is a tendency in members of the same Church to unite, not merely in confession and belief, but also in political views.'[1] Murray wrote a public letter in which he forthrightly disagreed with such a perspective:

> I do not know how I can best define the divergence between these thoughts and my own conception, than by saying that I cannot in the least see that a schism in the Church is unavoidable because

---

1. Du Plessis, *The Life of Andrew Murray*, p. 431. Malan went on to become a champion of Afrikaner nationalism. He served as Prime Minister of South Africa from 1948 to 1954. His National Party government was responsible for the comprehensive implementation of apartheid.

there exist within it two parties with different political convictions. The Church surely is a spiritual body, specially created by the Lord with the purpose of uniting, in the power of a supernatural love which derives its strength from Christ through the Holy Spirit, all His members, drawn even from nations which may have hated and despised one another. Paul gave expression more than once to the thought: 'In the new man there is not Greek and Jew, circumcision and uncircumcision, Barbarian and Scythian, bondman and freeman; but Christ is all and in all' [paraphrase of Col. 3:10-11].

... [As regards present dissensions] the Church must allow the voice of God to be heard above all the roaring of the waters: 'Love one another, forbearing one another in love; as Christ hath forgiven you, even so do ye likewise' [John 13:34; Col. 3:13]. If the Church is faithful to this duty it will be impossible that there should be any thought of disruption because of political differences.[2]

Immediately after the outbreak of World War 1 a number of Christian ministers and university professors in Germany issued a manifesto that sought to justify the German Government in having declared war. On 4 October, 1914 Murray wrote a charitable letter of response that again demonstrated his unflagging commitment to promoting Christian love and unity within the Body of Christ:

To the Brethren who sent from Berlin a letter to 'The Evangelical Christians abroad.'

Beloved Brethren – I am in receipt of your letter of August, and desire to send an answer, expressing the deep and divine unity in which God's children in the nations that now are at war know that they are the members of one body in Christ Jesus.

In regard to the contents of your letter there will of course be very great differences. But this is not the time or occasion for entering upon them. It is our great duty as beloved in Christ Jesus to love each other through all the misunderstandings and estrangement that a war causes. ...

And my one object in writing these lines is to send you my brotherly greetings in Christ Jesus. The members of the body

2. ibid., pp. 431-2.

of Jesus Christ, whether in Germany or in England, are bound together in the love of God, in the mighty love of Calvary, in the love of the eternal Spirit. For a moment national or personal differences may stir up unholy feelings, but the moment we return again into the secret of God's presence and hide ourselves under the shadow of His wings we are brought back to the place where we are really one, and where our love and prayer pours itself forth on behalf of all who are one in Christ Jesus.

Accept the assurance of my continual daily prayer that God may help me and you, dear Brethren, and all who are apparently utterly separated from each other by the war, ever to take our refuge in the High-priestly prayer of our beloved Savior, and in the power of His grace to pray, in the fullness of faith and love, with our Lord Jesus: 'Father, that they may all be one, as Thou, Father, art in Me and I in Thee – I in them and Thou in Me – that they may be one even as we are one, that they may be made perfect in one' [John 17:21, 23].[3]

During the war years Murray's daughters often overheard him praying aloud in the middle of the night. On one such occasion they heard him offer a long, beautiful prayer for peace in which he made requests for the rulers of the nations and for all the world powers locked in the conflict. The next morning at breakfast he related a vivid dream that he had had during the night. While traveling by cart he met a certain magistrate who asked Murray to pray with him. A gale-force wind was raging, so Murray descended from the cart and they found a sheltered spot in which to pray. He then offered up the earnest prayer his daughters had listened to in the night. When Murray awoke, the dream seemed so real that he at first thought the magistrate was still in the bedroom with him.

Murray closely followed the progress of the Great War. When the campaign in German Southwest Africa[4] commenced he purchased a map and had one of his grandsons mark on it such things as railway lines, the most important places and all the stages of the conflict.

---

3.   ibid., p. 503.

4.   German Southwest Africa (modern Namibia), located directly north of western Cape Colony, was a colony of the German Empire from 1884 to 1915. During World War 1 it was invaded by British and South African forces.

Murray also took an 'intelligent interest' in airplanes and submarines, which were then being used for the first time in warfare.

Throughout the final decade of Murray's life three grandsons lived at Clairvaux while pursuing their education. They were the sons of Murray's son, John, who was serving as a missionary to the Basuto of northern Transvaal. The children of Murray's nephews and nieces who visited Clairvaux now and again also called him 'Grandpa', or 'Oupa' if they spoke Dutch. The younger ones were especially attracted to his stout black walking-stick which had been made in the Boer prisoners' camp in Ceylon. Murray would playfully poke the staff at the youngsters and allow them to use it as a hobbyhorse.

Annie testified of her father in the final years of his life:

> Up to the very end of life his interest in everything was intense – in his work, in the visitors who called, and in the quiet beauty of nature. 'Do look at the exquisite green of those trees,' he would frequently cry. At the close of the day's work he would take all the physical exercise in which he could indulge in those years of increasing bodily infirmity – two turns along the road in front of Sunnyside on the arm of one of his daughters.[5]

Some time earlier one of Murray's other children had written of him:

> Father speaks very quietly now, with very little exertion, but with great spiritual power. It seems like a voice on the verge of eternity, of one just ready to go on living while God wills. Glad to live to deliver God's messages, but he talks little and spares all his strength for work. Yet he was never more bright and joyous in his whole life, so restful and peaceful. The world and all its interests are in abeyance; God's kingdom and its interests absorb his thoughts and heart.[6]

After returning from a Good Friday church service on 2 April, 1915 Murray declared to Annie, 'I must begin a new book.' He promptly

5. Du Plessis, *The Life of Andrew Murray*, p. 494.
6. Douglas, *Andrew Murray and His Message*, p. 238.

dictated the titles of twenty chapters for a booklet published later that year on *De Liefde* (Love). In the final three years of his life, 1914-1916, Murray published one book (*De Geestelijke Toestand der Kerk* [The Spiritual State of the Church]), some fourteen booklets (including four in the Pocket Companion Series), and several brief pamphlets.

Despite his declining bodily strength the warm final months of 1915 were active ones for Murray. In October he attended the reunion of current and past students of the Theological Seminary in Stellenbosch. Near the end of that month he spoke at a meeting of the Women's Missionary Union at Wellington, at which time he promised to send a copy of his newest booklet, *De Genadetroon* (The Throne of Grace), to each member of the WMU, including those in the Free State and Transvaal. On Wednesday 3 November he was invited to address the DRC Synod in Cape Town on what had been designated as 'A Day for Missions'. That Saturday he traveled to Worcester for a missionary festival at which he preached twice the next day.

On Monday 15 November, the forty-second anniversary of the arrival of Misses Ferguson and Bliss at Wellington, Murray spoke to all the students of the Huguenot College and Seminary in Goodnow Hall. At a Christian Endeavor Meeting in Goodnow Hall on Sunday 5 December he addressed the young teachers who were leaving at the end of the year and enlisted fifty of them as members of the Teachers' Christian Union. The following Sunday he spoke at the communion service of Wellington's DRC.

That December Murray was also working diligently on two of his Pocket Companion booklets, *Het Kruis van Christus* (The Cross of Christ) and *De Heilige Geest* (The Holy Ghost). In addition, he had become very interested in a new ministry prospect that had only recently been suggested to him: holding one-day ministry conferences. He no longer had the strength to carry out lengthier conferences that involved a number of sessions over the course of several days. But he was still able to present two or three messages on a single day. Before year's end Murray produced a leaflet in Dutch, delineating the benefits of churches holding one-day conferences and suggesting suitable topics for such gatherings. His proposal was favorably received and, as a result, a number of such conferences were held at various locations.

On Christmas Day Murray preached and officiated at a communion service in nearby Paarl. He was invited to deliver a thanksgiving sermon there on Old Year's Eve but preferred, instead, to speak on the confession of sin. Early in the New Year, 1916, Murray started composing a new booklet, *The Supreme Need*, to address 'the sin of prayerlessness'. January and February found him writing extracts from William Law for two other booklets: *God in Ons* (God in Us) and *The Secret of Inspiration*.

During the past several years Murray had repeatedly been encouraged by various people to write an autobiography of his spiritual experiences. Alexander Whyte, minister of Edinburgh's Free St George's Church, had encouraged Murray to produce such a work, especially one that shared his personal experiences as a man of prayer. Whyte even went so far as to send his own publisher a suggestion for a suitable announcement of the hoped-for volume: 'Grace Abounding Again: The Spiritual Autobiography of Andrew Murray. *In Preparation*.'

While Murray was making selections from Law's writings for *The Secret of Inspiration* Annie again raised the subject of her father composing his spiritual memoir. 'Well,' he responded, 'if I could pass through Law's experiences, I might be persuaded to set down something, but not otherwise.' When Annie suggested that his experiences may have been equally deep and vivid, though not along the same lines as Law's, Murray shook his head and stated, 'No, my child, God has been very gracious to me. But in this matter I must have something more to go upon before I can venture to write.' That continued to be Murray's perspective throughout the closing years of his life.

The month of February was spent at 'Patmos', a seaside cottage at Kalk Bay. Patmos had come to serve as the Murrays' 'usual seaside resort' for a temporary break from the stifling summer heat. While there Murray preached one Sunday morning in Dutch and one evening in English. 4 March found him back in Wellington for a special occasion when about sixty members of Parliament were served tea at the Huguenot College grounds. Murray delivered a short speech 'with something of his old fire' on the subject of education, with his remarks being 'much appreciated and loudly cheered'. That same month he preached one Sunday at Paarl and spoke at the monthly prayer meeting of the Huguenot College teachers.

At breakfast on 4 April Murray quoted aloud from a daily prayer calendar that he used, 'Carelessness about the friendship of Christ the crying sin of the Church'. He then remarked, 'But for the cultivation of such a friendship you need time.' Pointing to a plate of bread on the table, he commented further, 'You could not have that plateful of bread without taking time to prepare the dough and bake the loaf. Everything we do needs time, and most of all does the exercise of fellowship with God demand it.'[7] At noon that same day he had 'a few words of prayer' for some friends who stopped by to visit. Annie revealed, 'He seldom let a visitor go without offering a brief intercessory prayer, either in the study or on the stoep.'[8]

In the latter half of April Murray preached in Wellington's DRC one Sunday morning and at the English service in Goodnow Hall another Sunday evening. He participated in the Laymen's Missionary Union meetings at Paarl the last week of the month, speaking several times during the conference and delivering the morning message the following Sunday 30 April. Four days later he attended a one-day conference at Stellenbosch as well as the induction service of Rev. J. du Plessis as professor at the Theological Seminary there.

Murray's eighty-eighth birthday was celebrated nine days later, with 'many visitors and a large party of relatives to dinner'. That afternoon he reminisced about his experiences in Scotland and Holland as well as at Bloemfontein and Worcester. In addition:

Mr Murray spoke of the lameness and deafness of his latter years as a kindly dispensation of God's Providence. God had shut him

7.   Du Plessis, *The Life of Andrew Murray*, pp. 498-9.
8.   ibid., p. 499.

out from the life of ceaseless activity which he led in former years, and had shut him in to a life of greater quiet, in which he could give more time to meditation and prayer. In the silence and the solitude precious messages had come to him, which he had endeavored to pass on to others. His closing exhortation, on this last earthly birthday was: 'Child of God, let your Father lead you. Think not of what *you* can do, but of what *God* can do in you and through you.'[9]

In response to the 200 or so birthday greetings he received by letter and telegram, he distributed an equal number of his just-published booklet, *God in Ons*. Just at that time he was working on two other booklets, *De Blijdschap* (Joy) and *Eendracht maakt Macht* (Union is Strength).

On Friday 9 June Murray traveled by car to Riebeek West, twenty miles north of Wellington, in the pouring rain. He preached there that evening and the following morning and afternoon. The next day, 11 June, he conducted the morning service at his old church in Wellington, in what would prove to be the final occasion he would ever preach there. It was raining heavily that day and the congregation was very small. He spoke from Galatians 4:6 on what the Holy Spirit expects from Christians and what believers may expect from God's Spirit.

On 16 to 22 June Murray undertook what turned out to be his last ministry journey, this one to Somerset West, Caledon, Villiersdorp and Worcester. His youngest brother George, the seventy-year-old minister of the DRC at Oudtshoorn, shared in that ministry venture with him. The brothers held a number of services at each of the locations they visited. People were touched at the sight of the two veteran ministers still so full of spiritual zeal.

Andrew Murray's daughter Kitty also accompanied him on that week-long trip. The morning after Murray returned to Wellington he informed Annie, somewhat apologetically, 'I am sorry, but as a result of my visit to Caledon I must commence a new book. I can't help it.' He then dictated that same morning eight chapter headings and two initial chapters for a booklet, *De Opwekking* (The Revival),

9.   ibid., pp. 506-7.

all of which Annie recorded in a half-used examination book of one of the grandsons.

At breakfast several days later, Murray revealed, 'I did not sleep very well, so during my waking hours I composed three chapters for a little volume on *Christus ons Leven* (Christ Our Life).' So those three chapters were immediately dictated and committed to paper. Around that same time he also composed an article on Mary 'Ma' Slessor for *De Kerkbode*.

30

DEATH AND ONGOING INFLUENCE
1916–1917

Murray preached the ordination sermon at the installation service of the new minister in North Paarl on Wednesday 26 July. He continued to work on *Christus ons Leven*, intending to have it ready in time for the one-day conferences he hoped to attend at Hopefield and Darling. Sunday morning, 20 August, Murray seemed in his usual health and went to church. During dinner he asked his family members to tell him the gist of the sermon that Rev. J. Rabie, one of the directors of Wellington's missionary Training Institute, had preached that morning. Due to his deafness Murray had been unable to hear any of the message. That evening Murray did not feel well and went to bed early. The next day a doctor was called to examine him. The physician stated that Murray was suffering from 'a slight attack of influenza and bronchitis'. But those quickly developed into a heavy cold. After that Murray never really recovered his health and strength.

A grievous blow befell the Murray family when news was received that Andrew Haldane had died on 16 September. At the outbreak of World War 1 Haldane had volunteered to serve in the British allied campaign in East Africa.[1] After rising to the rank of lieutenant he was killed in action while attempting to save the life of a wounded comrade. He died at age fifty and left behind a wife and

---

1. German East Africa was a German colony that had been established in the African Great Lakes region (modern Burundi, Rwanda and mainland Tanzania) in 1885. After World War 1 the territory was divided between Britain and Belgium.

three children. For 'some weeks' the news of Haldane's death was kept from the ailing, elderly father. When Murray was informed he bore the intelligence 'with Christian resignation and fortitude'. 'But there can be no doubt,' du Plessis asserts, 'that the passing of this beloved son cast a burden of grief upon Mr Murray's heart, and served to hasten the inevitable end.'[2]

By late October Murray seemed a little stronger so arrangements were made for him to spend all of November at Kalk Bay. That proved to be an exceptionally hot summer, and when Murray returned to Wellington in December it soon became apparent that his strength was flagging. He lamented the fact that he was too weak to resume his writing.

On 26 December he thought it was New Year's Eve so wished to hold a devotional service. He stated:

> God loves to give, and we should open our hearts wide to receive Him. We have now to close the book of the year. On one side, which is full, we have the record of the prayers offered, and the answers of help or grace supplied. The other page is blank, and there are two columns. Above one is written, 'Prayers not offered'. Above the other, 'Graces not received because not asked for'. Oh, how much we have missed of blessing this year, because we have not opened our mouth wide for God to fill [Ps. 81:10]. Let us seek in the New Year to have our hearts open, and our prayers, our petitions made deep, to ask and receive more from God.[3]

The 11 January, 1917 edition of *De Kerkbode* reported:

> The following communication has reached us concerning that old and revered servant of God, Dr A. Murray. He continues weak, though his heart is still fairly strong, and he is generally up each day. The great heat affects him unfavorably. His mind is not always perfectly clear, and in his wanderings he appears to be always occupied with his fellow ministers, asking them repeatedly to give themselves to more prayer. ... He dwells frequently upon the

---

2.   Du Plessis, *The Life of Andrew Murray*, p. 508.

3.   Douglas, *Andrew Murray and His Message*, pp. 242-3.

necessity of taking more time to contemplate the wonderful love and grace of God, of which we have so feeble a conception. The condition of our people weighs heavily upon him, and impelled him to cry one night, 'Pray, pray, pray, that our people may be strong in righteousness.' On another occasion he said, 'We are perishing through selfishness. What we need is men who will really sacrifice themselves for the cause of education, and will so devote themselves to the poor that the problem of "poor whites" will be solved.'[4]

In another moment of mental confusion and concern near the end, Murray turned to one of his daughters and said, 'The wind is blowing a gale and the tempest is raging. I think you must ask the captain to put into the nearest port.' Du Plessis comments, 'His voyage had been a long one, and not free from heavy storms; but he was nearing the harbor, and quiet water lay ahead.'[5]

On 13 January a fresh set of thoughts stirred in Murray's mind which he dictated to Annie. As it turned out, they were the last perspectives he had recorded in that way:

(1) Everything in us must be like God.

(2) Everything can only be like God by partaking of His nature.

(3) Everything must have the nature of God.

(4) Nothing can be like God but God Himself.[6]

While preparing for bed on Wednesday 17 January, on what proved to be the final night of his earthly life, Murray paused and remarked, 'We have such a great and glorious God, we ought to be always rejoicing in Him.' Then he spontaneously prayed: 'Oh! ever blessed and glorious God, satisfy us with Thy mercy that we may rejoice and be glad in Thee all our days. Satisfy me that I may rejoice and be glad always in Thee.'[7] 'Good night, my child,' he tenderly stated

---

4. Du Plessis, *The Life of Andrew Murray*, p. 509.

5. ibid.

6. Douglas, *Andrew Murray and His Message*, p. 326.

7. ibid., p. 243.

to one of his daughters who kissed him on the forehead before he fell asleep that evening.

At 3:30 the next morning a 'Sister Brown' who was helping to care for Murray awakened his daughters,[8] stating, 'I think your father is going, his pulse is so weak.' The daughters got up and gathered in his room. But after a time Murray seemed to revive, so all the sisters except Emma went back to bed. As Emma continued to watch at her father's bedside, he was sometimes conscious and stated more than once, 'Have faith in God, my child. Do not doubt Him.' Later Murray said, 'Ah, it is my little Emmie, my eldest child.' He stroked her hair and then relapsed into unconsciousness. After awakening awhile later, he said, 'God is worthy of trust.' Those appear to have been Murray's last recorded words.

Emma had been kneeling 'in the attitude of prayer' at her father's bedside when he made those statements to her. She continued to kneel there till 5 a.m., at which time she opened the shutters and said, 'Father, the day is just dawning, and it will soon be light.' She then retired to rest, leaving him in the care of the nurse, Sister Brown.

Throughout the day Murray was restless but as the afternoon progressed he became peaceful. At the very end his daughters were gathered silently around his bed. They saw his forehead contracting, as it always did when he closed his eyes to pray, but no words came from his lips. A moment later, at 6:45 p.m. on 18 January, 1917, he had peacefully stepped into the heavenly presence of his God and Savior. At eighty-eight years and eight months of age, Andrew Murray's long earthly course of fervent, fruitful service of his beloved Lord had come to an end.

Murray's funeral took place two days later, on Saturday 20 January, at Wellington's Dutch Reformed Church. Shops and other places of business were closed as 'all Wellington' gathered at the church around four in the afternoon to pay a final tribute to

---

8. The three grandsons who lived at Clairvaux for a decade were 'away for the holidays' at the time of Murray's death (Du Plessis, *The Life of Andrew Murray*, p. 502).

the town's most venerated citizen. Rev. D.G. Malan, the minister of Wellington's DRC at that time, officiated the service while Rev. J.R. Albertyn, Murray's former associate pastor at the church, described the work and influence of Murray's life. Professor P.J.G. de Vos of the Stellenbosch Theological Seminary presented the funeral message.

Murray's body was buried in the DRC churchyard, his grave being immediately to the right of the church's main entrance. Some sixty DRC ministers as well as prominent citizens from many area towns attended Murray's funeral and graveside service. Telegrams of condolence and commemoration were received from all parts of the country and from a number of its highest officials.

In the final year of Murray's life Dr J.I. Marais, a professor at Stellenbosch Theological Seminary and a close associate of Murray in 'many ecclesiastical and social undertakings', wrote in tribute of him:

> Emerson has said somewhere: 'Every man is a cause, a country and an age. ... All history resolves itself very easily into the biography of a few stout and earnest persons.' These words may fitly be applied to Dr Andrew Murray; for few men in South Africa have had an influence more wide-spreading than he, few have left such an impress upon their time and their generation. That influence has been extensive as well as intensive. The Dutch Reformed Church, which claims him as her own, and to which his best energies have been devoted for many years, has felt the intensiveness of that influence, has been, and still is, under the spell of his wonderful personality. There is hardly an institution – ecclesiastical, educational, philanthropic, religious – within the purview of the Dutch Reformed Church, which has not benefited by his advice, or received a strong impulse from his prayers; few of these institutions have not been initiated by him. For his sympathies are wide as his religious life is deep. Even in feeble old age, with a body bent and frail, he takes the keenest interest in whatever good is done or attempted by the Church of his fathers, or the Church of God in any corner of the globe. ...

And yet Andrew Murray has never sought fame. Apparently he is a man without ambition – except perhaps the ambition so characteristic of St Paul, … 'to preach the Gospel' and to be 'well-pleasing to God'. He was, and is, essentially a preacher. In the days of his prime, his appeals have stirred thousands; for his influence in the pulpit was magnetic. His tremendous earnestness has swayed men's minds as the wind sways the cornfield. … Set speeches he has never delivered; an oration from his lips would be an anomaly and an impossibility. He was, and is, as he professes to be, a minister of the Gospel; and in no other capacity has he ever appeared before the public.

No one can understand Andrew Murray without reckoning with two things. He is essentially 'a man of prayer' and, at the same time, 'a man of affairs'. The eternal world is to him an intense reality, not a matter of speculation; things spiritual in his case dominate the temporal. The 'new life', which in his books is discussed in various ways, is developed by prayer, which to Andrew Murray means unbroken communion with the Unseen, intercession for others, fellowship in feeling and suffering with the Church of God in all portions of the globe. … He is essentially a mystic. Life for him means simply activity, 'permeated and purified by the sense of the Eternal Presence …'

But Andrew Murray is not a mere anchorite, a mystic dreamer of dreams, whose 'otherworldliness' lies beyond the influence of earthly stress and strain. He is essentially a man of action. At eighty-eight years of age the keenness of his intellect and his amazing vitality are a marvel to his friends. The *joie de vivre* [zest for life] is his in the truest sense of the term. He feels that he has a mission given him by God, a task to be performed, a message still to proclaim, a book or two still to be written. Some years ago a friend approached him with the request, 'Will you not give us some of your reminiscences?' The answer was characteristic: 'I have far better things to do than to talk and write about myself.'[9]

After Murray's death Rev. G.S. Malan, editor of *De Kerkbode*, similarly paid tribute by delineating some of his primary character traits:

---

9. ibid., pp. 515-16.

[W]e think first of all of the passionate earnestness which filled his soul. This impressed every one – those most of all who came into closest contact with him. At all times and in everything he did there glowed the fire of this deep earnestness. His calling and responsibility – both as a Christian in private life and as a servant of God in the interest of the Kingdom – were to him matters of the holiest moment, which he strove to perform with all the strength of his being. ... His was an earnestness which half affrighted and half repelled; but all who knew the tender soul and humble heart that beat within him were speedily arrested and overcome by it.

A second trait which characterized him was his lofty nobility of character. Who ever discovered anything low or mean or ignoble in his conduct? Who ever heard him mingle in the idle talk that gloats over the faults and defects and sins of another? Who did not feel instinctively in his presence that he had to do with one who led an exalted life, was occupied with exalted matters, cherished exalted ideals, and exercised an elevating influence?

After elaborating on Murray's courtesy, humility, unselfishness, love, sincerity, fidelity and 'perfect rectitude', Malan continued:

His courageous faithfulness to the truth and to his own conscientious convictions procured him many adversaries, but never, to our knowledge, did he make a single personal enemy through any lack of Christian courtesy.

Another trait of character may be mentioned – his absolute devotion to his calling and his work. He had laid himself upon God's altar, body, soul and spirit, with all his gifts and talents, with all his time and strength and possessions. He had no worldly by-ends; he knew no personal ambition. Everything was placed at the service of his Savior. He was always and everywhere, first and foremost, a minister of the Gospel, who had consecrated himself wholly to this high calling, and regarded the ministry as his greatest honor and privilege.[10]

According to du Plessis one of Murray's final accomplishments near the end of his life was the establishment of an Intercessory Union

---

10. ibid., pp. 513-14.

of Christians who were willing to devote at least fifteen minutes daily to interceding for others and for the advancement of Christ's cause throughout the world. Following his death the alliance was renamed the Andrew Murray Prayer Union with the hope that it would be 'a lasting memorial to his profound influence as a man of prayer, and his earnest advocacy of the place and power of prayer in the scheme of redemption.'[11]

In appreciation of the nearly three decades of support and advice that Murray had given the South Africa General Mission, the SAGM established a new mission in Portuguese West Africa after his death, naming it in his honor the Andrew Murray Memorial Mission. Murray's interest in and support of various missionary enterprises had remained vibrant to the close of his life. During the thirty years from 1886 to 1916 some seventy DRC missionaries went out to sundry fields of service. Of that number twenty-one were sons of DRC ministers and missionaries, including fifteen male members of the Murray clan. Three of Andrew Murray's own children served as missionaries: Mary among the Bakhatla in Bechuanaland (northwest of Orange Free State); John among the Basuto of northern Transvaal; Charles in Nyasaland then later in Bechuanaland.

For many years Murray's oldest daughter, Emmie, worked in Cape Town with the Salvation Army, rising to the rank of staff captain. In 1902 she left the SA in order to become the director of the Magdalena House, which rescued 'young girls and unfortunate women' from degradation and abuse. Murray's daughter Catherine (Kitty) devoted herself to educational work, serving as principal first of the Branch Huguenot Seminary at Bethlehem, then of the Girls' High School in Graaff-Reinet. Annie, the youngest daughter, was her father's 'faithful and zealous private secretary' for the last twenty years of his life.

In 1922 'a remarkable centenary gathering' was held in Graaff-Reinet to commemorate the arrival of Andrew Murray, Sr, in South

---

11. ibid., p. 361.

Africa. There 220 of his 486 descendants gathered for the special reunion. With humble gratitude to God it was duly noted:

> During the hundred years now ending, over fifty ministers have been connected with the family by birth or marriage, and about the same number of men and women have given the whole or part of their lives to work in the foreign mission field. Some of the young men are now attending the Theological Seminary and others are expecting to enter it in due time, some are studying medicine in the hope of becoming medical missionaries. … Looking over the past one could only adore the goodness of the covenant-keeping God and entrust to the same God the keeping of the future generations.[12]

The following year, in 1923, a marble statue of Andrew Murray, Jr, was erected outside the Wellington DRC. The statue portrays Murray sitting in his study chair with his Bible on his lap; his stone face looks out ponderously over Church Street. So great was the lingering respect for Murray, even years after his death, that town drunkards feared to pass by his stone likeness as they staggered to their homes. 'Ou minheer sal ons sie,' they said ('The old minister will see us')![13]

In the two years immediately following his death, 1917 and 1918, five short new works written by Murray were published posthumously. A number of projected volumes were left uncompleted at his passing. He was greatly interested in the missionary endeavors of Zinzendorf and the Moravian Brethren. Murray had researched several books about them in both English and German, and desired to write a biography on Zinzendorf in Dutch, but was unable to carry out the work. The same lot befell an 'elementary treatise on education' he had also hoped to compose in Dutch. Yet another volume Murray left unfinished was one on the inner life of the Apostle Paul.

Murray's prolific writing output, especially through the final thirty-three years of his life, was astounding. Rev. D.S.B. Joubert's

12. Douglas, *Andrew Murray and His Message*, pp. 23-4.

13. ibid., p. 132.

chronologically-arranged 'Bibliography of Andrew Murray's Published Works'[14] comprises nearly 240 leaflets, booklets and longer books.[15] Sixteen of those were produced during the twenty-six years from 1858 to 1883 while all the rest were published in the thirty-five years from 1884 to 1918. Seventy-three of Murray's books were over 100 pages in length while his longest work, *The Holiest of All*, was 552 pages. 'Murray did not write all of his books from start to finish as intended books; some were reprints of articles that appeared in [*De Kerkbode*]; others were compilations, by Murray or others, of his messages on certain themes.'[16] Still, the massive amount of material Murray produced and had published was indeed impressive.

Through his writing ministry Murray was able to reach a world-wide audience consisting of hundreds of thousands of individuals. Besides being published originally in Dutch and English, during his lifetime his works were translated and circulated in thirteen other languages, including French, German, Italian, Spanish, Swedish, Danish, Russian, Yiddish, Arabic, Armenian, Chinese, Japanese, Telugu and Malayalam.

Through the years Murray received scores if not hundreds of appreciative letters from readers of his books all around the world.[17] 'What I owe to you eternity alone will reveal,' a woman corresponded from New South Wales. A gentleman from Ireland wrote: 'I have read all, or nearly all, your books, some of them twelve times. Next to the Bible, they have been more helpful to me than any books I have ever read.' A minister's wife in Australia similarly shared, 'Now, as for so many years past, your books, beloved Father

---

14. That bibliography is recorded in du Plessis, *The Life of Andrew Murray*, pp. 526-35.

15. That number includes all Murray's works published in Dutch and English. Some of his volumes were published in both languages, with both the Dutch and English version being included in Joubert's bibliography.

16. Choy, *Andrew Murray*, p. 253.

17. Du Plessis personally examined some 150 such letters (Du Plessis, *The Life of Andrew Murray*, p. 474).

in God, are next to God's Word my very greatest spiritual help.' A missionary in China wrote to report of Murray's *The Spirit of Christ*: 'The book passed through many editions, and we often heard of the good it was doing. In one city a revival broke out through the book; in another case a pastor preached on it Sunday by Sunday, taking a chapter each Sunday as subject.'[18]

Many of those letters contained not only expressions of gratitude for Murray's writings but also requests for his prayers. His intercession was requested for the conversion of beloved children, for the healing of sick relatives, for individuals to be delivered from spiritual doubt or from alcoholism, for church and missionary work, as well as for philanthropic and literary ministries.

Murray's many published works have continued to bear much spiritual fruit around the world down to the present day. Throughout the nearly 100 years since his death countless Christians have been inspired, instructed and edified through his writings. Still today scores of his volumes are read with great appreciation and benefit by innumerable believers across the globe.[19] Such will doubtless continue to be the case for decades to come, should Christ delay His return.

Given Murray's Christian catholicity and his intense desire to help all believers grow strong in their spiritual life and service, it seems wondrous and fitting that God continues to use the written works of this choice servant to profit His children throughout the world. As was the case during his earthly ministry, so now Murray would desire all admiration and glory to be deflected away from himself to the Savior who empowered him to serve so devotedly and effectually.

---

18. The above testimonials and several others are cited in ibid., pp. 473-6.

19. Choy, *Andrew Murray*, pp. 253-74 provides synopses and background information on fifty of 'the major books' of Murray to be printed in English in more recent decades.

For Further Reading

Choy, Leona. *Andrew Murray, Apostle of Abiding Love*. Fort Washington, PA: Christian Literature Crusade, 1978.

_____. *Andrew and Emma Murray: An Intimate Portrait of Their Marriage and Ministry*. Winchester, VA: Golden Morning, 2000. This is a slightly expanded version of Choy's earlier Andrew Murray biography, containing several pages of additional information on Emma.

Douglas, W.M. *Andrew Murray and His Message, One of God's Choice Saints*. London and Edinburgh: Oliphants, 1927.

Du Plessis, J[ohannes]. *The Life of Andrew Murray of South Africa*. London and Edinburgh: Marshall Brothers, 1919. This voluminous work (553 pages) is the original 'official' Andrew Murray biography.

Farwell, Byron. *The Great Anglo-Boer War*. New York, Hagerstown, San Francisco and London: Harper & Row, 1976.

Hansen, Collin and Woodbridge, John. *A God-Sized Vision, Revival Stories That Stretch and Stir*. Grand Rapids: Zondervan, 2010. Chapter 4 summarizes the Prayer Meeting Revival that took place in the United States in 1857-1858 before spreading to South Africa in 1860-1861.

Lindner, Jr., William. *Andrew Murray*. Minneapolis: Bethany House, 1996. This is a brief (144 pages), introductory Murray biography.

McMullen, Michael. *God's Polished Arrow, William Chalmers Burns, Revival Preacher*. Fearn, Scotland: Christian Focus, 2000.

Murray, Joyce (Ed.). *In Mid-Victorian Cape Town, Letters from Miss Rutherfoord*. Cape Town: A.A. Balkema, 1953. This work chronicles Emma Rutherfoord's family life from 1852 to 1856, as well as her courtship with Andrew Murray.

Murray, Joyce (Ed.). *Young Mrs. Murray Goes to Bloemfontein, 1856-1860*. Cape Town: A.A. Balkema, 1954. This additional collection of letters written by Emma Murray relates her first five years of marriage to and ministry with Andrew Murray.

Neethling, Maria. *Unto Children's Children*. London: T.H. Hopkins & Son, 1909.

Nel, Olea. *South Africa's Forgotten Revival: The Story of the Cape's Great Awakening in 1860*. Longwood, FL: Xulon, 2008.